There I Was ...

The Wartime Memoirs of a Fledgling Birdman

Robert S. Crouse

Order this book online at www.trafford.com
or email orders@trafford.com

Most Trafford titles are also available at major online book retailers.

Printed in the United States of America.

ISBN: 978-1-4269-3845-0 (sc)
ISBN: 978-1-4269-3846-7 (e)

*Our mission is to efficiently provide the world's finest, most comprehensive book publishing
service, enabling every author to experience success. To find out how to publish your book,
your way, and have it available worldwide, visit us online at www.trafford.com*

Trafford rev. 10/08/2010

 www.trafford.com

North America & international
toll-free: 1 888 232 4444 (USA & Canada)
phone: 250 383 6864 ♦ fax: 812 355 4082

DEDICATION

To Laverda, my wife of, now, *67* years, who gave up the
comforts and security of home and family to follow her soldier
husband as he moved from base to base in his quest
to be an airman.
She endured hardships and anxieties far exceeding those
of her mate just to provide a few precious hours of love and brightness
each week, to spend time together that had a finite chance of
never being redeemed.
For that devotion, I shall be forever grateful.

HIGH FLIGHT

Oh! I have slipped the surly bonds of earth
And danced the skies on laughter-silvered wings:
Sunward I've climbed, and joined the tumbling mirth
Of sun split clouds---and done a hundred things
You have not dreamed of---wheeled and soared and swung
High in the sunlit silence. Hov'ring there.
I've chased the shouting wind along, and flung

My eager craft through footless halls of air.
Up, up the long, delirious, burning blue.
I've topped the wind-swept heights with easy grace
Where never lark, or even eagle flew—
And, while with silent lifting mind I've trod
The high untrespassed sanctity of space.
Put out my hand and touched the face of God.

John Gillespie Magee, Jr.

(John Gillespie Magee, Jr., a young U.S. pilot officer in the RCAF, wrote this hauntingly beautiful poem in a letter to his father during the Battle of Britain. Six weeks later he was reported killed in action when his Spitfire collided with another plane in a cloud.)

Contents

THERE I WAS.........

A Wartime Memoir

PROLOGUE

The first recollection I have of seeing an airplane in the air is one of those fleeting images that seem to reside in your memory banks unrelated to much of anything, they are just there. Kind of like the image on a postage stamp. It was a 1910 Curtis pusher biplane that landed out on the Hopper farm just south of my hometown, Rutherford, TN. It was probably flown by a barnstormer or someone on cross country who needed a place to light for a while. Anyway, I can see it now in my mind's eye, gliding in from the east and going down behind the trees about a mile from our house. I don't even remember how old I was, but it was probably in the late 20's, so I was about 5 years old. I got very excited about it and wanted to go see it but that was out of the question. No one was at home who could take me, and I was too little and it was too far away. This is not to say that this incident was what set me on the path to becoming an Army aviator, but it certainly initiated an interest in me that continues to this day. Then again, who can say for sure that it wasn't? Doesn't the theory of chaos say that the movement of a Monarch butterfly's wing in the wilds of Mexico may ultimately result in a typhoon in the Indian Ocean?

Mama has written in some of her reminiscences that I saw a plane go over when I was about five and stated to all present that I was going to fly one of those, some day. I can recall that all through my childhood, the sound of an airplane going over would bring me out into the yard to try to watch it. Thus began a fascination of a lifetime.

From the time I could read, I was fascinated with stories of WW I. Someone gave me a book entitled "Thrilling Stories of the Great War." It was quasi-history of WW I, written by the victors. It put all the actions of the Allies in the most heroic light and cast the "evil Boche" as the minions of Satan. Just the thing to stir the blood of an impressionable youth. I read it from cover to cover several times, paying special attention to the stories of the air war.

As I grew older and would occasionally have a nickel or dime in my pocket, I would buy a pulp magazine called "G-8 and his Battle Aces." These were thoroughly contrived thrillers of WW I that bore essentially no resemblance to the real war, but served to further enthrall me with the idea of someday being an army aviator. These came out once a month, so you can see; my mind was under constant, delicious assault. Comic books just added to my store of aviation lore of a highly adventurous and romanticized nature. There were "Smilin' Jack," "Barney Baxter," "Capt. Desmo," Terry and the Pirates," "Steve Canyon," and many others.

The thirties were a time of extraordinary worldwide interest in aviation. The military; Army, Navy and Marine Corps; were busily promoting their aviation arms, and like all new industries, plane manufacturers were equally zealous in keeping the latest developments before the public eye. In the midst of the Great Depression, all this brand new, highly exotic activity served as an escape from the drudgery of the day. A goodly portion of the older generation didn't believe flying was here to stay. If God had meant for man to fly, He would have built him with wings like a bird. All this foolishness was bound to eventually go away. We adventurous youth knew that aviation was the wave of the future, and many of us wanted to be in on the ground floor, so to speak.

Just about every magazine but the women's publications, and the confessions sheets, carried aviation stories and pictures. Popular Mechanics was especially into aviation, and that made it one of my favorites. I managed to inveigle Papa into buying a subscription for me and I was on pins and needles each month about the time it was due to come out. It was always full of the very latest. It once ran a series on Army aviation entitled "The West Point of the Air," featuring a picture story about Randolph Field in Texas. I think that may have been what crystallized my desire to fly for the Army. I realized that it was just a dream, but all youth need to have an impossible dream to take them away from the humdrum. To have something to reach for that is attainable, but only with extreme effort and lots of luck, is what drives most of us.

My interest in aviation never flagged. I began what I called my aviation scrapbook, that consisted of every picture of any type of flying machine that I could find, even some very futuristic ones from Buck Rogers comics.

Although the materials of the book are suffering the ravages of time, they are still around and constitute a veritable treasure trove of thirties aviation history.

At some point in my youth, I must have realized that circumstances were militating against my ever becoming a pilot for the Army. In addition to a congenital heart condition that limited my physical activities, there was the problem of getting the college education requisite to getting into the Army aviation program. Very few kids in Rutherford in the thirties had the wherewithal to go to college, and besides, the family farms required our help and marriage seemed to come into the picture, as well. Single men with a college education and in perfect physical condition were the only candidates considered by the Army at that time.

As the world situation worsened and moved ever closer to war, I began to think in terms of getting into some sort of military service when out of high school. This was not a driving desire of mine, you understand, but it did occur as a random thought from time to time. For the most part I was busy just being a kid going through school, developing my social skills, overcoming adolescent awkwardness, fighting zits and occasionally learning a little something from my teachers. I think I can say, without equivocation, that my high school years were probably the happiest of my life. The world was my oyster and the future would take care of itself. But big changes were on the horizon.

Chapter I

DRAFT CANDIDATE

Class Picture- 1942   Not a care in the world-yet.

World War II started for the United States on December 7, 1941. At that time I was a 17 year old high school senior.   War had been very much in our minds for several years, because of all the happenings around the world. Most of my generation, when we thought about it, was certain that the United States would sooner or later have to go to war with the Germans and/or the Japanese. I am not sure that our parents generation was as certain because they, exercising vain hope, thought we had fought the "war to end all wars" with World War I. My generation had little connection to that time and assumed that it would all have to be done over.

The military draft that was instituted in 1940 had been renewed by one vote in Congress in 1941. All males at age 18 were required to register for the draft, and although I was not yet 18, I was eagerly looking forward to it with all the patriotic fervor I could muster, and that was a lot. I was outraged by the Japanese attack on Pearl Harbor and the subsequent declaration of war by Germany and Italy. I could hardly wait to get into uniform.

My parents were a little perplexed by my attitude, but expressed little concern that I would ever serve because of the congenital heart condition. When I was 5 years old, it was discovered that I had something wrong with my heart. When I would get excited or exert myself strenuously, my heart would beat too fast. This was diagnosed as "leakage of the heart" by our family doctor and was thought to be serious. I was forbidden to do things that would cause an "attack". This restriction lasted about two days and Mama gave up and figured that I would just have to learn how to live with the condition, if it didn't kill me first. It turned out that that was the best course of action. I very quickly learned that I could not play games that required a sustained high level of exertion, such as basketball. That, as it happens, was the only sport in which I didn't participate in school. I played baseball, softball, ran track and played all of the childhood games our generation engaged in, some of which were very strenuous. I learned how to pace myself and how to take a break if my heart began to race and how to force it back into a normal rhythm. Playing basketball is the only thing I missed in high school. The best I could do in that venue was to be the first boy cheerleader in school history.

I graduated in May of 1942, and when my 18th birthday rolled around in June, registered for the draft. Many of my peers volunteered as soon as they could get their parents permission. My parents, of course, refused to even consider my pleas to volunteer because they were certain that I would never have to go. I looked into a lot of possibilities, but secretly assumed that I would not be able to pass the physical, so I didn't press very hard. I reconciled myself to doing my patriotic duty on the home front.

In 1943, things were not going real well for the U. S. on many fronts, so the draft requirements were made increasingly lax. The demand for warm bodies was high. It was said that to qualify for the draft one only had to show up at the draft office, let a doctor shine a light in one ear, and if no light came out the other, you were in. That is an exaggeration, but not by much.

The Selective Service System had a standard form letter that they sent out to all registered males. It began:

"Greeting:

You have been selected by your friends and neighbors…" and it went on to tell us where and when to report for our first physical. For many people that became a frightening letter; while for others, like me, it was eagerly anticipated.

My preliminary examination, when I was finally notified in early 1943, consisted of the doctor at the county seat looking in my ears and mouth and listening to my heart to see if I had one and pronouncing me fit for the next step. This meant that, for the moment, at least, I was classified **1A**. The next step was to wait for a call to report for a pre-induction physical at some induction center. At this point, my parents were surprised, but certain that a more thorough physical would reveal my bad heart and I would be sent back home.

There were a number of draft classifications that determined whether or not you served in the military. The top one, the one that assured that you would be called up for a pre-induction physical and likely be drafted was 1A. The one that assured that you would <u>not</u> serve in any capacity was 4F. There were a number of others that denoted various exempt classifications, i.e., farmer, defense worker, miner, sole support of a family, married with children, limited service due to partial disability, etc. I don't know what any of them were because I didn't qualify under any of them.

The order came for me to report to Ft. Oglethorpe, GA, by March 27, 1943, and with a combination of excitement and dread I made ready to go. Papa took me aside and offered to try to get me a farming exemption, and probably could have done so, but I asked him not to. I had not been farming on any sort of regular basis. I helped out when needed, but my full time job was working as a bundle boy at the local garment factory. I knew of a few men in the area that had gotten such an exemption who had <u>never</u> worked on their farms. When the draft began, they suddenly began wearing overalls and work shoes and driving dirty cars, when previously, they dressed in suits and ties and had their cars washed every week. They were not looked upon with favor, to say the least. I decided that I would take my chances with the draft, secretly hoping that somehow my tricky heart would be overlooked. I'm sure my parents were secretly hoping that the doctors would spot it, first thing.

About the only way to get to Ft. Oglethorpe from Rutherford was by bus via Jackson, Nashville and Chattanooga. As I recall, it took me most of a day to get to Chattanooga, where the buses were met by the Army. There was a constant stream of buses for carrying potential cannon fodder coming into the station where we were loaded into Army trucks like so many cattle and hauled off into the night. We had no idea what we were getting into and the Corporals and Pfc.'s herding us knew we were scared poopless and they did everything they could to frighten us even more. I had made up my mind before I left home that I was going to do everything I was told by anyone in uniform until I learned enough to know better. That philosophy served me well. There were a few wise guys that shot off their mouths and lived to regret it. They became targets for all the abuse that veteran non-coms are expert at.

It was near midnight when we were dumped off somewhere in the confines of Ft. Oglethorpe. We were assigned to an unheated, bare bones barracks and told to "hit the sack", my first encounter with Army jargon. The area to which we assigned was called the "Bull Pen". I have never known why it was called that, and until now, had never given it any thought. I guess it was part of my self-imposed conditioning not to question, but to go along. It <u>was</u> separated from the rest of the post by a chain link fence, and did resemble a pen where you might keep bulls to separate them from the cows. That may have been to keep us apart from the 10,000 WAC's (cows?) who were in Basic Training there.

We were rolled out at about daylight the next morning and "marched", more like "straggled", over to the mess hall for breakfast. It was probably a typical Army breakfast, dry cereal, scrambled eggs, bacon, toast and coffee, all thrown together on an ice-cold stainless steel tray, which succeeded in further congealing the already stiff eggs. My memory of such things is somewhat hazy after 60 years. Specific dates and instances are only vaguely recalled, but generalities are crystal clear. I remember that the men pulling KP all seemed to be either somnolent or irritated. They certainly were not friendly. Little did I know that I would be both somnolent <u>and</u> irritated within two weeks, doing the same thing in the same place.

After breakfast, we were "straggled" to the beginning of the ordeal of physical examination. The first thing we did was get checked in against the master list of draftees just arrived. When it was determined that we were, indeed, supposed to be there, we were given a clipboard with papers on it and ushered into a locker room where were told to strip to the skin, including removal of shoes and socks. Talk about a shock! We all sort of stood there looking at each other, and wondering if we heard the man right. When assured in no uncertain terms that we were to get "bareassed, <u>now</u>", we began to remove our clothes, wondering if we would ever see them again. That was our first experience with the Army's process of stripping us of our civilian individuality and replacing it with military uniformity. We each tried very hard to pretend that we were in the room alone and no one was sizing up our inadequacies. Thus began the great leveling process.

The first order of business was to give a urine sample. Most of us, myself included, had never done that before, being old country boys away from home for the first time. We were given a bottle and shown to the urinal, which was a long trough with water flushing through it. We lined up shoulder to shoulder, not actually touching, but without our three feet of space. Being very careful to concentrate on our bottle only, once again pretending to be the only ones there, most of us managed to produce an adequate sample. The running water and a lot of coffee for breakfast stood most of us in good stead. All except one poor guy. His sphincter muscle tightened up and the harder he tried, the less likely he was to succeed. There was absolutely no sympathy on the part of the Army personnel. In fact, I'm sure they were secretly enjoying the guy's misery. He was told to stand there until he drew a sample, and believe it or not, he was still standing there in the afternoon when the rest of us went to get dressed. I've often wondered if they rejected him for not being able to pee. I never saw him again.

We went from one station to another for a battery of examinations. Every bodily opening was pried open and peered into. We were stethoscoped, both heart and lungs. We turned our heads and coughed and learned about "short arm" inspections. Our eyes were examined, our hearing tested, our teeth counted; a few guys were rejected for not having enough, and our wrists X-rayed. I found out later that the wrist X-ray was to determine if we had fully matured. Some were sent home to finish growing up. That's how near the bottom of the barrel they were getting in 1943.

The day was one of organized confusion. We were shuttled from one station to another, still naked and carrying our papers. One startling and ultimately hilarious thing happened while we were waiting to be X-rayed. Bustling into the room of naked male civilians came a technician who, at first glance, looked like a rather homely woman. You should have us seen frantically turning our backs or covering up with our clipboards. "She" ignored us and continued on through the room. We later found out that "she" was a male civilian X-ray technician with a horribly disfigured face from over exposure to high intensity X-rays that made him look like an ugly woman. That was my first encounter with the possible deleterious effects of ionizing radiation. Who would have thought that I would eventually make a career of working with and around even more lethal radiation?

As part of our physical, we had to fill out the usual medical history forms. It was there that I told about my congenital heart condition and described it as well as I could. This surfaced later in the final interview with a doctor. There seemed to be some skepticism in the doctor's attitude, but he did follow up on it. He told me that I needed to have an EKG, but that the center's unit was down and they would have to keep me in the hospital and check me out while the machine was being repaired. This was something of a letdown because I was anxious to learn my status. I wanted to either be drafted or go home. There didn't seem to be much of a choice for me at the moment, since the Army had me and could pretty much do with me what they chose. When I left home, I had resigned myself to failing the physical, so this delay did nothing to set me at ease.

By the end of the day, all the physical examination was finished and I was admitted to the base hospital for observation until the Army could determine if I was a slacker or if I really did have a heart condition. I was by this time beginning to have some faint hope that I might be drafted, after all. That was really what I wanted. At age 18, in the middle of a war where my country was in peril, I felt invulnerable and wanted to fight. There appeared that I just might get a chance to fulfill at least part of a lifelong ambition and serve in the U.S. Army Air Corps. We were told when we started through that most of that group would probably end up in the Air Corps because they had first call for qualified men for aircrew. **Oh, happy day!**

The hospital was quite an experience. It made me resolve that if I did get in the service, I was not going to get sick or hurt the whole time I served. That was one of the most boring interludes I have ever experienced. The first thing they did was to get me into hospital pajamas and a robe. That was what I wore for five days. I was in a ward with a bunch of GI's, none of whom seemed to be sick or hurt. That was my introduction to the good old Army pastime of "goofing off".

I was assigned a bed next to a sergeant who was a real nice guy. He sort of took me under his wing and showed me some of the Army ways of doing things, such as, making up a bed with hospital corners. He knew that any officer not a doctor with my chart would not know I was a civilian and would come down on me if my bed was not GI. I needed to write home and with no money and no way of getting a stamp, he introduced me to "free mail" for servicemen. Servicemen did not pay postage on their mail during the war. They put their name, rank, serial number and station in the upper left corner and wrote "Free" in place of a stamp. He let me use his name for the time I was in the hospital. Laverda was understandably perplexed when she got a letter from me with an Army sergeant's name on the return address.

Each morning, the doctor would come around and have me run in place, jump up and down and otherwise exert myself, trying to induce my heart to race. I knew that was never going to work, but I didn't suggest that I go outside and run until it acted up. The EKG machine never seemed to become operable, so each day the doctor went away becoming more convinced that I was making up my heart problem. The rest of the day was spent killing time. There was a PX there and a recreation room where we could play ping-pong and read books and magazines. That whole time there remains pretty vague. After five days of finding no evidence of a heart condition, the doctor declared me fit for duty and released me for induction.

We were given two choices before induction, Army or Navy. Very few chose the Navy. I was sworn in on 3 April, and sent on a seven-day leave to settle my affairs at home. I was to report back to Ft. Oglethorpe on 10 April, for active duty and further assignment.

I only had one significant affair to settle and that was to get married to my one and only love, Laverda King. Rather than stick that episode in the middle of my Army career, I think I will treat it by itself. It was so significant that it deserves to be a chapter by itself.

Chapter II

RAW ROOKIE

On 10 April 43, I again boarded a bus in Rutherford for the long trip to Ft. Oglethorpe, GA. Laverda and I had gotten married secretly the day before and here I was starting out our married life by leaving her to go into the Army. What a rotten start for a long-term relationship.

The bus left at about 6 AM and my brother Jab took me to meet it. I had said my goodbye to Laverda the night before and to Mama and Papa at home that morning. Jab was not the demonstrative type and, frankly, I was a little bit afraid of him. That seems a strange thing to say about your own brother so perhaps a short explanation is in order. He was sixteen years older than I and was by nature stern and reclusive at home. He had never married and was more than a little impatient with rambunctious younger siblings. He seemed to feel that our parents were unnecessarily lenient with me and my sister before me, and took it upon himself to discipline us, rather severely I might add, when he was around and we did something he didn't like. Unfortunately for us, our parents tolerated this. Although in looking back on my life, I can recall many good things he did for me because I was his little brother, but they somehow didn't stand out as vividly as the discipline he administered, occasionally. Suffice it to say I was, even at eighteen and going into the Army, still pretty reserved in his presence.

Jab, by age, might have been marginally eligible for military service except for the fact that he was nearly blind in one eye and was crippled. He had suffered from osteomyelitis as a child and had lost one of the bones in his right leg, which caused him to limp. Strangely, this never seemed

8

to hinder him athletically because he was on the high school basketball team and was a cracker jack baseball catcher. This meant that he would stay at home while his little brother went to war. That may have bothered him a little. I'll never know.

Not much was said while we sat in the car and waited for the bus. We just sat there, each with his own thoughts. I don't suppose either of us could think of anything that would be adequate to the situation. The bus came and when I got out of the car, Jab came around to me and shook my hand and nearly crushed my knuckles. He only said, "Good luck and take care of yourself." It was when I saw the tears in his eyes that I realized that he really did love me and that I loved him. Now, 67 years later, it is difficult to recall and write down because the computer screen is suddenly all blurry.

I arrived at Chattanooga late in the day and once again was bused to Ft. Oglethorpe. This time I was no longer a civilian but an Army private in civvies. I was put up for the night in the same old ratty barracks as before. The next morning I started through the process of converting from civilian to military by drawing clothes and equipment. I was issued all new clothes from the skin out, at least two of everything; underwear, socks, shoes, fatigues, shirts, pants, belt, blouse, ties, hats, mess kit and barracks bags. There were several miscellaneous items of toiletries and the like. All my clothes were too large for me, except my shoes and hats, but the supply sergeant assured me that the Army would fatten me up until they fit. That seemed likely because at that time I was 5 ft., 91/2 in. tall and weighed 121 pounds. Mama said I had to stand twice in the same place to make a decent shadow.

One of the first things we were issued was our Army serial number. We were to brand that number on our consciousness so that if awakened from a deep sleep we could recite it. It accompanied our name everywhere we went and the last four digits were stenciled on everything we owned. The first four digits identified where we were inducted and the last four identified us. After 60 years I can repeat it instantly, **34728841.**

The next few days were occupied with getting oriented. There was some attempt to teach a few items of military courtesy, like how to salute and whom to salute, how to pack our barracks bags and make up our beds. There was no close order drill other than a half-hearted attempt to teach us how to form up and march to the mess hall. Most of the time was taken with testing and interviews to see where we should be assigned for basic training. There was a fair amount of time when we had nothing to do but hang around the barracks or PX or watch the WAC's take their basic training. The Bull Pen was separated from the rest of the post by a cyclone fence ten feet high. Fraternization was not allowed, officially, that is. Those who wanted to fraternize managed to find ways to do it. Being newly married and very much in love I stayed away from the WAC area. Hanging around the barracks got me assigned to pull KP in the Bull Pen mess hall. That was quite an experience.

All Army mess halls in the WW II era were pretty much the same. The tables were just like picnic tables seating 8 – 10 GIs. You got in line, picked up a stainless steel tray, some flatware and a huge ceramic mug without a handle. As you went through the line the KPs on the serving line filled your tray with the food of the day. For breakfast you got dry cereal, juice, scrambled eggs, bacon, ham or sausage, toast and coffee or milk. For lunch and dinner you got a meat, bread, two or three vegetables, dessert and drink. The quality and quantity of food available depended on the expertise and dedication of the mess sergeant. If he was an old-timer and had been a mess sergeant for a long time, the food was pretty good. Otherwise, you could get anything from barely palatable to disgusting.

The first thing I had to do on KP was peel potatoes for lunch. There I was introduced to a mechanical potato peeler. It was a machine very much like a corn sheller where you put about a peck of potatoes in a hopper and they were spun, tossed and abraded by two toothed disks in running water until the skin was all off. You then dumped that load and put in another one. If you left them in too long, they came out about the size of marbles.

My job at mealtime was to take the dirty trays and brush off the food scraps under running water and stack them in the "China Clipper". That is what they called the dishwasher. This mess hall was the one the inductees ate in and the food was particularly unappetizing, especially to guys used to their mother's cooking. Most of the guys couldn't cope with the masses of greasy greens, and ice cream in the potatoes and gravy, so they came to my station with most of their food still on the tray. They had to scrape the trays out into a garbage can before turning them over to me. A corporal at the end of the line took delight in screaming at them for wasting food. His favorite line was, "Don't you (expletive deleted) civilians know there's a war on? There's GIs in North Africa that would kill for the food you're throwing away."

The only thing good I could say for KP was that you ate better than those you served did. Otherwise, it was hot, tiring, dirty work, especially if you got garbage detail, which always seemed to be my luck. By the end of the day I was bushed and ready to "hit the sack." That's just a little more GI talk.

Along about now, I began to lose track of the days. They began to run together, what with the push to get us classified and assigned to a basic training post. I just went from one place to another, answered the questions, performed the tests, and spent a lot "hurry up and wait" time. I really was not getting the full flavor of being in the Army because I was not yet a part of an organization. It seems like there was about a week of this routine before we were all sorted out and aimed at some part of the Army training system. The majority of us were told that we had three choices at that point, aerial gunnery, aerial gunnery, or aerial gunnery. In any event, we were all going to some Air Corps basic training camp for 12 weeks of basic, whereupon we would be sent to different schools to further our training. There is nothing like being certain of your future.

I almost forgot one of the most traumatic occurrences of my Army career that happened at Ft. Oglethorpe. I got my first GI haircut. I had long, wavy, blond hair that I had very carefully cultivated into a "ducktail"(That was the style in the 40s.). I was walking across the post shortly after I got my uniform with my little "Go to Hell" garrison hat cocked over on the side of my head and my wavy blond locks blowing in the breeze, when I encountered the First Sergeant. He said, "Soldier, the barbershop is over that way. Get that hair cut before morning."

I began to put my philosophy of instant compliance with all orders into action and headed for the barbershop. I was not the only one who had gotten the same order. That was one of the first of many lines in the Army.

I truly think there was a streak of masochism in those Army barbers, even though they were all civilians. He asked me how I would like my hair cut, and almost before I could finish telling him, most of my hair was lying on the floor, and he was chuckling with sadistic glee. The only consolation was that everyone else looked just like me. After I got over the shock of seeing my pride and joy scattered on the floor, I began to like the short hair. I have never allowed my hair to get that long again.

Houston Morgan, a boy I had gone to school with, was drafted about the same time I was and we were at Ft. Oglethorpe at the same time. Our schedules were not the same because he shipped out at a different time and to a different place. I remember that I loaned him 50 cents because he had no money and a money order he couldn't cash on the post. He shipped out owing me, but he got back home on leave during the summer and gave it to Laverda. She wrote me about it when I got to college, later.

There is one unlikely image emblazoned on my mind that can be called forth in perfect clarity any time I choose. Why I retain this truly insignificant event, I do not know. The Sunday before I shipped out, I was walking past a ball field where a pickup game of softball was going on. The batter was Houston. In high school he had never shown any interest in sports that I could recall and never played ball with the rest of us. But there he was, taking a cut at the ball that looked like he had done it all his life. Our schedule must have been out of sync because that was the last time I saw him until our 25th class reunion in 1967. Even now, as I write, the image is perfectly clear. The sunshine, the temperature, the dusty ball field, and Houston striding into the ball just like a big leaguer. This is truly weird!

On a Monday morning in April, 1943, exact date unknown, a very large group of us brand new draftees were herded like cattle onto a troop train and headed south. We were all speculating about where we were headed, but none of us knew enough about the Army to know where any of the camps were, so we could only guess that it might be somewhere in South Georgia or Alabama. There was the inevitable GI with the inside scoop who got his information from someone who heard it from someone who heard it from the mess cook who knew the officer in charge. That's how rumors go in the military. He was sure we were headed for Maxwell Field. The true destination will be revealed.

Chapter III

BASIC TRAINING

My first experience with a troop train was the trip from Ft. Oglethorpe to Miami Beach. Yes, Miami Beach. That was to be our home for the next 12 weeks. No Maxwell Field.

A troop train was a conveyance like no other in the world. It was long, slow and dirty. It had no priority, and any other train could force us onto a siding to wait for what seemed like hours. Fortunately, we did a lot of our travelling at night so it didn't seem too long. The excitement of being in the Army and going to our first real post for real training in the art of soldiering diverted the boredom that came to be a part of our lives on subsequent troop trains.

The cars on this train were made especially for transporting troops. The bunks were stacked four high and folded up in daytime and bench seats appeared. The mess car was at the front of the train and we ate out of mess kits. That was an experience! The food wasn't bad, as I recall. I was already getting into a wake/sleep routine different from the one I was in before the Army and was courting Laverda.

We no sooner got started than the poker and crap games got started. Most of us had very little money, so the stakes were not very high. By the time we got to Miami, most of the money in the games was in the possession of just a few GI's. I have never been much to gamble, so I stayed away from them.

We got to Miami Beach just before daylight, on some day of the week, and were dumped off the train right in the middle of the most posh winter resort in the country. That was truly a shock to this old country boy for whom Reelfoot Lake was the biggest body of water he had ever seen. Most of us, it turned out were from Tennessee with a few Chicagoans thrown in. Watching the sun come up over the Atlantic Ocean was a sight I shall never forget. That was the first body of water I had ever seen that you couldn't see across.

Perhaps a little explanation about this basic training base is in order. In the rush to get training facilities for the millions of troops needed for this war, all sorts of expediencies were developed.

Since travel was severely restricted and vacations at the beach frowned upon, the Beach, as it came to be called, came on hard times. Some enterprising soul in the Air Corps came up with the idea of using the nearly empty hotels to house troops. There were numerous vacant lots and parking lots that could be used for drill, calisthenics and lectures in the balmy Florida sunshine. The idea was first floated for Officer Candidate School (OCS), and later for basic. OCS stayed in the midtown hotels and drilled on a golf course. Draftees stayed in the smaller hotels in the south of town and drilled on the vacant lots and took calisthenics on the beach. There were still permanent residents there and they seemed to merely tolerate the military. They went about their daily routine as though we were invisible. Many of them were relocated Yankees of the Jewish persuasion and, if you watched closely, you could see the distaste in their faces at all these brash, energetic young men who were disrupting their neighborhood and cluttering up their beach. The war and its inconveniences were things to be just tolerated until we all went away and left them alone.

Despite the seemingly idyllic setting, I'm here to tell you that the Army can turn the Garden of Eden into a facility you would like to get far away from. Take all the furniture and carpets out of a hotel room in Miami Beach, put in three double decker army bunks and you have a barracks. All in all, I guess we did have it pretty good compared to some of the other Basic posts. From what we heard later about Sheppard Field in Wichita Falls, TX, and Jefferson Barracks in St. Louis, I guess we did have it easy. I learned to feel sorry for the fellows who had to endure those places, but never sorry enough to want to change places with them.

I was billeted in the Lord Balfour Hotel at Fourth and Ocean Drive. There were two training flights in the Lord Balfour, H and F, about the equivalent of an Army company of 200 men. I was in Flight F with the above mentioned Tennesseans and Chicagoans. Flight H consisted of Bostonians. Right away you can see the potential for intense rivalry and even conflict. None of us had ever been very far from home, but I believe the Bostonians were more provincial than the Tennesseans. I don't believe many of them had been out of their neighborhood. That didn't keep them from looking down their noses at us "hillbillies." I discovered that Bostonians look down their noses at everyone. This fact was confirmed in later years as I encountered Bostonians in other settings.

There were other flights in other hotels. I don't remember just how many there were, but the whole basic training class consisted of several thousand men. We all came together occasionally for a large review formation to see how we were coming along with our close order drill training. For the most part, my life was pretty much circumscribed by flights F and H. We drilled together, we attended class together, had PT (physical training) together, went to chow together, pulled KP together, all the while maintaining the individual flight identity. We even took our breaks together, and that is when the Civil War was fought all over again. The South won that version of the war because we had been more thoroughly indoctrinated by our culture to the injustice that was done to us by the Damyankees. Besides that, most of the fighting had taken place in the South and we knew in intimate detail how the battles were fought. Most of us had forebears in that war and many of us knew veterans still living. The Bostonians really only knew what they had been taught in history class by Yankee educated teachers. They didn't have the advantage of having the Civil War taught by teachers whose parents and grandparents had fought on the losing side. I had Civil War history in the eighth grade and my teacher was the daughter of a veteran. I didn't know the South lost the war until the last day of school.

As I recall, my room had four bunks in it, which gave me three roommates, all from Chicago. They were Roland Torma, Jim Sills and Tom Gregg. Gregg applied for A.S.T.P, which I think stood for Aviation Student Training Program. Anyway, before he got very far into Basic, he was shipped out to The Citadel for testing and classification to determine his acceptability for the program. I got a letter from him some time later telling us he was going on to college for 39 weeks, after which he would go to OCS to become an officer. I think Gregg had had ROTC in college, so the Army thought he could dispense with the rest of Basic. All through Basic, men would sort of not show up for roll call, and we would find out later that they had been shipped out. On rare occasions, a man might be discharged with a section eight (undesirable) discharge.

Torma and Sills were really nice guys from different backgrounds. Torma was a first generation Yugoslavian whose father worked in the steel mills, and he, Roland, had come from the foundry of one of the carmakers. Sills was from Evanston, which made him from the upper middle class, and I believe his father was a professor at Northwestern, where Jim was a freshman. Despite our vastly different backgrounds, we got along well. There was never any friction. When everybody has the same haircut and wear the same clothes, differences are pretty well submerged. We were all learning how to be soldiers together and we all were pretty much starting from the same point.

Jim Sills finished out Basic and was assigned to the testing and classification center at The Citadel like Tom Gregg. We corresponded for awhile and I still have his letters. They bring back a lot of memories when I reread them. In one of Jim's letters he thanked me for paying the $2.00 I owed him from Basic. I remember that I had to borrow from him when my wallet was stolen from our room one afternoon while we were at chow. I had left my wallet and money belt with $75.00 in it in my room after taking a shower. I remembered it at chow and told the sergeant and he said had better hot foot it back to the hotel before it was stolen. I didn't make it. We found them behind the blinds in another room, both empty. I borrowed from the guys until I could get some money from home. Payday was too far away.

I was able to do Jim a favor after the loan when he was scheduled for guard duty on Sunday night and couldn't make it because he had gone to sleep on the beach that day and gotten second degree burns on his back. I took his place. He was pretty grateful for that.

From the very first formation at Ft. Oglethorpe, we were constantly being taught something, and it really intensified when we got to the Beach. We had to learn how to fall in, first. When the order came to "Fall in!" we, as a group of newly uniformed civilians, would likely be just milling around in the area, not knowing what to do, waiting for some kind of order. At that command, we at first had to be almost placed by hand in some sort of order. The non-commissioned officer in charge would tell us to line up facing him in four lines. You just got in line somewhere, usually behind another line. It was a little difficult for everyone to be in a line behind another line, because not everyone can be in the rear rank. This led to some pretty choice language by the non-com, but sooner or later, we managed to form four more or less equal ranks facing the same way. This, I think, is called a "company front". We were then told to "dress right".

Dress right? What the heck does that mean? Patiently, we were told that everyone but the first man on the right was to look to the right and then stretch out our left arm parallel to the ground and touch the shoulder of the man to our left. This led to a lot of shuffling, pushing and stumbling until the formation was stabilized with each man in a row an arms length from his neighbor. This was the basic formation and was the one we assumed when we fell out for anything.

Once we were organized into flights, our real basic training began. The first time we fell out in Miami Beach we were arranged in our permanent positions. The tallest man in the flight was always on the right in the front row. The second tallest was behind him, and so forth until the shortest guy was way down at the leftmost position in the back row. Once we were in formation, we were told to memorize the men around us, side to side and front to back, and always get into that position. Believe it or not, it didn't take long for us to form up like that, automatically. Sometimes we would dress right or left by placing our hands on our hips and closing up the formation until our elbows touched the man next to us. This made for a very closed packed formation.

Although the normal cadence was 120 steps a minute, you must realize that there was a significant between the length of a pace of a tall guy and short one, although the Army specification on paces is 30" each. You can imagine that the little guy in the rear of a formation had to really stretch his step to keep up if a really tall GI led the whole formation. In a large formation doing a left turn in a review, the man on the outside end literally had to run to keep up, and that didn't look too good to the brass.

Each flight had what is called a guidon. That is a staff about six feet long with an identifying pennant, in our case, a blue triangle with a white "F". The Guidon Bearer in front of the formation carried it and he set the pace. It was the practice of most flights to make the shortest GI in the flight the Guidon Bearer. That helped take some of the pressure off the rear of the formation.

The next command we learned was "Right Face" or "Left Face". This required a little footwork that had to be demonstrated and practiced. It was a simple heel and toe pivot, but you would be surprised how many men had trouble getting it down right. With a "Right Face" command we found ourselves in a column of fours and the next logical command was "Forward March", or "**Fowaaahd Hahch**". Before long, we found that none of the commands from the drill instructor came out sounding like the printed word in the Army Field Manual, and sometimes you had to guess what he was saying based on the next logical command from the formation you were in. A failure to guess right on the part of one or two men resulted in a thoroughly screwed up formation.

At the "Forward March" command, we all stepped smartly off with our left foot first to the cadence count of "Hut, hoop, heep, ho", or "one, two, three, four" in English. Actually, it was <u>not</u> so very smartly. It was more of a stumble start, but with a little practice and a lot of blue vocabulary on the part of the DI, we could approximate a drill formation. In this basic column of fours formation we marched everywhere; to chow, to the drill field, to class, or anywhere else we needed to go as a flight.

When we arrived at the Beach, there was a basic class already there about half way through their twelve weeks, so they could already march fairly well. I was astounded to hear them singing as they marched. Man, I thought that was the greatest sound I had ever heard. I could hardly wait to get a chance to step off to the **U. S. Army Air Corps** song. Among the first things we were issued when we got there was a list of the songs we would be marching to. We were instructed to learn them as soon as possible. Singing as we marched not only helped us keep cadence it also was a great morale booster. It gave us sort of panache that helped ease a little of the homesickness we all felt, and made us feel more a part of a larger group and gave us a special feeling about ourselves. It also brought us to the attention of the civilians about us to let them know that we were getting ready to go off and protect them. After the war, I read an interview of some people who lived in Miami Beach and they told of how they enjoyed hearing the soldiers sing as they marched. I'm sure they didn't interview any of the people I mentioned earlier. For the rest of the war, all the small formations I marched in sang as we marched. In addition to the Air Corps Song, some of the songs we sang were:

> The Field Artillery Song
> The Marine Hymn
> She Wore a Yellow Ribbon
> Someone's in the Kitchen with Dinah
> I've Got Sixpence
> Oh, Mom, I Wanta go Home

And many, many more; some of which had fairly ribald lyrics. We weren't allowed to sing them except on a regular base, away from civilians. Notice how quickly I have begun to distinguish between GI's and civilians? Sometimes, the word "civilian" could take on a rather pejorative connotation, depending upon the tone of voice and situation.

> One of our <u>own </u>songs went like this:
> "Flight F's the best flight on the Beach,
> This we all know.
> Whenever we go out,
> The people always shout
> Flight F's the best flight on the Beach."
> Da, da, da, da, da, da, da, da."
> And then repeat the refrain, endlessly.

The first formation of the day was immediately after reveille. We fell out in the street beside the hotel for roll call. The sergeant would call our names in alphabetical order, and it was sometimes hilarious to hear him mangle the names. One he especially had trouble with was Wojeihowski. After a while, Woj would just answer, "Here" after the name just before his, because the sergeant would always pause trying to figure it out. It was sort of a standing joke in the flight. Woj didn't think it was particularly funny, but he took it good-naturedly. What else could he do?

Each month, we had to sign the payroll voucher before we could get paid. Under our name there was a box that would just about contain our signature, if you were careful. There were certain things that could get your pay redlined, which meant you did not get paid that month. You didn't forfeit any pay; you just drew it the next month, if you didn't get redlined again. In signing the payroll you had to keep your signature completely in the box, or get redlined. The ink could not touch the box anywhere. I never knew the reason for that, if, indeed, there was a reason. Some things you had to do had no reason, you just had to do them. Woj's full name was Gilbert C. Wojeihowski and he couldn't get it all in the box properly. I know that he was redlined the first two pay periods, at least. We didn't need much spending money and at $21/mo, we didn't have much, but there were a few things that we had to buy, like toothpaste, shaving cream, soap and other toiletries. Sometimes we could go out to movies or to soda fountains or juice stands, or bars. Most of us took pity on Woj and treated him until he could get paid. As I recall, he paid all of us back.

We soon settled into a routine of drill, classes and PT. In drill we learned to execute all the necessary movements on command and without thinking. Forward March, Column Right, Column Left, To the Rear,

Right Oblique, Left Oblique, Double Time and others that I don't recall at the moment. At first, we seemed to all have two left feet and no sense of rhythm, but fairly quickly, we began to shape up. From time to time, certain of us would be chosen to drill the flight. I was never quite sure what the criteria were for temporary DI, but I think it had something to do with size and loudness of voice. I was never chosen and did not miss it a bit.

There were classes in military justice, military courtesy, organization of the Air Corps, why we were fighting, some infantry tactics, and other fairly useless things. Since we were all, or most all, destined to become air crewmen we learned about aircraft maintenance, radio and armory. We were told that since we were all going into aerial gunnery, like it or not, we needed to be able to choose one of the three specialties above. Somewhere in our basic training stint we were tested and retested to determine our aptitude for these specialties, and then they placed us in the specialty that needed warm bodies without regard to test scores, mental or physical capabilities or other qualifications. The ways of the military are mysterious, indeed.

One of the things that came as a great shock and surprise to most of us civilian soldiers was the Army's insistence on extreme cleanliness and orderliness in the barracks, or rooms, in our case. There was one way to make up a bed, the Army way. There was one way to pack our footlockers, the Army way. There was one way to clean our floors, one way to shine

our shoes, one way to tie our tie and tuck it in, one way to wear our hats, one way to line up our shirt fly, belt buckle and pants fly. **The Army Way!**

It was often said, not entirely facetiously, "There are three ways to do everything. The right, the wrong way, and the Army way." I'm sure the Navy and Marines said the same thing, substituting their particular service.

There was a daily inspection with increasingly severe criticisms and tongue-lashings as we began to slowly learn how to do things the way the Army wanted them done. On Saturday there was "white glove" inspection by the CO, and on the outcome of that inspection depended how you would

Window Cleaning for
inspection

spend your free time that weekend. I was never confined to quarters, but some of the less meticulous types were. Fortunately, my roommates and I were quick studies and we never had one person screw it up for the whole room.

PT was an integral part of our daily routine. Most of us were in pretty lousy shape, all things considered, and it was up to the PT instructors to get us into fighting trim as quickly as possible. Each session started out with calisthenics; toe touches, deep knee bends, torso twists, side straddle hops, sit-ups, push-ups and lots of other torture tricks. We had one instructor that liked to show off by doing more one-arm push-ups than we could do on two.

Most of the time, we took PT on a drill field, but occasionally, we went to the beach in the soft Florida sand. That felt pretty good until we had to run in it. That killed your legs in a hurry. Fortunately, PT on the beach also meant that we got to finish up the session in the water. That was my first experience with swimming in the ocean and to my surprise, it really was salty. This was a far cry from the muddy old pond or even the Milan swimming pool. I liked it.

The combination of regular hours, plenty of good food and sunshine, lots of marching and the PT were really making me feel good and putting some pounds on my skinny frame. By the end of Basic, I was up to 145 lbs. of fightin' muscle.

As a hangover from WW I, the Army had a thing about soldiers learning how to use a gas mask. This device became a part of us. We put it on just like we put on our shoes and socks. We were not allowed to go anywhere without it when on duty. It hung on our side not unlike a book bag in grammar school. It had to be packed just right or you couldn't get it out and on your face properly in the required amount of time. The technique for removing it and placing it on your head as quickly as possible was drummed into our heads, again and again. If someone yelled *"GAS"*, you stopped whatever you were doing, snatched the mask out of its bag, and as quickly as possible, affixed it to your head, all the while holding your breath.

As part of our training, we would occasionally be unexpectedly tear gassed to test our reaction time. You only dawdled or were haphazard once. After that, you did it the Army way.

Part of our military training was learning to handle and fire a rifle. This was done at a camp in the dunes of the north end of the beach. That area was totally undeveloped and consisted of sand, scrubby bushes and flies. They had set up a "tent city" there with field kitchens, slit trenches and a rifle range. This was to introduce us to living in the field. This place was twelve miles from our hotel and we were required to march up there carrying our rifles, gas masks, mess kits and canteens. Fortunately, being in the Air Corps, we didn't have field packs like the infantry, but it was uncomfortable enough with what we were carrying. We were issued rifles just before the march and given some instruction in the manual of arms. Having teethed on guns, most of the Tennessee boys took to this like ducks to water. The kids from Chicago and Boston were mostly unfamiliar with rifles although some of them might have known about submachine guns, the favorite weapon of the underworld.

Around the turn of the century, the U. S. Army converted from the Krag rifle to the 1903 Springfield, .30-06 caliber. This was the standard piece for the Army and Marines until 1936, when the Garand rifle was adopted. At the same time, the British were using the Lee-Enfield rifle, which was very much like the Springfield. Somehow, our army had come into the possession of a large quantity of these rifles, and this was the rifle that the Air Corps trainees had to use. There were not enough of the new Garand rifles for our ground troops, let alone Air Corps types, so most of the remaining serviceable Springfield's were in the hands of "real fighting men". That left us with British WW-I cast-offs. Don't get me wrong, we were glad to have any kind of weapon, even if we only got to carry it and use it on the range. Come to think of it, that gun went pretty well with the horse cavalry hats they issued us at the Beach. Apparently, there was a large supply of these hats and guns lying around in warehouses somewhere and somebody in the Quartermaster Corps hit upon the idea of using them in Air Corps basic training. I guess that was a pretty smart thing to do. We needed the arms training and the Lee-Enfield was a serviceable enough piece for that and the hot Florida sun required some sort of head covering with a brim so the cavalry hat sufficed there.

For some reason, all basic trainees in the Army were required to qualify with, or at least, be exposed to four different types of firearms. We first had to learn how to shoot the rifle before progressing on to other guns. This first trip to Tent City was for the purpose of exposing us to long marches, field conditions and teaching us to shoot. As I recall, four flights made the trek to Tent City. We fell out in our fatigues with gas masks, canteens, mess kits and rifles early one morning. We started off up Collins Avenue with our rifles at right shoulder arms and marching in step. We were looking good! I think this was a show for the civilians and the brass up at the National Hotel, base headquarters.

It's been said that the Lee-Enfield rifle weighs 8.6 lbs., at first, but after about five miles, the decimal drops out and goes home. I believe it! It didn't take long for that gun to get very heavy. From time to time the sergeant would let us go to left shoulder arms for a rest. This marching in step didn't last long and we were allowed to sling our rifles and go to route step, which meant we just walked with no attempt to stay in step. That also made the march a little easier. Every hour we were allowed a "take ten, smoke if you got 'em" break, whereupon we would collapse on the side of the road in the shade, if we could find any. That break is the shortest ten minutes known to man.

When we arrived at Tent City we were assigned to tents, four to six men to a tent. They were very rudimentary accommodations. The only amenities were canvas cots. We had each packed a barracks bag with clean clothes and toiletries to do us for three days. These were sent ahead by truck and we collected them and set up housekeeping.

It was here that we learned about slit trench latrines. These were located away from the camp and generally down wind. They consisted of narrow trenches dug in the sand, and to answer the most basic call of nature required one to straddle the trench and assume a squatting position. This was no place for modesty. (My Vietnam vet son-in-law tells me that they were still using slit trenches in Nam at the forward artillery positions. And the feminists today want women in combat roles. What do they propose, His and Hers slit trenches?) They did provide toilet tissue and a trenching shovel as well as a supply of quicklime to "flush" with.

At chow call, we grabbed our mess kits and headed for the field kitchen. The Army mess kit is truly a great invention. It has remained pretty much unchanged since just after the Civil War. When folded up, it is about the size of a salad plate. When opened, it consists of two shallow pans hooked securely together with one of them having two compartments. A fork and a spoon and maybe a knife, I'm not sure about the knife, were inside the kit. Our canteen, which we carried slung to a web belt, sat inside an aluminum cup with a folding handle and this cup was used for drinking. You held the open mess kit in one hand with your flatware and the cup in the other as you went through the chow line. Your food was ladled into the compartments of the mess kit. True to form, the KPs managed to mix the most unlikely food items by just throwing the food at the kit. They seemed to get a perverse delight in screwing up the arrangement of your food. A fastidious eater either got over his squeamishness or went very hungry. After being served, you sat down in the sand away from cooking odors and raced the flies for your food.

After eating you washed your mess kit thoroughly in three barrels of very hot water. You first scraped out your kit in a garbage can and there was usually plenty of food to scrape. Field kitchen food is not a gourmet's delight. The first barrel had a GI brush and soapy water and you were supposed to give the kit a good scrubbing with the GI lye soap. The other two barrels were for rinsing. The last one was actually boiling. We were constantly admonished to clean our mess kits thoroughly. If we failed to get all the grease off, we could be sure of getting dysentery, or more commonly the GIs and you would become more familiar with the slit trench latrine than you wanted to.

The primary reason for the stay in Tent City was for us to fire on the range. The range was laid out facing the open ocean. The target butts were just behind the dunes that paralleled the beach and the firing line was about 100 yards inland from the butts. The targets were about four feet square wooden frames covered by a paper bull's-eye. They were arranged in pairs that could be raised and lowered to change targets. As one went up the other came down. These were manned by GIs not scheduled to be firing and were under the command of a non-com who was in communication with the firing line by phone. As each shot was fired, the strike was noted and the position indicated to the firing line by holding a large round disk mounted on a long pole over the bullet hole. This was to show the shooter just how far off the bull's-eye he was. Believe it or not, the target was missed completely sometimes and then a white flag called "Maggie's drawers" was waved across the target. I was never embarrassed that way.

The name of each shooter was relayed to the target crew before he began to shoot so one of the spotters could record his score on a target sheet. When a shooter finished a set, the target was pulled down and a spotter recorded the hits positions by crosses on the record sheet. These were sent to the firing line after the shooting was done for the session.

There was a large number of firing stations along the line, so when firing started it sounded like a small war because the .30-06 is a very noisy round. This was a very exciting time for me and the rest of the Tennesseans, because we were in our element. The men from Boston and Chicago were not very comfortable and had to be coached carefully or they could get in trouble.

We were required to fire from four positions, prone, sitting, kneeling and off-hand. Each of us had an instructor behind us to make sure that we did everything right. The sling had to be adjusted, our position made right and the gun held just so. As I have said before, the Tennesseans needed very little instructions. We settled right in and got ready to fire with a minimum of direction. We were shown how to load the clip of rounds, snug the stock against our shoulder and squeeze the trigger, not jerk it. About the only thing new that I learned was that you do not grasp a high powered rifle with your thumb <u>over</u> the stock like you can a .22. You essentially cradle the stock in your trigger hand. Failure to do that may put a thumb in your eye on recoil. Some people had to learn that the hard way by getting a black eye.

After all the shooters had learned how to hold and dry fire the rifle, we were told to stand back of the firing line and hold our piece muzzle up. The order was given to, "Move up to the line." We would move up to the line and take our position and be handed our ammo.

Once all the shooters were ready, the line non-com would call out, "Ready on the right? Ready on the left? Ready on the firing line. Commence firing!" That was when the young war started. When all rounds had been expended the order to cease firing was given, and everyone moved off the line and another batch took our place.

I had a pretty good rifle because most of my shots were in or around the bull. My instructor said, "Where you from, soldier?"

Tennessee", I said.

"That explains it", he said. "You handle a piece like you've done it before."

I said, "I grew up with a rifle in my hand."

"Most of you Tennessee guys are good. We won't have teach you much" he replied.

Some time later, the instructor brought a Bostonian over to me and told him to, "Watch how Tennessee here does it, and see if you can't learn something from him."

Needless to say, that made me swell with pride a little. It was just a little more proof to me that the "superior" Bostonians were superior only in their own minds. I already knew that I could do anything they could do, and some things I could do a lot better. My day was made.

Although I had used a rifle from before I was six years old and was a pretty good shot, I had never fired a high powered rifle, and the Lee-Enfield was definitely a high powered rifle. I was not prepared for the kick that gun had. A shotgun was mild compared to the .30-06. The recoil is entirely different. The shotgun gives you sort of an abrupt shove in the shoulder and can be pretty rough on a first time shooter. The rifle feels like someone has slammed the muzzle with a sledgehammer driving the stock back into your shoulder. That kick is what disconcerted most of us at first because it was so unexpected. It took considerable self-control not to flinch as you squeezed the trigger. As the day wore on, the scores tended to get more erratic as our shoulders got sorer. The second day out many of us brought a towel to pad our shoulders with. That helped a great deal. One of the trainees said that each time he fired he had to crawl back up from the ready line. That was a bit of an exaggeration, but the recoil was pretty scary.

I learned a little bit about rifle design through my experience with the Lee-Enfield. I had a chance at the range to examine a Springfield. There were some there, but we were not allowed to shoot them, just look at them. I noticed that the Springfield had a considerable drop at the comb, the part of the stock just back of the bolt. The Lee-Enfield had practically no drop at the comb. This meant that the recoil of the Lee-Enfield went straight along the stock transferring all of the jolt into the shoulder. The Springfield recoil causes the muzzle to rise, thereby lessening the jolt to the shoulder. This might seem like it would cause inaccuracy during rapid fire, but the effect was easily compensated for. Those with experience with both guns said the Springfield was much the better, more accurate rifle.

Although we did not shoot to qualify as marksman or expert marksman, I think I could have qualified with a rifle that I had been allowed to sight in. Mostly, we just shot with the piece we were issued and compensated as we learned where it shot. Some of them were pretty badly off. The objective was not to qualify us, but to familiarize us with firearms we might be called upon to use someday.

After three days on the range, we struck camp and marched back to our hotel. The trip back was just as tiring and miserable as the trip up. We cleaned our rifles and turned them in and, at that point, I was glad I was in the Air Corps and not the infantry. I would have hated to have to be responsible for the care and upkeep of a rifle, not to mention the other things that ground pounders had to put up with. Twenty-mile hikes with forty-pound packs on your back and twenty pounds of mud on your boots were not my cup of tea.

We had one other trip to Tent City to fire other types of weapons; the .30 cal. carbine, sub-machine gun and .45 cal. automatic pistol. The carbine was fired on a 1000-inch range instead of the 100-yard range. By comparison to the .30-06, the carbine was a popgun. Being gas operated and with a light load, there was very little recoil, so it was a joy to fire. It was designed as a close-in weapon for use in street fighting. That was the weapon most used by the GIs in all branches.

The submachine gun was quite a surprise. It could be fired on full automatic or single fire. Full automatic was fun, but most of us sprayed our rounds all over the range before we learned to fire in short bursts. There were two types of submachine guns, the Thompson and the so-called, "grease gun". The Tommy gun was a precision piece of machinery that was expensive and prone to jamming if not kept scrupulously clean. This was not easy in combat, so the Army came up with the grease gun. It was made much lighter and without the Thompson's close tolerances so it took mishandling better without jamming. It also was not particularly accurate, but that didn't seem to matter since that weapon was designed for "hosing down" an area with sheer volume of lead.

The .45 cal. automatic pistol was the sidearm of most officers and was carried mostly for effect. It looked good. Most people couldn't hit the side of a barn from the inside with it, but I found it to be very easy to fire and hit pretty much what I aimed at. Twenty-five yards was about the maximum range at which you could expect to hit a man-sized target. At that range, I could put six out of seven rounds in a silhouette. Thank heavens, I never had to fire one in anger.

Those two trips to the range pretty much did it for firearms training for Air Corps trainees until they got into their aerial gunnery specialty. Since we were not going to defend ourselves on the ground, at close range, familiarization was all that was thought necessary. A few unlucky souls that washed out of flight training may have ended up in the infantry, but not many. I hope they got some more range training.

Willie B.

As we made our way through basic training, certain shortcomings in the system began to manifest themselves. Some people were just not suited to the aviation environment and were slated to end up in ground jobs. Some were not even suited to be in the military, at all. One such case was Willie B. In today's "politically correct" climate, Willie would be considered to be developmentally challenged. How he ever got past the initial evaluation was a mystery. Either he was not all there, or he <u>was</u> all there and was the greatest actor I ever saw, because he was finally sent home with an unfit discharge.

Willie couldn't march. He couldn't stay in step and he couldn't count cadence. It was useless to try to teach him the close order drill movements, because he didn't seem to know his left from his right. He never learned the different ranks, so he resorted to calling everyone, "Mac", even officers. The DI's couldn't get mad at him, because he was just about the most good-natured guy you ever saw. Willie loved Roy Acuff and would sing "The Great Speckled Bird" or "The Wreck on the Highway" at the drop of a hat. Occasionally, we would have to miss a drill session because of a rain shower, so we would gather with our DI's under cover somewhere and have a bull session. We probably learned more about being soldiers in these sessions than in the formal classroom sessions. Everybody but Willie, that is. He was often called upon to entertain us with an Acuff tune or answer questions put to him by the DI's. At first, they thought it was hilarious to poke fun at him, but before long, Willie won them over and they began to protect him. They didn't make him drill or do any of the onerous things that are part of early Army training, because he would thoroughly screw up a formation. The non-coms must have alerted the brass to the fact that Willie never should have been drafted, because about halfway through basic, he got a discharge and was sent home. About eighteen months later I met one of Willie's home town buddies who told me Willie had gotten a job at a defense industry and was making $2.40 an hour. That was a princely sum in 1944. I've often wondered just how retarded Willie was.

The subject of Willie brings to mind a story that I heard while in basic. It seems there was a draftee that developed a peculiar idiosyncrasy early in his basic training. He was seen walking around the drill field at every break, picking up pieces of paper. He would pick one up and examine it very closely. Then he would say, "That ain't it," and throw it down.

He kept doing this every free minute. Pick up a piece of paper, examine it, say, "That ain't it," and throw it down. This went on day after day until the DI's got fed up with it and decided he was crazy and recommended him for a Section 8 discharge. The post psychiatrist examined him and agreed, the guy was nuts.

Headquarters processed the discharge and called the private in and handed him the paper. He examined it carefully and exclaimed, "This is it!"

I have often wondered if Willie took his discharge and said,
"This is it!"

Among the commands that we soon learned was, "Fall out! Police the area. "Police up the area?" What in the world did that mean? This was immediately followed by, "If it's on the ground, pick it up. If it moves, salute it. If it doesn't move and it's too big to pick up, paint it." This was the Army's unique way of telling us to clean up the place. That meant to pick up every piece of paper, cigarette butt, over sized rock, miscellaneous wood chip, box, or can. Anything that did not appear to belong on the ground was to be picked up and put in a proper trash container. This seemed a bit excessive to me, at first, but as I became more experienced and saw what pigs uncontrolled crowds can be, it made sense. Just imagine how many cigarette butts alone would accumulate in an Army compound over a few days time. The Army's intent was to leave an area cleaner when it left than it was when it came in. By and large, it succeeded.

Another command was, "GI your butts." This rather vulgar command meant to split your dead cigarette butt, scatter the tobacco, roll up the paper into a tiny ball and throw it away. Cigarette paper, being tissue-like would dissolve in the first rain and the tobacco would become part of the ground. A few GI's were already into filter tips and they ended up with something the Army didn't allow on the ground. When they asked the DI what to do with the filter he told them to eat it. They finally resorted to putting them in their pockets for disposal later, or changed their brand of smokes.

There were two duties that no GI ever liked or looked forward to, but could always count on having to pull, sooner or later. KP and guard duty were always around for punishment for "goof offs" and malingerers, and for the rest of us to experience as part of our total military training.

Each squadron, or pair of flights, was scheduled for KP at least twice in the basic program. Each mess hall was under the supervision of a mess sergeant who had several cooks and other permanent party under him. The KPs were the guys who literally did all the dirty work. We cleaned up the place, washed the dishes, prepared much of the food for cooking, served the food, and collected and disposed of the garbage. We reported early for breakfast and stayed until the evening meal was disposed of and the mess hall cleaned and shaped up for the next day. The only good part of KP duty was that we got to eat early and sometimes got some goodies that the cooks had prepared for themselves. These were dishes that were generally better than you found on the serving line. By the time the day was over, we were all very tired and very dirty and ready to "hit the sack".

I seemed to always get the garbage detail. This meant that I first had to clean the garbage cans from the previous meal so they would be ready to receive the next onslaught of garbage. I was equipped with a stiff brush and a bar of GI soap. This was probably the strongest lye soap that could be found anywhere in the world. It would literally take the skin off your hands after a day's exposure. With plenty of hot water, soap and elbow grease I was expected to get the cans so clean you could "see your face in the bottom". Slight exaggeration, but not much.

Just like a lot of Army ways, this seemed at first to be a useless exercise, and it was overdone by some mess sergeants, but it did have sound reasoning behind it. Just imagine how filthy a greasy garbage can could get in a very short time of not being cleaned. The smell alone would be awful, and they would be a breeding place of all sorts of flies and disease. Good personal and corporate hygiene were demanded by the Army.

One kid from our flight was assigned to garbage detail with me and as soon as the mess sergeant went inside the mess hall, the kid took off, rented a row boat and spent the rest of the day floating around in Biscayne Bay, in sight of the mess hall. Somehow, he never got caught and I ended up with the detail to myself. It just as well the guy beat it, because if he had hung around I still would have had to do it all and there just might have been a fight.

Guard duty at the Beach was sort of a sham, in the sense that we were actually guarding a sensitive facility. It was mainly a training exercise. Certain beats were laid out and we trainees were required to patrol an assigned beat, armed with a billy club that looked like about two feet of hoe handle. These beats were around hotels, beside drill fields, and other miscellaneous "military" sites. Just what we were guarding or guarding against was never clear to me.

We were required to be in Class A uniform; khakis, dress shoes and garrison cap. Our post was numbered and we were expected to remember that number so that we could sing it out in case we needed the corporal of the guard. The post had limits, say, from one corner of a block to another, or along one side of a drill field. We had to walk slowly back and forth the length of our post for four hours, or until relieved. Routine guard duty was usually from Retreat until Lights Out.

If trouble arose, which was unlikely, we were to call out, "Corporal of the Guard. Post number 8." This was relayed up the line to Post 7, Post 6, etc., until it reached the guard headquarters, which was Post number 1. Whereupon the corporal of the guard would jump in his Jeep and rush down to Post number 8 to see what was up. About the only thing we might have to call the corporal of the guard for might be a civilian trying to go into a hotel. This happened to me one time. I was on duty in front of the hotel one Sunday afternoon when a civilian tried to walk up on the front porch where some of the squadron permanent party were hanging out. I had been told that the hotel was off limits to civilians and tried to stop him. He ignored me and kept going. Not knowing what else to do, I tried to restrain him and call the corporal of the guard. Just before I was about to rap him on the head, one of the sergeants told me to let him go. It turned out that he was the civilian barber and he was going into his shop in the lobby. The nom-coms were getting a big kick out of my dilemma until they saw I was getting agitated. I don't know if I would have hit him, or not. I'm sure glad I didn't have to find out.

One of the pluses of being stationed at Miami Beach was that my sister Julie and her brand new husband, Major J. R. Young were stationed at Coral Gables, and we got to spend quite a bit of my off duty hours together. As soon as I found out that Julie was in the area, I called her. We were both delighted; because we were both far from home in a strange land of strange people. Having her near made my stay there more enjoyable, and I hope it had a similar effect on her.

I had never met Rog, and hadn't seen Julie for a long time. The first Sunday that Rog had some time off they drove over to the Lord Balfour to see me. I was lounging around the front of the hotel when this 1940 Buick convertible pulled up and stopped, and this sharp looking Major and very attractive young lady got out. All conversation among the non-coms on the porch stopped when this scrawny buck private strode up, threw the Major a sharp salute and hugged the girl. From that day forward I was sort of a marked man. I seemed to get a bit more respect than was normally accorded basic trainees, who were generally considered lower than dirt by the permanent party personnel.

Julie and Rog lived off post in a neat little, typical Florida bungalow in Coral Gables. I had Sunday dinner with them a few times, and we went riding about the area some. We didn't ride around much because gas was in short supply, and Rog was somewhat tight fisted, a characteristic that he still has. I guess that is one of the reasons he is a millionaire a few times over. Needless to say, their being there certainly proved to be a boon to me.

Early in my stay at the Beach, my oldest sister, Mozelle, came to visit Julie and Rog, and we were able to spend some time together. It was out of this visit by Moz that my Army career took a decidedly different turn. At this point,

Mozelle and I in Rog's Buick

I had reconciled myself to following the course the Army had laid out for me; finish basic, go to technical school, gunnery school and then overseas as an enlisted air crewman. I realize that it must seem most unlikely that a country woman lawyer from the county seat of Gibson County, Tennessee, could so profoundly affect the course of history as to change the career of one of the Army's budding heroes, but she did.

The war had an impact on the lives of most people, in all walks of life. One such was Hal Holmes, a lawyer from Trenton, TN, who was a friend of Mozelle. He, being a lawyer, took a commission in the Army Air Corps and was stationed at the headquarters of the Beach training command. Moz knew this and had promised to look him up when she came to visit Julie. I had often talked of my desire to become a pilot and fly for the Army. The whole family knew this and was sure that it would never even be a possibility, that is, until I ended up in the Air Corps. The subject came up while Moz was there, and she suggested that since we were going to see Hal and he was in headquarters, maybe he might be able to give me some pointers on how I might get into the cadet program.

While we were visiting with Hal one Sunday, I asked him if there was any way I could get into the aviation cadet program. We had all been told by the Army to forget trying to get into some other program. We were going to be aerial gunners, and that applications for transfer to some other program would be ignored. Hal said that he would look into it and see what he could do. That was all I could ask. I didn't want any special favors, just a chance. If I could somehow get my foot in the door, I felt I could take it from there. I wanted to make it on my own merit.

Early in the week, after I talked to Hal, I got a call to the First Sergeant's office. He said, "I don't know how you did it, but you have orders to report to headquarters to be tested for entrance into the Aviation Student Program."

He knew that I had not applied through his office, but Flight Headquarters did not oppose Training Command Headquarters, so off I went.

So far in my army career, I had not had an episode of tachycardia, but I had not been faced with something that meant so much to me. I was afraid that I might get excited enough for it to start up, so I exerted every ounce of will to stay calm. I kept telling myself that if I didn't make it into the Aviation Student Program I at least I had made it much farther than I had ever hoped. I really wanted to stay in the Army and I wanted something besides my heart to keep me out of the program.

Just as I had expected, one of the first things they did was listen to my heart and take my blood pressure. The technician was taken aback by how low my pressure was. Apparently, in my efforts to stay calm I had overdone it and depressed my blood pressure. He asked if I never got excited, and I assured him that I did. I guess he was used to men coming in a high state of anticipation and their pressure would show it. I had artificially depressed mine. I guess there is something to the Hindu mystics' abilities to mentally control some of their bodily functions. I had apparently affected mine.

He suggested that I exercise a little and let him take it again. I went out and walked around a bit and carefully eased up on my efforts to stay cool. It must have worked because the next time my pressure was more normal. I was given a few visual tests to check my eyes and depth perception, some aircraft recognition tests, and had an interview with a psychologist. They reviewed my test records from the beginning and apparently decided I had the makings of a flying officer. They told me that they were sure I would be accepted into the program and that I would be hearing from them soon. I floated back down to the Lord Balfour. Once again fate had treated me kindly.

I resumed my regular training the next day just like nothing had happened. No one seemed to particularly interested in what transpired, so I just went about my business. In a few days, I was notified that I was accepted into the program and would not be shipping out with the rest of the flight. I was to finish up the basic course and wait for orders.

At the end of twelve weeks, the basic course was over and most everyone shipped out to where ever it was that they were assigned. I packed up and moved into the Hotel Charles across the street from the Lord Balfour. Since I was between assignments, I had nothing special to do so the Army took care of that by putting me on KP or guard duty most of the time. Generally, I just goofed off and tried to stay out of the sergeant's sight. I made a few new acquaintances among the other casuals that had not been assigned, but nothing lasting because I was the only one going into the Aviation Student Program.

Remembering the move to the hotel across the street recalls to mind an incident that decidedly unnerved me. To set the scene, I need to go back and recount something of the situation at Miami Beach dating back to early 1942.

When the war started, the German submarines were pretty much in control of the American Atlantic coastline. It was not unusual for them to sink ships in sight of land. It was obvious that they were surfacing where they could see the Beach and could be seen by a sharp-eyed observer. There were all kinds of stories about German U-boat crew bodies washing up on shore with Miami theater ticket stubs and souvenirs in their pockets. It was assumed that they could come ashore with impunity. These stories are completely apocryphal, and have been summarily denied by the Germans. Nevertheless, the East Coast was in a high state of alert from December 41 until I was there in 43.

As part of the defense against saboteurs coming ashore from subs, the Army had a system of beach guards patrolling the entire coast. They went on duty at sundown and off at sunup. They worked in pairs with trained attack dogs, usually German shepherds or Doberman Pinchers (Poetic, eh, what?), one at the water's edge and the other up on the dunes. The guards were armed with submachine guns and sawed off shotguns, and were directed to shoot first and ask questions later.

One evening, about dark, I remembered that I had a pair of fatigues drying on the patio rail out by the beach. Without thinking, I went out to get them, and had just reached for them when I heard the most blood-curdling growl I had ever heard. I froze in my tracks. All I could see were white teeth four inches long and blood red eyes. There was a Doberman the size of Shetland pony, just dying to get at me. The guard said, "Soldier, you'd better get back inside. I don't know how much longer I can hold him."

Suddenly, I was quite sure those fatigues were not dry and needed to stay out there overnight. Besides, if they were stolen, the Army would issue me some more, and I was sure they would not like for one of their future air heroes to end up dog meat. This future air hero certainly had no desire to contest the issue.

I was not as successful at avoiding KP and guard duty as I would like to have been and was occasionally stuck on that bane of all basic trainees, 24 hr. guard duty. For this duty, you were trucked away to some other site on the Beach where temporary sleeping and eating facilities were set up. There you would be assigned a post to patrol for four hours, at which time you would be relieved for four hours, and then back on patrol for another four. This went

Ready for guard duty

on for 24 hours, and to what end I was never able to determine. I think this may have been to prepare us in case were ever assigned to the MPs.

In Florida, the wind generally blows in from the ocean and is relatively comfortable, even in the dead of summer. On occasion, however, it blows from the west over the Everglades. This happened once while I was in basic. For about a week a west wind blew mosquitoes by the gazillions right over the beach. They were little and black and extremely thirsty, and they must have thought they had died and gone to mosquito heaven, with all those GI bodies to feast on. It was pure torment to be out at night. There was run on oil of citronella at the drug stores, but all it did was make you smell like a fairy. The skeeters loved it.

Sunday off courtesy of
Maj. Young

One GI on guard duty one night swore that he had to take off his socks and burn them as a smudge fire to keep the mosquitoes off him. I could believe it, because you could see them in black swarms around the streetlights. It was in this infestation that I had to pull one of my stints on 24-hr. guard duty. It was not a pleasant time.

I got this duty twice during my month between assignments. One Sunday morning as I was in my second four hour tour, the first sergeant came charging up in his jeep with some luckless GI, and said, "Here's your replacement. You're coming with me."

I was totally confused, but willing to go along just to get off guard duty. As soon as he got me in the jeep he said, "Why didn't you tell me your brother-in-law was a Major in Coral Gables?"

"I didn't think it would make any difference, and besides, I wasn't looking to get out of anything," I told him.

What had happened was, Julie had called the flight headquarters and identified herself as Maj. Young's secretary and wanted to speak to Private Crouse. When informed that I was on 24-hr. guard duty, she said, "What a shame, Maj. Young wants him to come to Sunday dinner."

The sergeant said, "That's alright, ma'am. I'll get him for you."

The sergeant then grabbed the first private he saw, piled him in the jeep and brought him to my post, relieved me and set the poor sucker to walking my beat. That was the last KP and guard duty I got at the Beach.

While I was between assignments, I struck up acquaintance with a couple of other unassigned GIs, Ray Maley and Aime LeBlanc. I don't remember why they were there, but we were a little like lost sheep, so we kept each other company while we waited. LeBlanc was by birth a French Canadian (A Quebecois [?]), who was living with his grandmother in Maine when he was drafted. Apparently, they could do that sort of thing then. Aime didn't mind. He said he would rather be in the U. S. Air Corps than in the Canadian infantry. Both of them shipped out before I did and got one letter from LeBlanc in Keesler Field, AL, but I never heard from Maley. Maybe that was because I never wrote to them.

For some reason, the Army felt like their aviators needed some college hours, so the Aviation Student Training Program (ASTP) was a way of getting some college credits before learning to fly. After about a month, I got orders to report to Beloit College, Beloit, WI. I was going to college!

It turned out that there were quite a lot of us that had made it into ASTP from the Beach, so there were a number of troops in the train north. Once again,

With Ray Maley

here I was on a train heading into a brand new adventure. By this time I was convinced that I could cope with anything the Army could throw at me, and although there was a certain level of trepidation in the air, I was excited and not apprehensive. From here on out, it was up to me to meet the Army's and my own expectations.

LEISURE TIME AT THE BEACH

Showing off my wedding ring

Mis-matched uniform. Wrong hat

relaxing before guard duty with Aimee LeBlanc

Chapter IV

OFF TO COLLEGE

I had no idea what I was getting into, but with the supreme confidence of youth, I was sure that I could handle it. I had made very good grades in high school and felt that I was as prepared for college as I could be. We had been told that the emphasis would be on math and sciences, and that the courses would be extremely accelerated so that in just twelve weeks we would get the equivalent of one year of normal college work. At least one year of college was thought to be necessary by the Air Corps for all their flying officers. There would be no classification as to pilot, navigator or bombardier until after ASTP.

Officially, the Army forbade basic trainees to have their wives follow them to camp, and, as far as I know, only a few intrepid souls did come to Miami Beach. In my case, it would not have mattered. Laverda and I had kept our marriage secret because of the objections raised by my family to my getting married. They thought that at eighteen I was too young. Chances are, since I was the "baby" of the family, they would have thought I was too young if I had been twenty-eight. We had eloped to Corinth, MS, the day before I left, and pretended not to be married. Only three people knew for sure, Laverda and I and Nell Johnston, who went with us to Corinth. I'm sure most everyone in both families felt we were, but it was not official.

With the transfer to a new duty station came a relaxation on the restrictions concerning wives. At this point, Laverda was determined to come to Beloit, which seemed, somehow, closer to Rutherford than was

Miami Beach. Of course, she told her parents and her mother insisted that we make our marriage public before she would let her come to me. The die had been cast. It was to become public knowledge.

After I broke the news to my family, my parents wrote me that they thought that we had eloped, and now that it was an accomplished fact, they no longer had any objections and wished us well and that Laverda was now a treasured new member of the family. With this revelation behind us, there was a new sense of freedom for both of us.

On August 9, I got a phone call in the barracks. It was Laverda to tell that me she was coming to Beloit. I don't know when I had been so happy. I ran back to my room whooping and yelling and one of my roommates, called "Double Time," said, "I'll bet that was Red's wife."

I said, "Yep, and she's coming to see me."

I had no idea where she was going to stay, and had no way to get out to make arrangements for her. She told me not to worry that she would find a place when she got there. How she did it I'll never know, but she found a room with a nice family just off campus, and there she stayed until I was shipped out.

Beloit College was a small Liberal Arts college in the town of Beloit, WI. It was just north of the Illinois line, with South Beloit being in Illinois. The population of the college at that time was about 1500, mostly women. The Army took over most of the facilities and instructors and fashioned them into an Army college. The dorms were converted into barracks and the campus and athletic fields into drill and physical training areas. There was essentially no contact with the rest of the college. It was just another Army training post, except this one was on a college campus. The program we were in was called, as I have previously noted, ASTP. The organization was referred to as a College Training Detachment (CTD)

Once we were settled in, a reorganization of the troops took place. Whereas, in basic we had permanent party officers and non-coms in charge of all our activities, in ASTP we were organized like the service academies, with cadets in charge of most everything. We were arranged in flights, squadrons and groups. Over the entire cadet corps was the cadet colonel. Under him was the whole Table of Organization (T.O) with all the positions found in the real Army, adjutants, executive officers, squadron commanders and their subordinates. I was never sure just how these positions were assigned, but we had to relate to these cadet officers just as though they were commissioned. This was get us used to the way things would be when we were commissioned ourselves and assigned to a combat or training operation. It also gave us experience in the various levels of command. There were commissioned officers there in charge of the training and they accompanied all formations and gave directions and guidance.

Orientation at Beloit, before starting academics, consisted of lectures on interior guard duty, military customs and courtesies, military sanitation and hygiene, and two periods a day of close order drill. The cost of notebooks, pencils, paper and athletic equipment, about $10, came out of our pay, which had just been raised from $21 a month to $75! That was the scale for aviation students. In 1943, that was a king's ransom.

Our days consisted of a half-day of academics and a half-day of drill, calisthenics and more classes of Army stuff. Of course, we marched everywhere we went with cadets in charge of the formations. There were the obligatory inspections every day and it was there that we experienced some of the hazing that has come to be associated with the service academies. All underclassmen had to be whipped into shape by the upperclassmen. We were completely at their mercy and had to do anything they told us to do with only "Yes, Sir! No, Sir!" and "No Excuse, Sir!" as permissible responses.

At the command, "Hit a brace, Mister!" you had to snap to attention with your back as straight as possible, heels together, arms reaching for the ground, eyes straight ahead and your chin tucked in until they could count wrinkles under it. You could never achieve the perfect brace. The bracer was nose to nose with the bracee screaming to the top of his lungs. This was supposed to make the perfect little cadet automaton. Most of the hazing took place after the evening meal and didn't last very long because most of us, cadet officers included, had too much studying to do to waste time with this foolishness. Besides, the officers were usually around in the background to see that it didn't get out of hand.

It was in college that I first came in contact with the demerit system. As part of our training to conform, there were certain things that would earn you a demerit, or several. Most frequently they were whatever the cadet officer wanted to "gig" you for. You could earn a gig if the officer didn't like the angle at which you wore your hat, or if your shirt fly, belt buckle and pants fly didn't line up exactly. These gigs were most often earned during inspection, either in formation or in the barracks. Our shoes and belt buckles had to be perfectly shined for inspection. If these didn't come up to the inspecting officer's satisfaction, you would likely hear, "Give this man five gigs." A certain number of gigs, usually 25, would earn you a "tour". This was an hour of marching back and forth across the quadrangle during your time off on the weekend. Some sad sacks never seemed to get any time off for walking tours. Fortunately, I never had to walk a tour in college.

Our bunks had to be made up every day to Army specifications. The corners had to be square and there could be no white showing under the mattress. This meant that the blanket had to be pulled tight around the mattress to the point that a half-dollar (they had half-dollars in those days) would bounce when dropped on the bed. My sergeant friend in Ft. Oglethorpe taught me well, because my bed was always one of the best in my barracks.

Our footlockers had to be arranged in the manner prescribed by the Army. Certain things were expected to be found in their proper places as well as the proper number of said items. Socks and underwear were to be rolled and tucked just so and be in the proper relationship one to another. This sort of nit-picking detail came to be known as "chicken s__t", or just "chicken". This terminology was applied to any and everything we found to be objectionable, including officers; especially, officers.

We had one man in our class that had been in the South Pacific and become afflicted with some kind of fever that caused him to lose all his body hair. He had no hair on his head, no eyebrows, or lashes, and no beard. Naturally, he did not have to shave. There was one cadet officer that everyone detested because he was so overbearing and unreasonable, and besides, he had a slight speech impediment that made the word "Mister" come out "Mishter," accompanied by a spray of saliva. This guy loved to get up in your face and shout, "Did you shave this morning, Mishter?"

With only "Yes, No or No excuse, sir," as our only authorized answers, this poor guy with no hair could only answer, "No, Sir."

The detestable one would gig him.

Finally, someone managed to get to the cadet officer and explain the situation to him. To his credit, he publicly apologized and lifted the demerits. He was a chastened man after that. We still didn't much like him, but the dislike was not so intense.

Now that we were in the cadet program, we were expected to march like the cadets at West Point; therefore, we spent a great deal of time in close-order drill. There was a weekly review on Saturday morning in which the entire corps of cadets marched past the reviewing stand in a massed formation. We were expected to keep our lines perfectly straight and be perfectly in step. At first, we were pretty pathetic because most of us had done very little parading in massed formation. We, also, had not marched together so we didn't know each other's marching characteristics. As we became more acclimated to the system and each other, our marching improved. By the end of my time in college, we looked pretty good.

Ulanoff

Everywhere I went in the Army that I marched in formation there was one or two men that just could not march in step. In basic it was Willie B. At Beloit, it was a kid named Ulanoff. Ulanoff was an immigrant from Russia. He had come over as a baby and seemed perfectly Americanized, because he had no accent at all. Just like Willie in basic, he was a very likeable guy, but unlike Willie, he was highly intelligent, he just could not march. Try as he might, he screwed up every formation he was ever in because he could not stay in step. Cadence seemed to mean nothing to him. To keep him from fouling up our formations, the DI's made him the mail orderly. Whenever we were to march anywhere, Ulanoff was excused to go to the mailroom and check on the mail. When mail was actually delivered, he was responsible for getting it and passing it out at Mail Call.

Because of his lack of marching capabilities, Ulanoff walked more tours that rest of us and spent most of his Saturdays on the quad. One day at break time, a kid from town riding his bicycle stopped to watch what was going on. Ulanoff asked if he could ride his bike for awhile and the kid said, "Sure."

It was then that we learned some things about Ulanoff that astounded us. He did more tricks on that bike than most of us could even think of. He rode standing on the seat, balanced on his head, backwards, balanced it in a stationary position and climbed all over it and never let it fall over nor fell himself. It turned out that he was from a family of circus acrobats and had spent his life performing acrobatic and balancing tricks. As a finale, he climbed up on the second story balcony rail of the dorm and did some amazing tricks of balance there. Although he couldn't march, he won the respect of all of the cadets and DI's and he walked no more tours. Someone speculated that the reason he couldn't march was because his feet were too big. They were size sixteen's. Could be, I suppose. They sure stood him in good stead in his circus life. I never knew what happened to him because he was still in school when I shipped out.

I had spent part of April and all of May, June and July at Miami Beach, and although many others were getting prickly heat, I never suffered from it. In August, in Wisconsin, the temperature reached 100 degrees and the humidity was almost as high, and I got the worst case of prickly heat I ever had in my life. There is something terribly inconsistent about that.

The college had the usual type of athletic and recreational facilities, including an indoor swimming pool. Now that was something for an old country boy who was accustomed to running the hogs out of the pond so he could go swimming. Believe it or not, it was in the pond that I learned to swim. Most of my aquatic activities had been either in the pond on the farm, or in the canal that ran east of Rutherford. Lest you get the idea that I was a total hick, let me hasten to assure that I had swum in a genuine pool before going to the Army. There was one at Humboldt and one in Milan, and we did go there, occasionally.

As part of our physical training, we were allowed to swim in the college indoor pool once a week, sans bathing trunks. Naked, folks. Many of the cadets were from a less enlightened part of the country than I was, and had never been swimming "jay bird" before. This came as a bit of a shock to them, but not to me. That was how we all swam in the pond and canal. I never owned a pair of swim trunks until I got to go to the pool in Humboldt the first time. They wouldn't let you swim naked there.

Early on, it was pretty warm in the pool house and we opened the door to get some air. It seemed like there was a fairly constant stream of coeds walking by that part of the campus, which was way out of the way for them to get from the classrooms to their dorms.

Lest I leave the impression that all our time was spent either in class, drilling or doing PT, let me assure you that there was some time off when we could pretty much do as we pleased. Each Saturday morning there was a review when we paraded past the brass to show how much our marching had improved and to give them, the brass, the feeling that they were still in the Army and in charge. After the morning parade we were on pass until midnight Saturday, unless we had a 24-hour pass, in which case, we could stay out all night. We were allowed one overnight pass during our stay at Beloit.

We then had all day Sunday off until seven in the evening, at which time we had to sign in and begin the Army routine all over again. The weekend provided a needed break from routine.

As I related earlier, Laverda had made known her intention to come to be with me, and come she did. Just having her there made the days shorter and brighter. Not only could we be together on weekends, there were a couple of hours in the evening when we could meet in the squadron ready room and visit. This was not forbidden, but it was frowned upon by some of the more intolerant officers. We were officially not supposed to send for our wives but they, being civilians, could go where they pleased, so many of them came to be with their husbands.

One evening we were in the ready room when one of the officers, a 1st Lt. came through and saw us. He didn't say anything at the time, but very soon a cadet corporal came and told me to report to the Lt. immediately. When I reported he asked me who the young woman was that I was talking to, and I told him it was my wife. After he chewed on me for a bit he told me that I had orders not to send for her. I told him that I did not send for her, but that she came on her own. This seemed to satisfy him because he dismissed me and no more was ever said about it. I never understood why he went through that exercise, unless it

Wedding portrait 4 months after the fact

was just to let me know that he had some importance and that I had better not forget it. Maybe he had not chewed out his obligatory cadet that day and I happened to be handy and doing something that had the appearance of a rules violation. I'll never know.

Laverda and I spent a lot of time going around Beloit, which was not a very big town, about 25,000, as I remember. We also strolled around the campus, and pretty much just enjoyed each other's company. It was in Beloit that we had our wedding portrait made, albeit, somewhat belatedly. As I look at that picture now, it is sort of unbelievable how young we were. Nineteen and twenty years old and with no idea what the future held for us, and not caring very much.

Each cadet was required to sign in by midnight on Saturday and seven PM on Sunday. We all tried to use as much of our time off as possible, so the first cadet to sign in did so at 2359 and 1859 with the rest of the squadron lined up behind him. That resulted in a chronological impossibility. Two hundred cadets all signed in at 2359 and 1859. Since it took a considerable time for all of us to sign in, a few daring souls showed up just in time to tack on to the line as the last man signed in. That was taking a chance, because the Officer of the Day (OD) had a habit of monitoring the sign in. I was never that brave. I got in line at 2359 and 1859.

Part of our ASTP program, in addition to academics, was some actual flight training. We were to have 10 hours of dual instructions in a Piper Cub or Taylor Cub, essentially the same plane. It was here that some elimination from the flight program began.

It is known that some people simply cannot fly an airplane. It is a matter of depth perception, coordination, lack of balance, fear, airsickness and a host of other things, including jackass instructors who hated what they were doing and hated cadets. They may be smart and good athletes and appear to have all the necessary attributes, but they just can't fly. These men began to fall by the wayside at this time.

Four weeks into the program, we began our flight training. At Rockford, IL, the school had a flight school set up, and it was to there they bused us each flight period. My first day of flying was 8 Sep, my last day was 21 Sep. During that time I had 14 lessons that added up to 10 hours flight time. According to my CAA flight records I was only an average student. I did my share of bonehead things and got chewed out by my instructor. Some things I did rather well. I seemed to learn and not repeat too many of my mistakes so there was a general improvement. I already knew that I was not a "natural", by any means, and that if I made it, I would have to pay close attention and follow the book. I aced my final check ride and got a "Recommended as excellent military pilot material" from my check pilot. I'm pretty sure my regular instructors would not have agreed. Fortunately, the check ride was pretty much all that counted.

The Air Corps identified the classes of cadets with numbers and letters that reflected the year and position in the year of each class. For example, the first class to graduate in 1944 was class 44A. The next class five weeks later was 44B and so on. At Beloit I was assigned to Class 44H although it was still 1943. This meant that I would start out in the eighth class to graduate in 1944. Eight weeks into my projected twelve weeks, I was notified that due to some washouts in 44G, I was being moved up a class. It seems that my grades and performance were good enough that I was chosen along with one other to move up. I took this as a good omen and a compliment since I would get on with my training a little faster. It also seemed to mean that the Air Corps might think I had what it took. I was eager to get away from Wisconsin, because, although it had been very hot when I got there, it had already frosted and we were in winter uniforms in early October.

Moving up to 44G meant that I was going in with guys I didn't know, but that didn't bother me much because I had not gotten real chummy with anyone. Most military friendships grew from off duty associations, and my off duty hours were spent with Laverda. I did, however, get acquainted with the other fellow who was moved up with me. His name was Harrie M. Taft, a tall, rangy, fast talking Yankee from Providence, RI. He was single and just about my age. He had a very quick wit and a set of principles the same as mine. We hit it off immediately, and spent the next several weeks palling around together. The fact that Harry was single and I was married didn't affect our relationship, because he was not one inclined to chase after women. He had a girl back in Providence named Florence that he was true to. He married her when he was in flight school.

For some reason, Beloit College was in the Western Flying Training Command (WFTC) and when Class 44G shipped out it was sent to Santa Ana, CA, for Classification. We were bused to Chicago and put aboard the Santa Fe Railroad and headed southwest. This was the famed Atchison, Topeka and Santa Fe Railroad of the then popular song of the same name. As I recall, the AT & SF went through Kansas City, Topeka, Amarillo, and Albuquerque on its way to Los Angeles. We were on board for four days and nights and were scheduled in such a way that we stopped at the famous Harvey House Restaurants in at least three places. These were restaurants that served meals for the riders of the AT & SF, and were staffed by the more famous, Harvey Girls. These were young, attractive waitresses who were all dressed in identical immaculate blue and white striped dresses and white aprons and caps. They lived in dorms together with housemothers that ruled just like their mothers. It was an honor to chosen to be a Harvey Girl, and no parent would object to their daughter going off to work for Mr. Harvey.

It was quite a treat to be able to get off the troop train and be greeted by people that treated us like the world saviors we really were. The rest of the meals were strictly GI and served aboard the train. This train, incidentally, had to be the slowest train in the entire Santa Fe fleet. We had no priority at all, and were sidetracked for just about every train on the road. I remember being on the siding out in the middle of New Mexico, for about four hours. Usually, when we stopped, sooner or later the reason for our halt would come flying by on the main line. This time the only moving thing we saw was an Indian on a burro off in the desert. In the time we sat there, he came into sight and went out of sight and we never moved. We also never saw another train come by.

Chapter V

CLASSIFICATION AND PREFLIGHT – JOY AND REGRET

Southern California in WW II was almost completely militarized. There were Army, Navy, Marine and Coast Guard camps everywhere with the accompanying concentration of uniforms. Civilians were in the minority, it seemed. Of course, that was only how it appeared because the uniforms were either on base or on pass with no individual homes to go to and the civilians could get in at night and leave the night to the uniforms. There was such a concentration of military looking for something non-military that the civilians began to take a distinct dislike for uniforms. Being off post was about like being on post except we did not march everywhere, because we were surrounded by uniforms. We got the feeling that the civilians we came in contact with would just as soon we would leave our money with them and go back to our posts. The Southern California of the cinema was not much in evidence, from what I could see.

Santa Ana Army Air Base, Santa Ana, CA, existed for the sole purpose of taking ASTP graduates and deciding whether they were to be Pilots, Navigators, Bombardiers or not. The "nots" might end up being non-commissioned air crewmen, ground echelon Air Corps or in some other branch, entirely. The "some other branch" was devoutly to be avoided, because this meant Infantry, usually.

Classification was just what it says. We were once again subjected to battery upon battery of physical tests, aptitude tests, psychological tests, endurance tests, altitude chamber tests, code tests, manual dexterity tests and tests for which there were no names. All of these were to determine whether we were suited to be pilots, navigators or bombardiers. They could have saved a lot of time by just asking each of us what we wanted to be. Then we would have had an air force of all fighter pilots; no navigators, bombardiers or gunners. That would have made for an interesting war.

The classification period was two weeks long, during which time we were restricted to the barracks area. We were in Squadron 55, Flight A; Commanding Officer, 1ˢᵗ Lt. Crabb. Lt. Crabb was really a nice guy, demanding but nice. He let it be known right away that he was in charge and did it without having to threaten or discipline us. By this time, most of the riff-raff had fallen by the wayside, or not made it into aviation training. The cadets, for the most part, came from good homes and upper middle class backgrounds and had been raised right. We were all pretty dedicated to becoming aviators and realized that screwing up was not part of the plan.

From my first days in the Army, as I recounted in the Basic Training chapter, barracks order and cleanliness were the order of the day. Santa Ana was the first real Army base I had been on, where the buildings were strictly GI. Our barracks was the typical two stories, frame building with the main door facing the squadron street and the showers and latrine on the other end. The sleeping areas were big open rooms with row upon row of double-decker bunks. Each bunk had a cotton mattress, one or two blankets, sheets, pillows and pillowcases. Each cadet had a footlocker that he lived out of.

All the things we had to do at the others posts concerning beds, lockers and personal effects were in effect here, too. Each post had certain things that were done a little differently than at your previous post, so there was always something new to learn and look out for. The inspection drill was pretty much the same at Santa Ana as elsewhere, except we occasionally had to GI the barracks floor. This meant you took everything off the floor but the bunks and with hot soapy water and GI brushes you got down on your hands and knees and scrubbed the floor until you could eat off of it.

It was at Santa Ana that we were introduced to latrine duty. Every day someone was assigned to make sure the latrines were scrupulously clean. This could be assigned as part of some kind of punishment, or, if there were no screw-ups, you were picked by the sergeant at random. This was in addition to your responsibility for your own area.

Because the barracks were always open, and all of us had some personal stuff, it was required that there be a barracks orderly on duty at all times. He was sort of a security person. Weekends were especially irksome because it kept you from getting a pass to L.A. Despite the level of responsibility, nobody relished getting barracks orderly on weekends. This duty was passed around. It was not a punishment.

I was tapped for barracks orderly on Christmas, and although I had no special plans, I was more than a little hacked off. This was when I came to have an increased respect for some of my Hebrew mates. One Jewish guy volunteered to take my place because he wasn't going to observe the holiday, and he had been allowed off on one of the Jewish holidays in the Fall. I thought that was extremely decent of him, and I came to have a great deal of respect for him. It humbled me.

There may have been some method to the evaluation of our test results, but it was not evident from the tests themselves. I think what really happened was, at the end of our classification period, the evaluation teams got together and went over what the Air Corps said it needed for that time and they drew our names from an old cavalry hat. "The Eighth Air Force is losing a lot of crews right now and that means two pilots, a navigator and a bombardier for each plane, so we'll make each third name a navigator and each fourth name a bombardier, and make the first two pilots."

"The fighter commands in all theaters are screaming for replacements. Maybe we'll take one hat full just for fighter pilots." "And," as Linda Ellerbe would many years later say, "so it goes."

I think the single most defining test was the psychological one. It was after that one that most of the "washouts" were posted. Contributing, also, were the manual dexterity and code tests. These seemed to have the potential for pinpointing certain characteristics that may have been defining in a way I don't yet understand.

Santa Ana was also a Pre-flight school where we continued different aspects of our training that had not been addressed before. One of the most stressful for me was the learning and passing of Morse Code, both aural and visual. We had to learn the Morse alphabet of dits and dahs. Each letter in the English alphabet has its own peculiar combination, and we had to listen to them over headphones until we could transcribe messages at the rate of ten words a minute to pass. I barely made it.

There was a method to efficiently taking code that I only rudimentarily mastered. That was to listen to groups of words and secure them in your mind before writing them down. You had to be able to write them while with another part of your brain received more of the message. Most actual messages are relatively short, so the accomplished code taker can save his writing until the message is over. The really good ones can write and receive simultaneously.

As it turned out, pilots were never required to be able to send code, only receive and read it. Fortunately, bombers and transports all had radiomen to do the long-range radio sending and receiving, so they were the crewmen who had to be proficient in all aspects of code.

Another part of learning and using code was visual, and this was by the use of blinker lights. Each multi-crew combat aircraft was equipped with a blinker light used for signaling vessels not equipped with radio. Six words a minute was the passing grade for this device. I barely passed that one, too. I only remember using the blinker light once in my career and that was on a training mission off the coast of North Carolina.

Physical training continued at Santa Ana just as it had at my previous two posts. I think it was there that I was introduced to the nonsensical expression, "Hubba, hubba, hubba." Now, I doubt that anyone knows how or where that word, "Hubba" started, from what it was derived, nor what it was supposed to mean. Actually, it came to mean whatever the speaker wanted it to mean, and was most frequently used to call attention to a particularly attractive female. Or just a female, depending on how long the GI had been away from female company. I didn't use the term in that context, being a recent bridegroom like I was.

While taking PT, at the end of some exercise like, sit-ups or leg lifts, the instructor would say, "Pull up your knees; pat your belly and yell, Hubba, hubba, hubba." And five hundred cadets would start pounding on their bellies and screaming to the top of their lungs, "Hubba, hubba, hubba." Surprisingly, that served as a physical release that actually made us feel better and more relaxed.

Axel

You remember that I said that in every formation there was at least one person that did not march well? At Santa Ana it was Axel. Axel was an easy-going, soft-spoken Swede from Minnesota, right off the farm. He was a unique physical specimen. He was about 5', 11", 185 lbs. and the same breadth from his shoulders to his hips, double-jointed, and strong as a bull.

One of the things we learned to do in marching was to set our steps by the movement of the man's head and shoulders in from of us. The only trouble with marching behind Axel was that his head and shoulders were out of step with his feet. His feet were in cadence but the rest of him wasn't and it threw those behind him out of step. Unfortunately, the man behind Axel was me. I got chewed on for being out of step every time we made formation until I learned to look past Axel to the man in front of him.

I liked Axel, as did everyone else in the flight. He turned out to be extremely intelligent with an almost genius IQ, but he was so quiet and self-deprecating that it took some time for me to come to appreciate his mind. He impressed me right away with his strength when he started doing push-ups between two foot lockers and going well below the tops of the lockers with his body. We also seemed to always get teamed up at PT when it came time for hand-to-hand combat. I was quick and wiry and might get behind him and grab him, but once I had him I couldn't do anything but hold on. There was no way I could throw him. He was patient with me and let me go through the procedures of learning the holds and moves, but I could never throw him unless he helped. When he became the attacker, I was amazed to learn that he knew jujitsu. The guy was full of surprises.

Axel drove the code instructors crazy. While we were in code class we were supposed to take down the exercise as it was given and at the end of the class take a test to see how we were doing. Axel would sit there with his headset on and his eyes closed like he was asleep, not writing down anything. The instructor yelled him at him, but he just smiled and pretended to take down the words. When we were tested at the end of the period, Axel was perfect and the fastest man in the class. It turned out that in addition to his many other accomplishments; he was also a ham radio operator, proficient in Morse Code.

I don't know what happened to Axel. I don't know if he ever made it to flight school, or not. He looked so little like an officer that his appearance alone might have worked against him. I'll bet he would have made a cracker jack navigator.

Among the demonstrations that we were subjected to was one on night vision and how to cope with observations in almost pitch blackness. We were gathered in a classroom that could be made as dark as a cave. We were shown conditions ranging from full moonlight to starlight to overcast skies in the dark of the moon. We were shown how to get our eyes adjusted to the darkness and how not to look directly at objects on the horizon, but allow our peripheral vision to register them.

51

Once the instructor showed us how staring at an object or light can mislead as to its movement. He showed us a GI flashlight with cover over the lens so that there was just a pinpoint of red light showing. He told us to take a piece of paper and our pencil and follow the movement of the light when the room was darkened. After about ten minutes of watching the light erratically drift slowly up and to the right, he turned the light back on, and the flashlight was sitting on the table. It had been there all the time. Our natural head movement had tricked us into thinking the light was moving.

Part of the screening process involved going through the altitude chamber to see how we handled the low pressure of high altitude. This was a huge vacuum chamber equipped with positions for about twenty men. We were herded into this device with an instructor and were literally sealed in. Each position was equipped with a regulation oxygen mask. We were instructed on how to put on and check the mask and were lectured on the effects of anoxia, low oxygen pressure, such as one would encounter in high altitude flight.

When the instructor was satisfied that we could all get into our masks properly, the pressure was gradually reduced. There was a large altimeter in the chamber so we could see just what our simulated altitude was at any time and could relate to the physical effects we felt.

We all started out without masks and as the pressure went down we could first feel the effects on our ears, they being the most sensitive organ to reduced pressure. Many of us had never been on an airplane that flew very high, or even on a moderately high mountain, so had no experience with variable air pressure. The airtime in ASTP didn't count because a Cub couldn't get high enough to make much of a pressure change.

We were told how to swallow and work our jaws to equalize the pressure and were warned not to worry if we heard popping noises. That was what was supposed to happen. We each had a pad of paper and a pencil and at each thousand feet of altitude change we had to write our name. As the effect of oxygen lack began to kick in, our handwriting would deteriorate. This would give us a clue to the deterioration of our physical faculties. Knowing this would help us to recognize anoxia if we ever encountered it in flight.

We were all required to go without masks until we could definitely feel the effects of low pressure. Most of us began to feel them at between fifteen and eighteen thousand feet. At the instructor's command we put our masks on and saw how quickly pure oxygen restored our condition to normal. This was a real revelation and an excellent object lesson. Having once gone through this exercise, I doubt that any of us failed to recognize anoxia in flight.

To see how our individual bodies would respond to very high altitude, we were taken to a simulated altitude of forty thousand feet. There is more than just oxygen deprivation to worry about at altitude. There is also the effect of lower pressure on the dissolved gases in the blood stream and the gases in the digestive system. It is not good to eat bran cereal or beans before high altitude flight.

On my first test I experienced extreme pain in my hip, knee and elbow joints at about twenty-seven thousand feet. I was in agony. We had been warned about "the bends," so I knew enough to alert the instructor. He stopped the test and took me out. That was not a good sign, but it didn't wash me out because it was not unusual for this to happen, occasionally. I was rescheduled. The second time I passed with flying colors.

Individuals have varying susceptibility to the effects of anoxia, but most of us don't perform well at all above twenty thousand feet without oxygen. Prolonged exposure above that altitude can kill most people. In each test one volunteer was asked to see how high he could go before passing out, and there was always some nut willing to give it a go. I, incidentally, was not that nut. The volunteer in our group had a phenomenally high tolerance for low pressure. At thirty-eight thousand he could still write his name legibly, although he acted like he was on a high drunk. The instructor finally put his mask on him and terminated the test, saying that no one had ever gone that high for him before. I always wondered if that particular cadet really had the requisite number of brain cells to be affected by anoxia. We were together through Primary Flight training and he sometimes acted like his ducks were not all in a row.

Among the other things we had to do while at Santa Ana was a day at the beach. This was a far cry from the duty at Miami Beach in that it was not the warm Atlantic, but the frigid Pacific. It was also not mid-summer, but Thanksgiving Day, 1943. That's right. Thanksgiving Day. Part of our pre-flight training was to undergo some water survival training and machine gun and trap shooting practice. This facility was set up on a desolate stretch of beach and sand dunes south of Long Beach. There they had a range set up where we could shoot clay pigeons with tripod-mounted shotguns and traveling targets with .30 cal. machine guns. This was to get us initiated into the art of deflection shooting which would be needed if we ever wanted to take pot shots at German or Japanese planes.

Just how much we were judged on our ability to hit the moving targets, I don't know. I never heard of anyone washing out because he was a hopeless wing shot. This was the fun part of the outing.

Water survival training involved learning how to jump into the water in our clothes, pull off our pants, tie knots in the legs and fill them with air, either by throwing them over our heads or going under water and blowing into them. The idea was that wet pants filled air would serve as a makeshift flotation device. They did work if you succeeded in not drowning before you got them off and filled. I was successful in making that procedure work.

Another exercise involved jumping fully clothed off a twenty-foot high platform into the Pacific Ocean and swimming fifty yards to a float. By that time, both Harrie and I had been in the water and knew how cold it was. I believe that if it had not been salt it might have been ice. We both found ourselves clinging to the railing of the tower trying to figure out how to avoid going into the water. When we were informed by the non-com in charge that it was into the water or stay there all night, I finally pushed Harrie and he grabbed me as he fell and we both went in. That is the coldest I have ever been in my entire life. By the time we got out and got into warm, dry clothes, I was beginning to have second thoughts about this Army life.

As I mentioned, it was Thanksgiving Day and they had a proper feast for dinner that night. There was turkey and dressing, roast beef, ham, potatoes, greens beans, and other vegetables, salad, and two or three kinds of desserts, and plenty of hot coffee. That brought all of us back to life and put a fine point on an otherwise dreadful day.

So far, my experience with Army food had not been bad. It was pretty good. Not up to my Mama's, of course, but not bad. I had gained some weight and you could no longer see my ribs like you could when I was drafted. The only dish that I remember that I really liked, mainly because I had never had it before, was meat loaf. The Army's recipe for meat loaf was very good, and it was the same at both posts at which I had been stationed. Another new taste to me was orange marmalade. Of all the jams and jellies they put on the table, my favorite was orange marmalade. It remains a favorite even today.

At Santa Ana my food experience was to take a turn for the worse, not so much in the quality, but in the quantity. The manner of serving changed from a cafeteria type line to table service. We marched in and sat down at the typical Army picnic type table and the KPs brought the food to the table and put it on the end. Each dish was passed down from man to man with each one taking his portion. We began to notice that the men on the end away from the start were not getting any food. The dishes were empty before everyone was served. The first men were not hogging the food. There was just not enough to go around. This was especially true at breakfast. There was, however, plenty of bread and gravy, so we didn't go hungry. One does not live by bread and gravy alone, but must have eggs and meat, occasionally.

This food shortage went on long enough for most of us to begin to get upset about it and to complain. It was obvious we were on short rations, for whatever the reason. Someone in this outfit had never heard of the Army mess hall slogan, "Take all you want, eat all you take." Then, before a full-scale uprising could ensue, the food suddenly got better and more abundant. The word came down that the Inspector General had been tipped off about our situation and launched an investigation. He discovered that the base Mess Officer, Mess Sergeant and several more Quartermaster personnel were engaged in a thriving black market of Army foodstuffs, making the troops suffer to cover up their thievery. Needless to say, they spent the rest of the war and then some at Fort Leavenworth.

Being in Southern California and near the fabulous Los Angeles and Hollywood of movie fame, made most of us eager to get on pass to see what it was all about. By this time, we had been in the Army for all of six months and were, we felt, men of the world and needed to find out all we could, while we could. After 7 weeks, we were permitted off post on weekends without restriction, so most of us loaded on the Pacific Electric (PE) train to L. A. as soon as we could. It turned out that most of the uniforms in Southern California had the same idea and headed for the same place, Pershing Square. This is in the center of L. A. and where the PE station was, and it was from there that we started out on our adventures. This was also where the homosexuals hung out, or so they say. One never accosted me, so I can't testify to that fact.

I actually don't remember many specific details about Los Angeles except that it was noisy, dirty and full of GIs looking for what most GIs look for when off post. With the town also full of women war workers, also looking for what they could find, it was not long before connections were made. I just felt totally overwhelmed by it all and since I was not looking for what most other GIs were looking for, I soon decided that my time could better be spent back on the base.

In the weeks I was at Santa Ana, I think I went into L. A. about three times. Overnight accommodations were very scarce. Hotel rooms had to be booked in advance, if indeed, they could be found at all. I spent one night in an all night movie, which featured vaudeville acts between shows. That was where I saw my first and last strip tease act. Another night was spent in a genuine flophouse, where the bed was a cot in a large room full of cots, each of which seemed to be occupied by a vagrant. Needless to say, I didn't get a lot of sleep that night. As soon as the first train back to Santa Ana ran in the morning, I was on it.

The post had just about all the amenities that one could want if you weren't looking for women. There were movie theaters with first run movies, ones that had not been released to the civilian public. There was a great recreation hall with a snack bar, library, reading room, ping pong tables, pool tables, piano and auditorium. You could read, write letters, play games or listen to some very talented GIs play the piano. They booked USO shows in there and I saw some Hollywood headliners. The one I remember most was a routine by Eddie Bracken. He did the usual stand up jokes and wound up with one made famous by Joe E. Brown. It was pantomime of a baseball pitcher with all the facial expressions and body contortions that Brown had perfected. It was hilarious. All this without leaving the post.

Harrie Taft and I spent a good deal of time together and became fast friends. We seemed to have pretty much the same tastes and enjoyed doing the same sort of things. Neither of us felt it necessary to try to impress the other and occasionally would go our own way. Harrie was with me when I went to L. A. and he was no more impressed than I was, so we pretty much wrote the place off and stayed on post. We did go to the famous Hollywood Canteen on Christmas weekend, 1943, along with half the uniforms in Southern California. We missed the early show where some of the Hollywood notables performed and mingled, so, despite the impression the movie Hollywood Canteen gave, we saw no stars. The place was so packed that you could have poured a little fish oil on us and we would have turned into sardines. That little bit of romantic history was a bust.

As I have mentioned, Santa Ana Army Air Base was right in the middle of a vast complex of war production plants, especially aircraft plants. The Navy and Marines had bases all over the place and there were planes of all kinds in the air constantly. It became sort of a game with us to see if we could identify the plane by the sound of its engine. Most of the time we could, because each engine, propeller, airframe combination had its own peculiar tone and rhythm. Even today, I can spot the familiar sound of the occasional C-47 (DC-3) as it lumbers past. It is about the only plane of that era that is still in use. All other Warbirds that are flyable are confined to air shows and don't go over here much.

I remember an episode that impressed me with just what some people can do with an airplane when challenged. One day, as we were walking across the post with no particular place to be, we saw two hotshot Navy guys in their brand new F6Fs jump a lone P-38 heading up the coast. That was not an uncommon happening in that area because of the abundance of training flights.

In light of what happened next, I think the Navy picked on a test pilot from Lockheed. Just about the time the F6Fs were in position to fire had it been a combat situation, the 38 flipped into an impossibly tight turn right into the F6Fs and they ran right by and found the 38 on their tails with all four fifties and one 20 mm cannon pointed right at their necks. They scattered and there ensued the wildest dogfight you ever saw. Every way the F6s turned, there were those awesome guns right on them. The Navy guys were good, but the 38 pilot was just a little better. This was probably a brand new P-38 with all the newest modifications, such as maneuvering flaps and dive brakes. This plane in the hands of a skilled pilot could turn inside any plane in the air at altitudes below 9,000 ft. It could also run away from most any fighter around. The Navy pilots were given a clinic that day and went home chastened and a little wiser. I'll bet, however, that the same pilots would jump the first P-38 they saw the next time they were out, just to see if they could take him. Each episode was a learning experience for all concerned and it was much better to learn without being shot at.

The F6F was designed to combat the Japanese Zero, the most agile dogfighter of the war, and had a remarkable record against the Zero, but not by trying to turn with it. The P-38, as well, had a fantastic record against the Zero, but also not as a dogfighter. Both American planes used their superior speed, firepower, and ruggedness to defeat the Zero.

All this aerial activity made us all the more eager to get this classification and pre-flight over with and into our flight training. Shortly after the classification period was over, those of us who were left, and that was most of us, I hasten to add, knew if we were pilots, navigators or bombardiers.

As the classification/pre-flight process wound down, a few unfortunates were being washed out and sent on to other assignments. Each day another man or two would be seen forlornly packing his bags for departure. It was sad and, at the same time, a relief if you were not the bag packer. We all knew that an unknown number of washouts would occur, and when someone left and it wasn't you, you knew your chances of making it were just a little better. One of the disconcerting things was to see someone you had picked as a sure thing to make it, packing his bags. You wondered just what the Air Corps was looking for and hoped that you had it.

Finally, all the ground testing and training were over and classification/pre-flight was complete. Most of the non-pilots already knew their classification before the assignments were posted, but there were a few surprises left to the end. Men who were sure they would be pilots were more than a little disappointed to find themselves assigned to navigator or bombardier school. Most of us, by the time we finished pre-flight without completely washing out, were just happy to be on our way to some kind of flying. After all, we were the next crop of junior birdmen.

Our Primary Flight school assignments were posted at squadron headquarters with departure and travel instructions. All of us had heard of some of the schools at such places as Twenty-nine Palms and Victorville in California, and Phoenix and Tucson in Arizona. No one had ever heard of Wickenburg, AZ, so guess where I was going? Wickenburg, AZ!

Harrie was going to Tucson, so we were parting company. We were a little disappointed not to be staying together, but by now, we were getting used to the ways of the Army and accepted it as our lot and promised to stay in touch. We made a bet on who would solo first and backed it up with $5. It turned out that when we did solo, we both soloed on the same day. We never did learn whether we soloed in different parts of the day, so I never did get my $5, nor he his. That exchange of letters was the last either of us ever heard of the other. That was the way of most military friendships. They remain fond memories and little else.

Chapter VI

PRIMARY FLIGHT TRAINING

First step into the wild blue yonder

Now that I had survived Classification and Pre-flight and come out in the pilot training program, the future looked bright, indeed. At last, I was going to get to fly real airplanes with real instructors that knew what they were doing. I was never sure the Cub instructors were really qualified to instruct or evaluate, but that was behind me and I was ready for the next step.

In order to expedite the training of the future birdmen, the Army hit upon the idea of using already existing civilian flight schools for Primary training. There were many of these all over the country with facilities and instructors. It was a matter of providing them with additional instructors, planes and ground school and maintenance facilities and there was a readymade flight school.

All of the civilian instructors had to go to Army instructor school to be trained in the Army teaching methods so there would be a uniformity to the overall training. Just how these methods might differ from the civilian way was never clear to me.

The Claiborne Flight Academy was my Primary Training Base. It was at what had been the Wickenburg municipal airport. They had built barracks around a quadrangle with a parade ground in the quad. That was also where punishment tours were walked, back and forth across the quad.

There was a regulation GI mess hall, but the cadets did not have to pull KP there. There were permanent party and civilians to take care of our culinary needs. We were much too busy and intent on becoming aviators to be expected to work in the mess hall. Also, in the Army's eyes we were a rank somewhere between Master Sergeant and Warrant Officer and actually rated a salute from enlisted men. Although that was what the Army regulations said, we were actually considered by the enlisted men as pampered playboys and not worthy of any sort of recognition. I suppose that most EM really didn't know about the salute reg. All this to say, we had enough rank to be exempt from KP and guard duty, and not enough to be respected by enlisted personnel.

The Claiborne Flight Academy staff consisted of both military and civilian personnel. The civilians were primarily responsible for our flight training and the Army personnel were there to see that everything was done the Army way and to check out the students to make sure they came up to Army specs. Before any of us could graduate, we had to pass Army check rides. All in all, I would say that the Army guys had a pretty cushy assignment.

The Army unit had the basic organization, Commanding Officer, Adjutant and other staff officers who did I knew not what. There were two doctors and five ground officers. There were seven flying officers whose primary responsibility it was to make the aforementioned check rides. There were also some miscellaneous enlisted men that really did most of the work, just like in the real Army.

The civilian contingent was organized along military lines and they even wore military style uniforms with insignia that identified them as civilian flight personnel. The "Commanding Officer" was Harry Claiborne, contractor and school owner. He was retired military and I'm sure that helped get him the contract. He had a Group Commander, Flight Commander, Asst. Flight Commander, two Squadron Commanders, and four Flight Commanders. Actually doing the instructing were thirty-seven flight instructors.

Thirty-seven may seem like a lot of instructors, but there were two classes on base at one time, 44F and 44G. There were 147 cadets in 44F and 164 in 44G. That is 311 cadets who had to be taught to fly over a period of 14 weeks. That is two overlapping 9-week classes. You can see that those thirty-seven men were kept pretty busy seeing that we got the requisite training and seventy-five flying hours.

Civilians handled the ground school, also. There were six of them reporting to the head of instruction, Major (Ret.) MacLachlan. It was said that he was a graduate of West Point, and I believe it. He looked about seventy years old, straight as yardstick and very lean and leathery. As I recall, he taught courses in military history and unit organization and discipline, including military justice. His was a commanding presence and we all respected him, probably more than the active duty guys.

One of the most memorable civilians at this school was not a member of the faculty or an instructor, but was the head custodian. He called himself "General" Tracey. He had gone out to Arizona for his TB, or so he said. It must have been cured, because he was addicted to big, black cigars. He was a short, fat, fast-talking little Yankee, who, for some reason, seemed to have quite a bit of influence around the base. He sold souvenir post cards of himself and autographed them. I still have mine somewhere.

After a short period of settling in and orientation, our life as primary flight trainees began. Each day was divided into a half-day of ground school and a half-day of flying.

Ground school consisted of courses in weather, navigation, aerodynamics, principles of flight, military organization and other things I cannot at this time bring to mind. PT was also worked into the ground school hours. It seemed like PT took up about two hours of every day. We had the usual calisthenics, but we also had competitive games. We played basketball, touch football, softball and ran track. Competitive sports were emphasized a means of bringing out our aggressive nature, which was supposed to sharpen our flying abilities. I can't say that I excelled in any of the games but I held my own with most of the cadets. I was unfamiliar with playing football, and only passingly familiar with basketball. I was as fast as anyone and usually came in first in the cross-country. Softball was my sport. I didn't take a back seat to anyone on the diamond.

There were some truly superb athletes in our group and they stood out. Strangely enough, some of the best athletes were not the best pilots. Some of them actually washed out of Primary. There didn't seem to be a noticeable correlation between raw physical ability and the ability to fly an airplane.

Among the things we were issued when we arrived at Wickenburg was a publication called the <u>Aviation</u> <u>Cadet Manual, Primary Stage.</u> It appeared to been put together by the school. It was a very comprehensive publication that covered a multitude of things that we needed to know. They were things that, if we studied the manual, gave us enough familiarity with terminology and procedures that our instructors would not have to spend valuable airtime teaching us. Such things as air discipline, fundamentals of flying, rules governing all the basic maneuvers, landing field locations and traffic patterns, forced landings, handling of parachutes, tower signals, etc. This was our bible for flight training, and as I re-read it now it brings back many once dormant memories.

The plane we were to fly in Primary was the Stearman PT-17. It was a classic two-place biplane with a 225-hp. radial engine swinging a fixed pitch propeller. It was a very basic airplane with only a few necessary instruments. It had an altimeter, a magnetic compass, airspeed indicator, tachometer, fuel gauge, and that was about it. There were switches for fuel and magnetos. A stick, rudder and throttle completed the cockpit. That is all that is needed to get a plane that simple off and on the ground. The student sat in the rear cockpit, the instructor in the front, and they were connected by a Gosport tube for communication from instructor to student. No verbal communication was allowed in the other direction.

The Stearman was the plane that most of us thought of when we thought of learning to fly. It was very much like the fighters of WW I, and stories of that air war were what we had grown up with. The image of the fliers of that time and the barnstormers of our youth with their helmet and goggles and white scarf blowing in the wind was what we all fancied ourselves as becoming.

Every day brought new revelations and wonders to this starry eyed future (?) birdman. I had to periodically pinch myself to realize that this was really happening to me. This was the fulfillment of a dream I had had all my life. The sounds

Walking a PT-17 to the taxiway

and smells of real airplanes that I was actually going to go off the ground in were almost intoxicating.

We had never been issued any flying gear, since until we finished Classification it was not certain we would be doing any real flying. On the day before we were to make our first flight we were issued helmet, goggles, gloves, A-2 flight jackets, fleece-lined jacket, pants and boots. The clothes we wore to fly in depended on the weather. When we started, we wore the fleece lined stuff, and by the time we finished the nine weeks the weather had warmed up enough that the A-2 jacket was plenty. We had to wear the goggles around our necks when on the ground until we soloed, then we could wear them on our helmets like real aviators.

We, four of us, met our instructor, Mr. Manchester, the day we drew our gear and were given a close up look at the Stearman PT-17. Among the things we were told about the plane was that it was very stable, so stable that a spoiler strip had to be added to the leading edge of the wing to make it stall. It was capable of withstanding 12Gs in a pullout, which is a lot more that the human body can stand. Looking back on it in the light of things I have learned over the years, I don't believe it is possible to dive a Stearman fast enough to pull 12Gs in a pullout.

The landing gear was quite narrow, which gave the plane a built-in ground loop on landing. In a Stearman, a ground loop was most likely to occur after a hard landing in a crosswind. Over controlling the rudder would cause the plane to begin to turn rather quickly and the wheel on the inside of the turn would leave the ground and the outside wing hit the ground. If you were lucky, you would only scrape the wing before you regained control. A really out of control ground loop could tear the wing off resulting in broken airplane and a washed out cadet. This sort of accident was usually the result of sloppy flying and inattention, neither of which is in the best interest of completing pilot training.

Another contributor to the propensity to ground loop was the free swiveling tail wheel. The tail wheel was steerable through 30 degrees by use of the rudder pedals. This helped guide the plane as you taxied or rolled out on take off and landing. If you happened to over control on landing and kicked the tail wheel into free swivel, the tail had a tendency to want to swap places with the nose, and you were well into a ground loop before you knew it.

At each flight line there were several interesting little devices called "Gink" trainers. These were little boxes about the size of a Stearman cockpit, mounted on gimbals and pivots, which made them very unstable. They had a stick and rudder pedals rigged up so that by properly manipulating them, you could keep the device balanced and headed in one direction.

If the Gink began to drift one way or the other, you could bring it back on line by using the same stick and rudder movements you would use in a Stearman if it began to ground loop. It was great fun to spin a cadet in the Gink and see how soon he could get it back in line. Believe it or not, that stupid looking little box helped most of us sharpen our ground loop recovery technique.

Ground loop prevention technique was so pounded into our heads that they seldom happened. I managed to lightly scrape a wingtip only once, very late in my primary training. The fabric over a spot about eight inches long was rubbed away, but the plane was still completely flyable, so nothing was ever said about it.

A cadet named Ernie Engstrom was taxiing back to the flight line one day when the wind was very gusty, and turned a plane over on its back right in front of all the cadets on the ground. A gust of wind lifted his left wing up and started him into a ground loop to the left. Ernie did the right thing when he put the brake to the right wheel to bring the left wheel back down. Unfortunately, he put the brake to the left wheel as well, and when it hit the ground, the plane essentially stopped in its tracks, rolled up on its prop hub and balanced there. After what seemed like minutes, it slowly rolled on over on its back and there Ernie hung on his seat belt with everyone on the line looking at him. He released his seat belt and fell out on his head, none the worse for the experience, except for a very red face.

Although washouts were fairly frequent in Primary, mitigating circumstances sometimes permitted a cadet to get through an otherwise serious offence safely. In Ernie's case, he was too good a pilot to let one slip up wash him out. Also in his favor was the fact that the field had just been closed because the wind was dangerously gusty, and that was why he was coming in. Aside from some kidding from the other cadets, no more was ever said about it.

The day we met our instructors, we were introduced to the flight line routine and the crew that manned it for us. There were two dispatchers, one for each of the two flights scheduled to fly, and two fuel truck drivers, all civilians, all women.

When the cadets and their instructors reported to the line, they were assigned planes by the dispatcher and sent on their way. Each instructor had four students for each flying period. Obviously, since there could only be one cadet in the air with the instructor, there were three on the ground. We spent our ground time helping get the planes off the ground, watching takeoffs and landings, reading tech manuals and other related military stuff in the ready room, training in the Gink, and just generally goofing off. Sometimes, an instructor or one of the officers would hold an impromptu critique, trying to pound as much aviation knowledge into our skulls full of mush as possible.

My first flight with Mr. Manchester began like this:

We drew our parachutes and he instructed us in how to get into it. It was the standard seat pack that one always saw aviators wearing in the movies. You carried the chute by the leg straps slung over your shoulder until you got ready to put it on. You put it on by slinging the harness on over your shoulders so the pack was on the same side of your body as your fanny. That put a buckle strap in position to be fastened across your chest. The leg straps on the pack came up between your legs and hooked around your legs to the harness, putting the pack in position to sit on. The "D" ring or ripcord was tucked away in a canvas pocket on the left vertical harness strap. There was a light cotton thread basting the pocket closed to keep the ring from falling out and getting fouled on something. The thread was not strong enough to keep a panicked flyer from pulling the ripcord in a bailout. As I recall, that was the one and only time that anyone showed me the "D" ring and said, "That is what you pull to open the chute."

From then on, you knew exactly where to grab if you needed to open a parachute. I never did, but even today, if you asked me to put my hand where the "D" ring would be, my hand would automatically go right to the spot. It was not by accident that the ring was positioned where one thinks of ones heart being located.

During our training I had occasion to talk to a cadet who had to bail out and I asked him if he had any trouble remembering what to do. He said that he didn't even think about it, he just did it like he had jumped a hundred times. He also said that he had no desire to repeat the process.

You didn't strap on the leg straps until just before you got in the plane. To walk around, you put on the harness and flipped the pack under and up so that it rode in the small of your back. This way, you could walk without the chute bumping on the backs of your legs. This also made you look like a real aviator, with your flight suit, helmet and goggles, gloves and clipboard. You looked like you had been flying all your life when you went out for your first flight. None of our equipment was new, so that even heightened the "look."

The first flight included a detailed "walk around" to check all the flight surfaces, tires, propeller for nicks and notches, engine for excessive oil leaks.

The PT-17 had a radial engine, and all radial engines drip oil constantly. If one doesn't, you had better call the crew chief. The oil tank is empty.

We had an external checklist on our clipboard, and we were taught from the first that the checklist must be scrupulously followed before every flight. Failure to do so could result in a broken airplane and a washed out, if still living, cadet. Check lists are a nuisance to a "bold pilot" but are the bible to "old, bold pilots."

Having ten hours in a Cub helped to know where to find the stick and rudder pedals and what they did when you moved them. Nevertheless, Mr. Manchester adopted the attitude that this was the first airplane we had ever been near and went over all the essentials again. The Army feels that in training you can never have enough repetition, which is good, because only about ten per cent of what you are told at first is remembered for more than ten minutes. If you are told something enough times and repeat it enough times, eventually, you'll get it.

Every airplane has its own peculiar entry procedure. The rear cockpit of the PT-17 had a stirrup for you to put your foot in, not unlike a saddle, and like mounting a horse, you always got in from the left. You climbed up on the lower wing, faced the tail, grabbed the edge of the cockpit, put your left foot in the stirrup and swung your right leg over into the cockpit and proceeded to sit down. All this after you had fastened your parachute across your butt.

Once in the cockpit, the <u>first</u> thing you did was fasten the seat belt. I learned this after an incident in ASTP that no one in the Army ever knew about, except me. One day the ASTP instructor asked me if I would like to spend the flight time seeing if he could loop the Cub. Never having been in a loop, I said, "Sure."

We climbed in and off we went. After getting air borne, he took over and climbed up to about five thousand feet. This took a good while, by the way. He proceeded to demonstrate that one could indeed loop a Cub. That was quite a thrill, but nothing like the thrill I got when back on the ground and tried to release my seat belt. <u>It had not been fastened</u>. Fortunately, the loop was a good one because I never left my seat. I later did loops where all that kept me from falling out was my seat belt. I would not have fallen out of the Cub, but I'm sure my head would have made a neat hole in the fabric covering over the cabin. And, in all likelihood, I would have been washed out on the spot.

Starting a PT-17 required at least three people. The pilot, in this case the instructor, and two people on the ground. At this point I was just a passenger. The pilot checked to make sure the gas was turned on and the switch was off and the throttle closed and cracked, and he would call this out to the crew on the ground. The plane had an inertial starter that required someone, usually two cadets, to wind up the flywheel by turning a crank located just behind the engine. One person would stand on the wheel and one on the ground and between them they would wind the starter up until it reached the right speed. With a little experience you could tell by the whine of the wheel when to start the engine. The ground crew would yell out, "Contact."

The pilot would answer, "Contact," and turn on the switch. The man on the wheel would pull on a cable that engaged the starter, the prop would begin to turn, and almost immediately the engine would start. That is, it would if the starter was turning up fast enough and it was tuned up well. We had very little trouble getting the engines started, most of the time.

Earlier, I said that there were usually cadets not flying, and they were the ones that cranked the starters. You could get pretty tired after starting three or four engines, because they required considerable strength and energy to get the starters wound up sufficiently.

Once the engine was running smoothly, the pilot signaled the man on the ground to pull the wheel chocks, released the brakes, and we were off. All the time this was going on the instructor was talking to me over the Gosport tube, telling me all the things he was doing and why. I was supposed to be absorbing this. He had me put my hands and feet on the controls very lightly and follow him through what he was doing.

In a plane like the PT-17, which is called a tail dragger as opposed to a tricycle landing gear, it is imperative that the tail be kept firmly on the ground by keeping the stick back in your gut, firmly. That was one thing instructors harped on continually. That was the first thing the cadet got yelled at about, because it was all too easy in the whirl of unfamiliar things going on around you to ease up and the plane could nose over under the right conditions. They told us that it could, but I'm not sure that would happen unless you completely let the stick go. I

Cranking up

think it was just part of the routine to get us in the habit of paying attention to everything the instructor said.

Like most tail wheel planes, ground visibility forward is very poor in the Stearman because the nose is in the way. To taxi without running into something required you to "S" along the ground. By using the brake on one wheel while moving forward, you turned the plane slightly to one side until you could see along the path you wanted to travel. Then you would turn slightly the other way until you could see along the track out the other side of the cockpit, all the time headed in the proper direction. If this seems complicated, it really isn't. In the Stearman, you could lean pretty far out if you had the seat jacked up high, which most of us did, and your "S" turns were shallow. We were supposed to apply the brakes with our toes and not walk the rudder. The brakes were not that easy to use and most of the time you would see a plane going along the taxiway with the rudder switching back and forth. At taxi speed, the rudder had absolutely no effect, but we felt like it did.

Mr. Manchester got us started out and lined up on the taxiway and turned it over to me. You could always tell when a new cadet was taxiing by, by the exaggerated turns being made. I made it to the end of the runway without running off the taxiway. Thank goodness for wide taxi strips! Just off the end of the runway we stopped and checked the magnetos by running up the engine to about 1200 rpm and switching from one magneto to another. A drop of 200 rpm on each was acceptable. More than that and you took the plane back for a checkup.

We lined up on the runway and he said, "You make the takeoff while I tell you what to do. I'll be on the controls with you and not let you get into trouble." And all the time I thought I was going to be a passenger on the first ride. I guess the Army felt like there was no time to lose, so they might as well start finding out who was going to make it and who wasn't.

With the stick firmly in my gut and Mr. Manchester's admonition to keep it there ringing in my Gosport, we advanced the throttle all the way. At first, you have to use a little right brake to overcome the torque effect, but very soon the rudder takes over and it's pretty easy to stay straight. I don't remember at what speed the tail wants to come up, but the takeoff roll had just started when I was instructed to ease up on the back pressure. The tail came up and, wonder of wonders, I could see where I was going. When the horizon was just on the nose, the stick was neutralized and we picked up speed quickly. As we gathered speed, I was told to apply just a little back pressure on the stick and the plane flew itself off the ground.

That was, and continued to be for all my flying days, the most exhilarating sensation that I could have in an airplane. Exhilaration accompanied each takeoff, relief accompanied each landing.

I wish I were a better word spinner, so I could put down on paper just how I felt as we parted company with Mother Earth. There was a sensation of lightness that I had not felt in the Cub. For the first time, I really felt like I was flying. There is something about sitting in an open cockpit with the wind in your face and the noise of the engine in your ears, those two big, old wings sitting out there sort of holding everything together. Man, that is living!! I could look out of the cockpit and watch the ground go rushing by, and then appear to slow down as we got higher and higher. This disconnectedness from the ground imparted, at once, a sense of freedom and also a feeling of genuine terror. I knew damn well I was not supposed to be up here, yet, here I was not only off the ground, but getting further from it every second.

Very quickly, Mr. Manchester's voice brought me back out of my incipient reverie, with, "Get the nose up." I had momentarily forgotten that this was a machine, not a living thing that operated on its own. It needed a human hand on the controls to tell it what to do and where to go. At the moment, this human hand had no idea what it was supposed to do next. A little more back pressure put us in the proper climb attitude, and easing back on the throttle established the right air speed rate and climb. Mr. Manchester was patiently talking all the time, and I could feel his hands on the controls. He never had to overpower me, so I guess I was following along properly. I had heard stories about cadets freezing on the controls and causing crashes. It was said that some instructors carried along an extra control stick to bash the cadet on the head if he froze. I never saw Mr. Manchester with one so I guess he had more faith in his cadets than some.

I don't remember much detail about that first flight, but I'm sure we spent some time learning the stall characteristics of the Stearman. That seems to be the first order of business when checking out in any airplane. You need to know the signs when a flying machine gets ready to quit flying, so you can do what is necessary to make it keep flying. The only times you want to let a plane stall is when you have enough altitude to recover, or no altitude at all.

After about an hour of orientation, we came in for a landing with Mr. Manchester doing the flying. With most tail draggers, the perfect landing is a three pointer; main gear and tail wheel on the ground simultaneously, and no bounce. Airplanes that don't stall abruptly, and the Stearman doesn't, will sometimes fool you in to thinking they are ready to quit flying when they aren't. That's when one landing becomes two or three or more. You have actually flown the plane into the ground rather than letting it settle of its own accord. The perfect landing requires a perfect approach and a deft touch on the stick and rudder. If you can get the plane in a three point position about three feet off the ground and hold it there with the power off, sooner or later, it <u>will</u> stop flying and plunk down and stay like it is glued. Needless to say, Mr. Manchester didn't quite make the perfect landing. A pilot never does when he is trying to show off for someone.

Each day of flying added a little to my proficiency and confidence. There was at least one take off and one landing each day, naturally, and most days there were several. The most important thing a pilot learns is how to get the aircraft back on the ground, safely, and don't believe the old saw that "any landing you can walk away from is a good one." It's possible to walk away from a totally wrecked airplane, but the Army takes a very dim view of broken training planes. We were expected to make a perfect three pointer every time. I must say, landing an airplane was something I did pretty well. I found that it was best to try to follow the instructor's direction to a "T". There is no place for individuality and innovation in putting an airplane back on the ground. Most of the planes I flew were fairly forgiving, but when you are dealing with your future, you don't experiment. It was important to remember that one should always have the same number of landings as takeoffs.

Early on, each flying period started by going over all the things I had learned up to that time; check list, start up, taxi out, run up, take off, climb out and fly out to a practice area. I learned to make turns without losing altitude, to stall and recover until I was doing them in my sleep. Pretty soon these preliminaries to more complicated maneuvers became pretty well engrained and the instructor didn't have to talk me through them.

Precision seemed to be the Army watchword for its pilots. When the instructor called for me to level off at 2700 ft., that didn't mean 2695 or 2703. It meant 2700! When he said to turn to a certain reference point on the horizon or on the ground, that's where the wings had better come level. A 1-½ turn spin did not mean 1¾. This insistence on precision taught me to anticipate and know when to start my recovery. I learned to do pylon turns around a point on the ground and stay right on my altitude. There were "lazy eights" where I would do climbing-diving 180-degree turns along a road or fence line and end up going the same way I started at the same altitude. I learned to do perfect 90 degree turns by picking a horizon feature on one wing tip and turning toward it and rolling out with the plane's nose right on it. Precision! Precision!

All the while I was learning these rudiments there was a constant drumbeat in my ears, "Look around! Keep your head on a swivel!" When we were up there, I seldom saw another plane, but we knew there were at least fifty other cadets out doing the same things. The last thing anyone wanted was to have two Stearmans trying to occupy the same airspace at the same time. It was absolutely essential that military pilots develop the habit of constantly scanning the skies for other planes. In combat those other planes would likely be the enemy. So, we were taught to look behind, down, up, left, scan the cockpit, right, up, down, behind and then do the whole thing in reverse. That was what was called keeping the head on a swivel. Not keeping my head moving was probably the one thing I got yelled at about most. From talking to other cadets, I assume that was what we all got yelled at about.

The average time of dual instruction was ten hours. Some cadets soloed in eight and some in twelve. Not many were allowed to go much over twelve before soloing or washing out. Usually, an instructor could tell if a cadet was going to make it in ten hours.

I began my flight instruction on 10 Jan 44. On 27 Jan, I soloed with ten hours of dual instruction. While I was in service and Laverda was in Rutherford, I tried to write to her every day. She kept many of my letters that seemed to her to be special, and the one I wrote on 27 Jan was special. Let me quote directly:

"I soloed today! Believe it or not, I took the plane up all by myself. We went up the same as usual and shot four landings. The first three were good, in fact the third one was perfect. When I set it down, the instructor grabbed the Gosport and said, 'Brother, that was perfect. I couldn't have done better myself.'

Naturally that made me feel good, but when I bounced and had

After SOLO. Now I can wear my goggles up

71

to gun it on the next time around I was sort of deflated. By then I had given up soloing and when he said to take it in, I was sure I wouldn't make it. When I reached the parking line and started to turn in, he kept me going straight. We taxied out to the take off line and stopped the plane. Believe me, honey, I was pretty shaky. Mr. Manchester got out and told me that he knew damn well I could fly that plane or he wouldn't let me try it, that all I had to do was remember what he had kept telling me and to use my head and I'd make it OK. Then he walked off and away I went. I taxied into position, got my green light and headed down the field. I could hear my instructor talking to me, telling me what to do. Every move I made came just as natural as breathing. I flew the pattern and came in for my landing. As I came near the ground, I began to wonder if I was doing all I should and then I came for a pretty good landing. Mr. Manchester waved me on around. I made three landings, each one better than the last and went in. Apparently he was satisfied because he didn't say much about my flying. Gosh, I didn't realize that flying could be so much fun until I got up there alone. It's so much different with no one in the front. The plane practically jumps off the ground and flies altogether differently.

The guys on the ground sweated out every solo flight made today. Whenever a solo came in they were right there, grinning from ear to ear."

That was written the day it happened. I'm glad Laverda kept some of my letters, especially that one. I could have never remembered the event in such detail.

The day I soloed was solo day for most of the class. We had all been flying about the same number of hours each day, so, naturally would reach the magic ten hours together. A few soloed later and some never did. One after another, most of us got to wear our goggles on our head instead of around our necks. This was the ritual that marked our passage into the ranks of the "junior birdmen."

If it appears that I am spending a lot of time on my flying experiences, it is because for me and most of the rest of us this was what we were there for. In the matter of time spent, more time was spent doing things on the ground than things in the air. There were the inevitable ground school, drill and PT. These really occupied more of our time than flying did. I remember writing to Laverda and complaining about having to drill in the moonlight one morning.

Just as at every other training post, we had to fall out for roll call first thing every morning. We were to get dressed, put on our winter overcoats, because it gets very cold in Wickenburg in January, and fall out in our normal order to be counted. There were always sleepy heads that tried to squeeze in every second of sack time they could, and while the rest of us were getting dressed, they would stay in their bunks. As we began to leave the barracks they would jump into their flying boots, put their overcoats on over their underwear and straggle into formation. When it was still dark, they could get by unnoticed, but as the days began to lengthen, their bare legs showed under the overcoat and the cadet officers would slap them with "gigs". A few tours on open post weekends helped to adjust their sleeping habits.

One particular sleepy head would place his flying boots on the floor beside his bunk where all he had to do was jump down from his top bunk, into his boots, pull on his overcoat and he was ready for roll call. One night, one of the practical jokers in the barracks put a condom full of water in each boot after lights out. When the cadet fell into his boots the next morning the water squirted up to his crotch. Needless to say, the air turned blue around him, but he had to fall out in the frosty Arizona morning, wet boots and all. He had not allowed any time for contingencies. We had an unusually long roll call that morning. I wonder if the officers were in on the gag?

Another ritual that I never fully understood occurred as we went out for PT. To get from the barracks quadrangle to the athletic area, we had to pass through an archway. In that archway, the doctors and medics stationed themselves and made each of us open our mouths so they could look in our throats, and pull up our shirts to bare our chests. I never found out what they were looking for and I don't think they ever found it, because it happened just about every time we went out. I guess maybe there might have been some early warning signs of some infectious disease, such as measles or chicken pox, and they were trying to head off quarantining an entire barracks. Nothing like that ever happened, so I guess we were a pretty healthy bunch.

Before very long, there was a noticeable sameness in our chow menus. We could anticipate what was going to be served a day in advance. One cadet observed that he knew when we were going to run the cross-country in PT by what we had for breakfast or lunch. If we had pancakes for breakfast and PT in the morning – Cross-Country! Chili for lunch and PT in the afternoon – Cross-Country! By and large, the food was not bad, but the menus were unimaginative, much more so than at later bases. I'll hold forth on that later.

Long before I was drafted, I had read as much about the aviation cadet program as I could find and one of the things always stressed was that cadets had to be unmarried. Since I had gotten married secretly and in haste, the Army did not know that I was married and in my naiveté I was afraid to tell them for fear they would take a dim view of my lack of candor. Little did I realize, the Army could not care less about such peccadilloes. They were far too busy getting us trained and into combat to follow up on any small inconsistencies in our records.

It was in Primary that Laverda's mother took things into her hands and wrote me that I should do the right thing and tell the Army that I was married so Laverda could get the allowance that she deserved. She was right, of course. I had been content to just let things ride and not muddy up the spring. Just to get some moral support, I talked to the chaplain, explained the situation and he told me to immediately apply for her allowance. The Army had no restrictions on married cadets anymore and would think we had just gotten married.

When I think back on what a wimp I was, it is obvious that I had a great deal of growing up to do. I should not have waited so long to tell my family and should never have lied to the Army. Laverda went almost a year before she began to draw her proper allowance. She never mentioned it to me and seemed content to let things stay as they were, too. Every time I think of that situation, I feel ashamed of myself.

I would have loved to have her with me, but Wickenburg was so small and isolated, there was no place for her to stay. I don't remember any married cadet that I knew who was able to have his wife with him. There were a few Arizonan's whose wives might come in for a weekend, but none stayed there.

I don't recall how long we were confined to post before we had a weekend out. The upperclassmen had passed their quarantine when we got there, and we watched in envy each Saturday at noon when "open post" was declared for them and they loaded on the busses for Wickenburg to be returned that night or the next day looking considerably the worse for the wear.

When we finally were granted open post, we all piled aboard the busses with great expectations. It was a treat just to get away from the confines of Claiborne Flight Academy for a few hours. I don't know what we expected to find in Wickenburg, but whatever it was we were sorely disappointed. I have never seen such a dump. There was one bar, as I recall, and not being a drinker, I spent very little time there. There were some small cafes, drugstores and a few other places of business that held little attraction for military types. The population seemed to be predominately Mexican or Indian and they pretty much stayed to themselves. In fact, the whole population seemed to stay away from the military. All in all, the only thing Wickenburg had going for it was that it was different from the base.

I do recall that there was a sizeable bridge over a dry wash in the middle of town. I was informed by a native that that was the Hassayampa River and it really did have water in it. It was just about three feet below the sand that comprised the riverbed. I never knew if he was pulling my leg or not. It did look like there had been water in it in the past, but there was certainly none in it when I was there. If you look at a map of Arizona, you will see the Hassayampa River drawn on it in a broken line. I guess that means there is water in it sometimes.

I guess you could say that open post in Wickenburg was not a highlight of my tour of duty in Arizona. The only excitement that occurred when we were there was when a battalion of tank drivers came in on leave from desert maneuvers one weekend. They pretty much took over the town and ran the cadets out of their favorite bar. They didn't have much respect for flyboys.

Once I soloed, my flying time was about evenly divided between dual instruction and solo. When I was up alone, I was expected to practice all the things I was being taught during dual instruction, and each dual period seemed to be devoted to drilling on the things I had already been taught, with some new things each time. It was the instructor's job to make sure I was proficient in all the basic maneuvers so I could pass my check rides. Every so often, we would have to be checked by one of the senior civilians. Interspersed along the way would be check rides by Army pilots. There were required checks at certain hours, with two civilian checks to one Army. It seemed to me that the civilians were a little tougher than the Army. I don't recall having any particular trouble on any of my checks, but some cadets were washed out on check rides.

There was one hard-nosed civilian named Ball that everyone hated to get. He had a reputation for chewing on his cadets the entire time they were in the air, and on the ground his mouth was constantly going. To listen to him, you would think we were the sorriest lot of prospects to ever pass an Army physical. When all was said and done, I don't think he washed out a single cadet in our class. There was doubtless method to his madness. I think he was deliberately trying to rattle his student to see how they performed under stress. You came away from a successful check ride with Ball feeling like you could handle anything.

I remember a critique session we had one day when flying was stood down because of weather. We all gathered in a hanger to listen to the instructors go over things that we needed to hear over and over. Ball was holding forth about an incident that had happened earlier. He was coming to land with a student and discovered another plane landing at the same time in the opposite direction. They appeared to be on a collision course. Both planes veered away from each other, fortunately, in opposite directions. He was practically frothing at the mouth as he recalled the incident. He used it to try to illustrate how to react to panic situations like that. He said he didn't get the other plane's number, or he would have washed him out on the spot. I'm just as glad he didn't get the number. I was flying that plane.

The day the above incident happened was one of those days, as happens in Arizona, that the wind had risen during the morning flying period and shifted directions. It was blowing hard enough that the ground crew had freed the wind tee to swing with the wind. This was supposed to alert us to unusual conditions. It seemed that everyone in the air, but Ball realized the wind had changed and appropriately changed their landing pattern. It turned out that I was in the proper pattern, and Ball was wrong. I'm sure he was so busy chewing on his student that he failed to check the tee and flew his pattern for the wind direction when he took off. Since there was no way he could ever find out who was in the other plane, I kept my mouth shut. I never told anyone about it.

I think most cadets enjoyed aerobatics in the Stearman more than anything else. I know I did. Loops, snap rolls, slow rolls, barrel rolls, aileron rolls, Immelmann turns, split S'es, four and eight point rolls, spins, chandelles were all great fun, and helped us become more familiar and comfortable with our plane. The Stearman had one disturbing little quirk that scared the pooh out of me the first time it happened. When the plane was rolled on its back, the engine died, dead. No sound, just the wind in the wires. I was unprepared for it the first time it happened, and was extremely relieved that it caught back up when we completed the roll. It seems it had a float bowl carburetor and upside down no gas went into the engine and it quit. I found out later that early models of the Spitfire did the same thing and it cost some pilots their lives.

One of my friends, Duane Adams, was up solo one day and started a slow roll. He had fastened his seat belt but had failed to pull it tight. He fell partially out of the cockpit, far enough that he couldn't reach the stick or rudder. There he was, upside down and the plane, being very stable, stubbornly remained on its back, slowly spiraling downward. He finally managed to pull himself back in far enough to kick the stick to one side and roll the plane back. Needless to say, he never needed to be reminded to cinch up his belt again.

One morning, I sprained my ankle playing basketball in PT. It didn't seem too bad. I just limped a little. That afternoon I was scheduled to go up solo and practice aerobatics. The ankle bothered me a little, but I was able to take off all right and climb up to altitude. My first maneuver was a snap roll. In a snap roll you pull the nose up and then sharply kick in full rudder one way and full aileron and elevator the opposite. The plane flips over on its back, and when upside down, you quickly reverse the controls and the plane is supposed to continue the roll and right itself. That is, it does if both ankles are in good working order. My bum ankle failed me, and there I was, stuck momentarily upside down. I about passed out from the pain. Very quickly, my snap roll became a half snap as I used my good ankle and rolled back the other direction. Right then, I decided that the best place for me was back on the ground, if I could get there. I did, and pulled in and parked it and filled out the plane's log. The girl who gassed up the planes came out and was topping off the tank when I tried to get out. As soon as my sprained ankle hit the wing, it gave way and I fell sprawling on the ground. She was off the truck and helping me up almost by the time I quit bouncing. That ended my flying for a couple of days. After soaking my ankle in hot Epsom salts water at the dispensary and having it wrapped in an Ace bandage, I was back on my feet. I was excused from drill and PT for a while. Fortunately, I didn't miss a significant amount of flying time.

The daily routine of flying, ground school, PT, drill and flight line activities went on. Each day we got better and better or we washed out. It seemed that about every other day some downcast cadet was seen packing his barracks bags and leaving the post. Actually, some of them weren't downcast at all. Flying was just not as thrilling an occupation as they had first thought and if they never saw another airplane, it would be too soon. I could sort of feel for them, because there were times after a particularly bad day, I wondered if it was worth it. I think the Army knew this would happen and deliberately staggered the flying periods so that we would have ground school and PT one day in the afternoon and the morning the next. This gave us a break away from flying to recharge our enthusiasm. It worked, because our class had a remarkably low washout rate.

With cadets, there was the potential for excitement any time they were in the air. I related the story of Ernie Engstrom nosing his plane over in front of the whole cadet corps. Another time there was an incident that demonstrated the sort of things that can happen when you have a bunch of airplanes in a congested area. On 14 Feb a cadet nosed his plane over on landing at the main field. This closed one side of the field and caused very heavy traffic on the opposite side. Three fellows came around for landings, but they overshot. Two of them went on around without even cutting the throttle. The third one went on in but saw he couldn't make it, so he gunned it and started climbing out without looking. Bill Brady, one of my flight buddies, and Rodney Bradshaw, also from my flight, stayed high while Basco, the third cadet, climbed right under Bradshaw. Brady frantically waved at Bradshaw to try to warn him. But he just grinned and waved back. Basco kept on coming up until he clipped Bradshaw's landing gear with his top wing. It tore off one of Bradshaw's wheels and caved in Basco's top wing. Basco immediately went into a glide and landed in the sand at the end of the runway. Bradshaw went on around for another try, unaware that one of his wheels was gone. Brady tried to make him realize what was wrong, but couldn't, so he came on in. He made one of those movie landings, on one wheel and went straight down the runway and didn't even scratch a wingtip. Bradshaw had no idea that he had only one wheel until the plane completely lost flying speed. Every time the wing would drop a little he would bring it back up with aileron until the landing gear stub dug in and stopped him. It was a great landing and even the instructors were raving about it.

The above description was taken from a letter to Laverda. It was in that same letter that I related the washout of four more cadets. Two got disgusted and quit, one couldn't fly and a check pilot told another that he was on his way out. That was the way it went. Every washout made the rest of us just a bit more careful and attentive and determined to mind our P's and Q's. And, as I've said before, we each secretly sighed in relief that we had survived yet another cut and felt better about our chances.

At the end of four weeks it came time for class 44F to graduate from Primary. Ordinarily, within a week of their departure, another class would roll in from Pre-flight, and we would become the upper class whose duty it was to impress the fledglings with our flying prowess. This time was to be different. With the war going better on all fronts and the training pipelines full of replacements, the Army began to close down its civilian operations. Ours was to be the last class to train at Claiborne Fight

Academy. The reduction in number of cadets meant a corresponding reduction in instructors, so I got a new one, Franklin Daley. Daley was a cherub faced young man with an infectious grin and a great personality. We hit it off immediately. His training approach was pretty much the same as Manchester's, so I made the transition very smoothly.

As we neared the end of our training, the weather in Arizona began to warm up and the flying became more enjoyable. This was due not only to the improvement in the weather but, also, in the improvement in our flying abilities. I certainly felt more comfortable alone in the cockpit. I assiduously practiced the lessons by my instructor, passed my check rides with very little difficulty. I began to feel that I was a little better pilot than my instructor at CTD thought I was.

I recall an experience one day near the end of my training that has stuck with me all these years. It was a beautiful day with about 4/10-cloud cover at 4,000 ft. The cover was little powder puff cumulus clouds that we called fair weather cumulus. They were all at the 4,000-ft. level with brilliant blue sky above. These were the kind of clouds that were just made for buzzing and stooging around in. The very thing that we had been admonished not to do. It was all too likely that if one cadet was up there buzzing clouds, there were others and the chance of an accident was not insignificant.

Despite having been warned of the dangers of cloud buzzing, I decided to go up there anyway. It takes awhile for a Stearman to climb to 4,000 ft., so I took off and straightaway began to climb. I circled above some familiar landmarks so I wouldn't get too far away from the auxiliary field we were flying from that day. Full of anticipation of some exhilarating cloud flying, I popped out on top of the cloud cover and immediately felt an overpowering sense of aloneness. All I could see in all directions was an endless sea of white, like the snowfields of the Arctic and above that, the bluest, most featureless sky you ever saw. There was not one wisp of stratus cloud to act as a point of reference, just inky blue emptiness. I felt like I had passed through some sort of time warp and was back at the beginning of time when all was "without form and void"(Gen. 1:2). All was not dark, as in Genesis, but all was blue and white. I got the weirdest feeling in the pit of my stomach, like I had become detached from the world. My plans to buzz clouds suddenly underwent a drastic change.

There was not familiar landmark to be seen in any direction, except down. I rolled up on one wing and down below was the familiar, old dirty brown earth. I did a split S back down through the clouds to where all the familiar stuff was. For a few moments I was a little shaky. I had undergone a bout with vertigo, not unlike that pilots experience when instrument flying. Lack of points of reference causes disorientation when the senses other than sight will take over. I finished my flight period below 4,000 ft. where I could see recognizable features.

The claim had been made that there were 300 days of flying weather in Arizona, which made it a great state for flight training. That was the claim. The last ten days of our nine weeks at Wickenburg were ten days of rain. Many of us did not get the requisite 75 hours of flying, but were graduated, anyway.

The days we could not fly were spent in critique sessions. It was at one of these that we got to know an interesting character among our fellow students. His name was Lyman R. Brothers, Jr. from Suffolk, VA, a first lieutenant of the Artillery. The Army permitted commissioned officers who had been on active duty for awhile to apply for flight training, if they chose. We had five of these officers in 44G. Lt. Brothers had been stationed in the Aleutians after the Japanese invasion. He had spent some very harrowing times there and as soon as the chance to get into pilot training arose, he applied. He told of some of the atrocities committed by the Japanese on our men at Dutch Harbor, and in relating it, he came to the brink of tears. His most fervent hope was to get through pilot training and be sent to the Pacific. I hope he made it.

Among the ground school subjects we had was map reading and dead reckoning navigation. We would study aviation maps and using the E6B navigation computer, and plot imaginary cross country flights. The E6B was actually a specialized slide rule designed just for aviators. With it you could do most of the planning for a cross-country mission. Knowing your airspeed and the wind speed and direction, you could figure the compass heading you had to fly to reach your destination. You could also determine the elapsed time between checkpoints and a myriad of other things you needed to know to properly plan. I found this course to be absorbing because I had always had a fascination for maps. I found that I was pretty good at relating a map to what I was seeing on the ground.

We were required to fly one round robin cross-country mission to satisfy our Primary requirements. We were given fresh maps of the area, told the destinations for each leg of our flight, handed our E6B's and told to plan our entire flight. We each filed a flight plan, just like the big boys. The circuit we were to fly was over unfamiliar territory, not where we had been practicing daily. This added a level of apprehension to already free flowing adrenaline. There is nothing like the prospect of getting lost over the Arizona wilderness to sharpen one's focus on the job at hand.

This was a new experience, but one which I had eagerly anticipated since getting into ground school navigation. I was ready to see if what we had been taught really worked. I knew I could fly the airplane, and now I was going to see if I could get from one place to another without getting lost. After all, that's why we were learning to fly, to get from a base to a target and back again.

I don't recall the route we were to fly, but there were two fields where we were to make touch and go landings for an instructor who was parked there. We were graded on how well we stuck to our flight plan and our technique in landing and take off. There was one field that was unmanned and we were to just circle it and proceed on our way. As I recall, none of us had any difficulty, and no one got lost. It was a lot of fun.

As training wound down, we began to speculate about where we might be sent for Basic. We knew very little about what Basic training bases were out there, but we all hoped not to stay in Arizona. We knew that the next step up was into the Vultee BT-13, a much larger airplane, but we knew little else about what lay before us. We were pretty sure we would go back to California, but we didn't know where. When the orders came down, it was Minter Field, Bakersfield, CA. So once again, we were off into a new adventure at a new base, with new planes and instructors and a whole new set of experiences.

Chapter VII

BASIC FLIGHT TRAINING

Having completed all the required curriculum of Primary and more or less the prescribed hours of flying and "mastered" the Stearman PT-17, we were now ready for bigger and better things. The bigger thing was the BT-13, a veritable brute of an airplane when compared to the PT-17. It was an all-metal, low-wing monoplane with a 450-hp radial engine with an enclosed cockpit, just like the fighter planes. It had flaps, trim tabs, a two-position controllable pitch propeller and a radio. We had learned the rudiments of flying and now we were to have the added responsibilities of more advanced equipment and other things to keep in mind as we moved further along the road to those coveted silver wings.

The better things did not necessarily include the BT-13, because it had a reputation of being a killer of cadets, or, that's what we had heard. Being bigger, faster and heavier than the Primary trainers, it was nowhere as nimble, nor as easy to fly. It was going to require a whole new set of parameters to adjust to, but not one of us of had any doubt that we would soon become the masters of the "Vultee Vibrator".

Troop trains always seemed to leave at night and arrive in the morning. This, I suppose, was by design so that the assignment of personnel to quarters and beginning the new base routine could take place in the daylight. So it was with the move to Minter Field. We disembarked the busses from the station at just about the time the morning flight period started. As we stood milling around on the post street, the BT-13's were taking off, one after another on parallel runways. What an awe inspiring sound! The props were in flat pitch and the engines were so much more powerful than we had been accustomed to that the ground fairly shook and our eardrums protested. We just stood there with our mouths agape.

The infamous Vultee "Vibrator"

These expressions turned to big grins as we began to realize that we were going to be doing that in a day or two. Although the prospect of moving into these bigger airplanes was a bit daunting, we were still looking forward to it. We had come to realize that the upperclassmen doing the flying were no different from us, just four or five weeks ahead. I think the brass in charge knew that this experience was part of our orientation and let us watch and marvel until the last plane was off the ground and the noise had subsided before they fell us in to be marched off to breakfast.

Bakersfield is at the south end of the San Joaquin Valley, 112 miles NNW of Los Angeles. It lies between the Sierra Nevada Mountains on the East and the Coastal Range on the West and just North of the Tehachapi Mountains. The San Joaquin and Sacramento Valleys extend through the middle of California and contain some of the driest, most fertile farmland in the world. They are, for the most part, relatively flat and quite wide, making them ideal for flight training fields, and there were dozens of them along their length. The weather was also a factor, because it seldom rains east of the Coastal Range.

The day we arrived at Minter was a typical March California day, bright, sunny and warm. After the last few days of cold rain in Arizona, we were ready for some pleasant weather.

Minter Field was a genuine Army base. It had been built some time before the war in anticipation of the need for training bases. It was strictly GI. All the buildings were of the classic, frame construction so prevalent on military bases. The streets were laid out on a grid alongside the airfield and the different areas, i.e., barracks, ground school, administration, headquarters, maintenance, engineering, etc., were all arranged to relate to each other so that they were separated, but accessible. This made for efficiency, but a distressing sameness. However, we were not going to be there long enough to become bored with the surroundings. We needed to get on with the war.

Our first surprise, albeit a pleasant one, came immediately. We were marched to the nearest cadet mess for breakfast. As we marched in and started to sit at our tables, we noticed that there was a crate of bottles of milk in ice at the end of each table. We were instructed to take one if we wanted milk for our meal. Needless to say, most of us did just that. After the experience in Santa Ana and the ho hum food at Wickenburg, we thought we had died and gone to heaven. The milk was not the only revelation. Civilians under contract to the Army ran the mess halls and they must have been very patriotic because there was never a shortage of food or a boring menu. We cadets were due only the best.

Since we were in the heart of some of the best fruit and vegetable farming in the country, we always had fresh vegetables and fruit on the table. At lunch and dinner there was always a bowl of fruit and olives on each table. It was there that I learned to like black olives. I had never seen anything but pimento stuffed olives from a jar and didn't know what a ripe olive was. It was love at first bite. There were apples, oranges, bananas, grapefruit, peaches and some fuzzy little green things that I didn't eat. It wasn't until well after the war that I learned that they were kiwis and that you had to peel them to eat them.

The tables were set with plates and stainless steel flatware and real cups with handles. Civilians served us and there were always seconds on everything. If they hadn't worked us so hard we would all have gotten fat. As it was, all that food was converted into muscle and expended in nervous energy. On Sunday and holidays there were special menus and the tables were set with white table cloths and silverware!! We never ceased to marvel at the chow at Minter Field. It was a true highlight.

Since Minter Field was a much larger facility than Claiborne Flight Academy, there were many more cadets there. It seemed to be a collection of the output from at least four primary schools. There were 459 cadets in 44-G, divided into eight squadrons of two flights each, A and B. Each squadron had 14 or 15 instructors and two flight commanders, all Army. Above all this was the usual Army hierarchy all the way up to the training wing commander, who was a full colonel. There were no civilians involved in our training anymore. Whether this was good or bad, I'm not prepared to say. When you get right down to it, we were all just civilians in uniform for the duration "plus six." We were not really full-fledged members of the military culture, and, for the most part, had no desire to be, beyond the end of the war. We just wanted to do our part and get back to our lives that had been so rudely interrupted.

The training routine at Minter was just about what it had been at Wickenburg. Drill, PT, ground school and flying were woven into a familiar tapestry, just the setting was different. A lot of what went on at Minter will be forever lost in my memory banks. Much of what I was able to recall about Wickenburg was retrieved from the letters to Laverda that she kept. When we were apart, we tried to write each other every night, so when she could be with me much of what I might have written is lost. That may be just as well, because I've found myself being caught up in the minutiae of too much recollection.

Graduating to a larger, radio equipped airplane required the learning of a more advanced means of communication between instructor and cadet and between plane and ground. Much of what we learned was on-the-job training, but there were ground school classes in the use of the radios in the BT-13. These rudiments carried over into the more advanced aircraft, because radio was radio in those days and most of them were pretty much the same. At least, the conversations were the same. Until we got into combat aircraft, we all used separate headsets and hand held microphones. Since we were now flying in enclosed cockpits, we no longer had helmets and goggles as our birdman badges. We wore our overseas caps and set our headsets up on the sides of our heads when they were not in use. That gave us that rakish, go-to-hell look that all of us tried to cultivate.

Radio discipline was stressed from the beginning. Unnecessary chatter on the air was frowned upon, to say the least. All pilots tend to get overly exuberant at times and fill the airwaves with extraneous conversation that can interfere with pertinent, even emergency transmissions. For this reason, we were commanded to use the radio sparingly. We had to call the tower for taxi, take-off and landing instructions, and occasionally ship to ship talk. The rest of the time we were to be on intercom with our instructor or monitoring our channel if solo.

One humorous episode was said to have happened at Minter, but I have a notion that this same story with variations was heard all over the Air Corps. A cadet was out doing his thing and talking to another plane when he was heard by the tower to say, "Oh, I'm all screwed up."(not quite the exact terminology)

The tower came on the air with, "Will the pilot who made the last transmission please give the tower his call number?"

To which the cadet radioed back, "I'm not that screwed up."

The microphone we used was the classic hand held unit that was designed just after the first radio went aloft. The mouthpiece was at right angles to the handle and the operating button was on the handle right where you could squeeze it as you held the mouthpiece alongside your mouth. Inattention to my radio procedure got me into trouble once. I was radioing the tower for taxi instructions when I forgot my plane's call sign. Without realizing I still had the mike button down, I said right over the air, "What the hell is this?"

When I remembered the right call letters, I finished my request for instructions. The tower immediately said, "The cadet in (my call sign) report to his squadron ready room immediately after returning to the field."

I knew I was in trouble, just what kind I was not sure. But, I went on with my flight and met my instructor at the door of the ready room. He was waiting for me. I got a thorough chewing out. He told me that I could be washed out for using profanity on the radio, and if I had to go to the commandant of cadets' office, that just might happen. He said that he had just happened to be monitoring the tower channel and caught what had happened and was going to punish me before the commandant got wind of it. Once punished, the higher ups could not do more to me. Double jeopardy works in the military justice system, too. His punishment was 25 laps around the ready room with my parachute on. I never heard any more about the incident, and needless to say, I was never again guilty of holding a mike button down while using profanity. That is not to say that profanity left my vocabulary. I just never let it go out over the air, again.

My first flight instructor at Minter was a Lt. Cozine. I remember him as a rather quiet, serious individual that didn't make much casual conversation. He was straight forward, but not overbearing. He really seemed to want his cadets to learn and become good pilots. That may seem like a funny thing to say about an instructor. You would think all of them would want their cadets to do well, but I can tell you that there were some that hated their job and the cadets that came with it. They seemed to think they were being wasted trying to pound flying skills into a bunch of thick headed numbskulls with two left feet. They would much rather have been flying combat and seemed to resent those who might get there before them. Fortunately, those were fairly few, and were weeded out before they could do irreparable harm. However, I'm convinced that some otherwise good pilots fell prey to these malcontents and ended up washed out. Usually, good check pilots could head off a washout if they were aware of an instructor's attitude. I have a story to tell about such an incident that happened to me later in Advanced Flight Training.

Actually, I remember very few details about my time in BT-13's, just some general impressions about the plane and some of the things we had to learn. In checking my old logbook, I find that I soloed the beast after about 5 hours of dual. That was about average, I guess.

There were quite a few horror stories floating around about how much trouble you could get into in a BT-13, from spins you could not get out of to half rolls on take-off. I never knew whether these were true or manufactured by the Army to make cadets stay on their toes.

As I said earlier, the Stearman was very easy to get off the ground. The control surfaces were so effective that you hardly got rolling before the rudder would control your direction down the runway. The engine/propeller torque was detectable but was easily overcome with just rudder control. The same was not true of the BT-13. If you rammed the throttle full open as soon as you started your take-off roll, there was a distressing tendency for the plane to veer off toward the boondocks. As long as you were on the ground right brake, full right rudder and back on the throttle would get you back on line. Where disaster occurred was when the pilot kept the power on and tried to horse the plane off the ground before getting sufficient flying speed. The plane could flip over on its back and dive into the ground. We were told again and again that this was a possibility, until we all refined our take-off procedure so as not to be the next statistic. I never heard of such a thing happening while I was at Minter.

The stall characteristics of the plane were completely different from the Stearman. Where the Stearman almost had to be forced to stall, the 13 stalled with authority. As you approached stalling speed, the whole plane began to buffet and shudder, thus the name "Vibrator." Instead of stalling straight ahead, like a good little bird should, this sucker would fall off on the left wing and you were in a spin before you could say, "Oh, s__t!" This characteristic was demonstrated to me on my very first ride, and spins must have been a big part of our training because I have notes in the margin of my logbook of the number of spins per flight and the total accumulation of spins. I learned that you can stall a BT-13 straight ahead if you are alert and manipulate the controls properly. An inadvertent spin occurred if you were careless and inattentive and could become vicious and a killer if you panicked or forgot your instructor's instructions.

On the day of my first check ride, 30 Mar, I was waiting in the plane for the squadron commander, Capt. Cowan, who was late. He came running out to the plane and jumped in with an apology for being late; explaining that word had just come in about a crash. He had me take off and once airborne and out of the pattern, he took over and flew out to the crash site. On the way, he told me that a cadet and an instructor had been practicing spins when the cadet froze on the controls. The instructor couldn't get him loose by overpowering him or screaming at him on intercom. The two seats were too far apart for the instructor to reach him, so finally he had to bail out and leave the cadet, who spun in and was killed. We found the site, which was at the edge of a plowed field. All that was left was huge crater and parts of BT-13 scattered about. My check ride was relatively short that day. According to my log I did one spin. As I recall, Capt. Cowan assured me that if I froze, he would leave me up there just like the other instructor did his cadet. I never got into a predicament where the instructor called for the controls that I was reluctant to give them to him. At "I've got it," my hands went up where he could see them, and he had it!

Aerobatics in the 13 were not nearly as much fun as in the PT-17, but all of the same maneuvers could be done. They just seemed a bit awkward. Snap rolls were sort of like snaaaaap rolls, it wallowed in a slow roll and loops were shaped like a fat, lower case "L". I learned all of the various maneuvers and became fairly proficient, but never enjoyed it as much as in the Stearman.

A new innovation came for us when we began to practice formation flying. We had never been officially allowed to do that in Primary, although I heard reports from other cadets about their instructors playing around with it. Mine never did.

In Basic, we flew formation as part of our training, and such flights were scheduled. I seem to remember one formation flight, although there is no mention of it in my logbook. This may have been impromptu, rather than scheduled. It seemed like fun and I know that other cadets got to fly formation more than I did, because halfway through Basic, I went into twin engine training, but more about that later.

Before I leave the BT-13, I have to tell you about Duncan. Duncan was a washed out naval cadet. This seems like the Air Corps was settling for second best to the Navy, but that was not quite the case. An instructor at a critique asked Duncan why he had left the Navy. His reply was, "Sir, I'm in the beginning swimming class in PT."

It seems that he had never learned to swim, and since naval Aviators spent a good deal of time over water, it seems a good idea for them the able to swim as well as fly. He had managed to make it all the way through Navy Advanced before he was found out. They gave him the option of becoming an ordinary seaman or transferring to the Army directly into Basic. Naturally, he chose to continue to fly and was probably a better flyer than some of our instructors.

The story was told about a time when three cadets, one of whom was Duncan, and their instructors were practicing formation flying, when the lead instructor decided to see just how good Duncan was. His intent was to see if he could lose Duncan by some wild maneuvering. He lost the other cadet right away, but Duncan stayed glued to his wing like they were one plane. After that, Duncan didn't have to go through some of the exercises the rest of us did. I never did know what happened to him, because our ways soon parted as our training regimens changed.

In addition to learning to use a radio as part of our flight routine, we began to do some instrument flying. The BT-13 was equipped with the basic blind flying navigational aids, or flight instruments. They were the same on all military planes and grouped the same way and in the same location on all instrument panels, right in front of the pilot. There were six of them and they were:

> Artificial Horizon
> Directional Gyro
> Turn and Bank Indicator
> Airspeed Indicator
> Rate of Climb Indicator
> Altimeter

Long before we had ever done any instrument flying, we had been told how to use these instruments, but not how to rely on them, exclusively. Although we had had some Link trainer time in Primary, it was minimal. In Basic we began to get serious about instrument flying, both in the air and on the ground. The 13 had a collapsible hood that the cadet could pull over his head and exclude the outside world, while the instructor in the rear cockpit directed his maneuvers and kept him away from other airplanes. At first, it was a very strange feeling not to be in contact with the horizon or ground, but dependent entirely on six little round dials to keep you from disaster. It took considerable will power not to rely on the feel in the seat of your pants determine your flight attitude. Being constantly reminded by the instructors and all our instrument texts that we <u>must</u> put absolute trust in those instruments began to have its effect and I began to feel more comfortable under the hood.

At first, we concentrated on flying straight and level, holding altitude and heading. We then began to do some procedure turns, left and right; altitude and heading changes, stalls and spins. I thought spins in contact flight were scary enough, I didn't know from nothing until I did a spin blind. All the flight instruments just went crazy. None of them are doing the right things in relation to each other. As I recall, we were supposed to rely on the turn and bank indicator, primarily, to get out of the spin. Once it was centered you could begin to get the others back in some sort of order. You had to sort of visualize what the plane was doing based on your experience in contact flight and make the requisite moves to right yourself. This was 54 years ago, and since I am able to write this, I must have done it right. Once the instructor even talked me through a blind landing. I didn't actually land, but I was on the approach and very close to the ground when he let me open the hood. This, I guess, simulated breaking out under the ceiling.

I earlier mentioned the Link trainer. This was the first flight simulator, and probably saved more pilots lives than any other one training device in the world. It was used to give pilots valuable training in instrument flying and radio range navigation without subjecting him to the hazards of actual flight. Externally, it looked like a stubby little airplane sitting on a pedestal. The wings and tail surfaces had absolutely no function except to amuse and to leave the student with the impression that he was getting into a real plane before he pulled the cover over his head. That was on the prototype used to impress the engineering brass that it was to be used for simulated flight training, since it looked like a plane. As sharp as they were, it might not have sold if it had been just a box on a pedestal with flight instruments in it. It would have performed the same training, but it would not have looked like an airplane. If I sound a bit skeptical about the mentality of some of the Air Corps brass, it is because I was and am. Some of the things the boys at Wright Field did to perfectly good airplanes that met all their specifications, just to see if they could improve them or make them do things they were not designed to do, would fill a large book. Specifications for combat aircraft were developed long before the military were real sure of just what they needed. When the manufacturers produced a prototype, it might or might not be what was needed then. Things change with time, experience and the input of real combatants. A good case in point is the P-38. It was originally designed as a high-speed interceptor of bombers, with high altitude capabilities and heavy firepower. Maneuverability and range were not in the specs. Before the war ended it had been modified and remodified until it was a superior long-range escort with exceptional maneuverability, capable of out flying just about any other plane in the air.

The Link trainer was a simulated, generic airplane cockpit. The instrument panel was complete with all the basic instruments, both flight and engine. There were both stick and rudder controls and they worked. Movement of the flight controls produced the proper response in the instruments, so that with the hood down you felt like you were actually in a real airplane. The only thing missing was the sound and vibration of an engine. There was a radio that connected you to the outside world, and at the other end of that link was your instructor who set up your problems, introduced simulated flight conditions, acted as tower and range control, and monitored your performance. For every hour under the hood in the air, there was at least an hour in the Link. All of the radio range problems we flew were first run in the Link. You could even spin a Link. Maybe you think that wasn't a sensation! I found the Link to be less responsive on its controls than a real airplane, and it felt less stable under you than the real thing. Otherwise, the simulation was very good.

There is about to be a break in my narrative where my career takes a decidedly different turn, so I think I will turn to spend some time away from the training regimen and talk about more pleasant things. I need to bring you up to speed on how I spent my off duty time.

Because Bakersfield is a much larger town than Wickenburg, most of the married cadets were able to have their wives with them. There were a lot of cadets from California and other western states, so it was not too much of a problem for them, but not many wives were as far away as Laverda was. I was hesitant to ask her to come out because of the distance and the difficult travelling conditions. That decision was taken out of my hands when she announced that she was coming out regardless of how difficult it was. There was no way I could get off the base in advance of her arrival to find her a place to stay, but she didn't let that deter her. She bought her train ticket, packed her bag and set out. Even in your wildest dreams you could never imagine the anxiety she must have felt getting on that train by herself and heading into who knows what.

Train travel for civilians during the war was extraordinarily difficult. Most of the passenger rolling stock was being used to move troops, and the railroads were making so much money that the train crews, especially the conductors, were very arrogant and impatient with all passengers, civilian and military alike. There was no such thing as reserving a seat. You got a ticket, showed up at the station when the train came in, usually late, and got aboard, if you could. Once aboard, you scrounged for seating as best you could. I have visions of the train she came out on looking like those trains you see in the travelogues about India, with people hanging all over it.

She boarded the train in Rutherford, went to St. Louis and changed to the train to Los Angeles, which, luckily, went through Bakersfield. The train was so crowded that she sat on her suitcase in the ladies restroom for **four days!** That is almost unbelievable. Looking back on it, I can see why our marriage has lasted 67 years. Love that would allow her to go through that sort of tribulation just to be with her husband the few hours a week he could be off base could never be extinguished. It just had to last. And my desire to be with her those hours was enough to permit her to make that trek, not that I could have stopped her if I had wanted to. She was not alone. Every civilian train that ran during the war was loaded with wives and wives to be going to be with their men. Our futures were uncertain, at best, and there was that burning need to be together as much as humanly possible.

There were no food services on her train so when it would stop the people would have to get off and desperately try to grab a sandwich and a drink before the train pulled out. There were usually "butcher boys" hawking food, so she managed not to starve, but it must have been nerve wracking for her. Not once in all our married life have I heard her say that she regretted making the trip. We both come from a background that taught us that you did what you thought you had to do, and made the best of whatever situation you found yourself in.

I don't exactly remember when it was she got to Bakersfield, but I think

Our first weekend in Bakersfield

it may have been on a Saturday because I met the train, and there she was. I was never so glad to see anyone in my life. She certainly didn't look like someone who had just spent four days sitting on a suitcase. I had gotten a motel room in town and the first thing she wanted to do was take a shower. She must have felt crusty.

Housing for dependents was a real problem in the towns near military bases. Fortunately, the Army did as much as it could to help. There was no new housing, so we had to depend on the good offices and mercenary proclivities of local homeowners. Many people opened their homes for servicemen to rent rooms for their families. They were paid, of course, and the Army was pretty good about screening them and seeing that we didn't get gouged. Most of the homeowners had someone in the service, too.

I immediately applied for a place, but for a couple of weeks we had to catch as catch could. Neither of us can remember much about

We had a room in this house

what Laverda did when I was flying, but I'm sure she must have had some anxious moments. We didn't have much money, because her allotment had not caught up with her. That alone would have been enough to deter a less determined person, but not Laverda. She managed to get a job in a blueprint plant, which she soon lost because she knew absolutely nothing

One of my favorite pictures

about that work. She had to call home for some money, and her father wired her $25, which was enough to get her through until she could get another job and the allotment caught up with her. Her next job was in a ten-cent store. It was not much, but it gave her a little money and something to do.

One weekend, we got together with one of my cadet buddies and his wife and stayed at a resort hotel in the Tehachapi Pass, between Bakersfield and L.A. The cadet's name was Bill Brady and he was from Hollywood, so he was not too far from home. He claimed his father was a PR man for the Crosby Enterprises. That's the Crosby as in Bing Crosby. He said he was acquainted with Bing and had sat in on recording sessions and watched the man perform. I was impressed.

Brady's wife had their car so she and Laverda drove up to the hotel to secure the rooms before we were able to get off post. We had to hitchhike up in a blowing dust storm. We spent a very long time thumbing before a kindly old couple picked us up. I was very glad to get there because I needed a bath as bad as Laverda did after getting off the train. It was not a real fun weekend, except that we were together, and that was what counted.

Somehow we managed to get over that initial hump and life sort of smoothed out when I got a room with kitchen privileges in a nice part of town. It was at that place that Laverda prepared our first home cooked meal of our married life. As I recall, we had fried chicken and the trimmings. Laverda was a nervous wreck, because she wanted it to be just perfect. By her own admission, she had never cooked much, preferring to work outside. She would trade places with her sister, Grace, and do her outside chores while Grace learned to cook from their mother. The

Caption: Sundays were great

dinner came off just fine, considering that she was a novice and was cooking in someone else's kitchen. It was probably the best dinner I had ever eaten.

Just like in Beloit, there was not much to do in town, since we had no transportation except our feet. We ate out some, palled around with some of the other married cadets and their wives, not forming any lasting relationships with any of them. Most of us were trying to squeeze as much time with our spouses as we could in the limited hours we had. Each weekend pass was only about 36 hours long, which didn't leave much time for anything but being together. Neither of us remembers much about that time, so I suppose nothing earth shaking happened. Being in California, I suppose nothing earth shaking is considered to be a definite plus.

As I said earlier, my flying career was about to take a decidedly different turn. Up to now, the normal training routine was for all cadets to complete Basic in the BT-13. When going into Advanced, decisions were made about who was to continue in single engine training and who was to go multi-engine. Single engine meant advancing to the North American AT-6, much more powerful and faster trainer with retractable landing gear and a constant speed propeller. This was the plane that prepared pilots for flying fighters. In fact, some small countries actually used the AT-6 as a fighter. Multi-engine training was done in Beechcraft AT-10's and AT-11's. The 11 was also use to train bombardiers, navigators and gunners. Due to the lack of twin engine trainers and facilities, it was not unusual for cadet to finish training in an AT-6 thinking he was going into fighters and end up in transition training as the co-pilot of a bomber. That was usually one disappointed cadet.

Many aspects of flight training were being looked at in a radically different light, now that the Army had a great deal of experience with the accepted methods and the pilots they produced. Some forward thinkers were convinced that the American boys were capable of moving into larger, more powerful aircraft faster than the accepted routine was taking them. It was thought that Advanced cadets could successfully train in combat type aircraft, which would give them a head start in combat training. With this in mind, a new approach was to be inaugurated with Class 44-G in the Western Flying Training Command.

UC-78

Halfway through Basic, half of 44-G at Minter Field was to train in a twin engine plane, the UC-78. Apparently the first half of the alphabet was to go twin engine and the rest to stay in the BT-13. This, of course, laid to rest all our dreams of becoming ace fighter pilots.

The UC-78 was small twin originally designed as a lightweight civil transport plane which became available in sufficient numbers at the beginning of the war to be converted to courier and training duty. It had space for two pilots and about five passengers. It was all wood and fabric construction with two small Jacobs radial engines, swinging fixed pitch, wooden props. It was designed for adjustable propellers, but manufacture of the props could not keep up with the production of engines and airframes, so wooden props were substituted. There were controls for props in the cockpit and we had to go through the motions of adjusting the props at the proper times so that we would know how when we got real airplanes.

The UC-78 was variously known as "the Bamboo Bomber", the "Double-breasted Cub" and the "Useless 78." Like many planes converted from civilian to military use, it had some interesting characteristics and a scary reputation. It was said to be fire prone and due to its wood and fabric construction, would burn to the ground in a distressingly short time. We were told we had about thirty seconds to get out and away from the plane should it catch fire on the ground. Fires were said to start when a careless pilot flooded the carburetor and caused a backfire in one of the engines. There were correct procedures for start up that would preclude such an incident, and these were paid strict attention to after we were regaled by our instructor about the fire hazard.

The landing gear and brakes were also tricky and needed alertness and proper technique to prevent bad things from happening. The gear was electrically operated and sometimes a switch would fail or a circuit short out and the gear would come up at a most inopportune time. To make things real embarrassing, one might come up and the other not. If you didn't have flying speed, you can imagine that things would quickly go from bad to worse. There was a limit switch that was supposed to keep the gear down as long as there was weight on the wheels. It was possible to throw the gear up switch and the gear was not supposed to come up until the plane was airborne. It was a favorite trick of the more adventuresome to flip the switch before getting flying speed and have the gear retract just as they left the ground. This was a "hot pilot" trick, and really looked cool if you got away with it.

One day a couple of cadets were doing solo work and the one playing first pilot did the "hot pilot" thing and flipped the up switch after starting his take off roll. The only problem was that the day was very hot and the plane tried to fly before it was really ready and made a little hop that was just enough to release the limit switch. Up came the gear and down went the 78. Before the pilot could react, the prop tips hit the runway and shattered. This left him with props that were a bit too short and not of even length. Fortunately, there were enough props left to complete the take off and fly fairly well. He climbed to pattern altitude and came around to land, thinking he had gotten away with something. When he throttled back, severe vibration set in and almost shook the engines out of the plane. **Panic time!!** After another circuit he decided he couldn't stay up there forever. He had to try to come down and take his medicine. He flew throttles open as long as he could, then chopped them and hoped for the best. He made probably the best landing of his life, with the plane threatening to shake itself to pieces any minute. He rolled off the landing mat, cut the engine switches and sat there trying to formulate a plausible lie. His story was that the limit switch failed and the gear came up on its own. Nobody believed him, but that very thing had been known to happen, so they let him get by with it. He was a very good pilot with a temporary lapse of good judgment. The Army's attitude was that he had probably learned a great deal that actually improved his flying, and that he would put that boner to good use. I was not that pilot, by the way.

My learning experience involved the brakes, which were prone to fail at inopportune times, also. I was flying first pilot with another cadet and was landing at the end of the morning flying period. It was extremely hot that day, too, and the thermals coming off the asphalt landing mat tried to keep the 78 airborne too long. I had made a good approach, but the plane wanted to keep on flying. My touch down was too far down the mat, so I had to get on the brakes pretty heavily. Just as I neared the edge of the mat, the right brake let go and I ran off the mat into the grass. Not knowing what else to do, I held the left brake on, executed a perfect 270 degree turn back onto the mat and taxied around to a parking place just like I had meant to do that all the time. My instructor was watching me and was waiting on the wing when I got out. "What the hell did you think you were doing out there?"

"I lost my right brake." I answered, "and that turn was the only thing I could think to do."

My co-pilot backed me up and the instructor bought it. I never heard any more about the incident. Crazy things like that were happening all the time in that plane, so it made us more alert and on the ball and probably made us better pilots. I think the UC-78 was a pretty good plane, if properly maintained, which it wasn't at training schools. We all thought that our maintenance people where those not good enough to go overseas and work on combat planes. The Army disliked losing anyone, but it was better to keep planes and crews in the air against the enemy, so there was where the real miracle workers among maintenance people were to be found.

Twin engine training in the dual phase had two cadets flying with one instructor. The flying time was split between the two cadets. The first five or six hours were spent in familiarization with handling two engines and learning the flight characteristics of the UC-78. Some of the time there were two cadets flying pilot and co-pilot with the instructor standing between us. It was necessary that each of us learn the duties of both seats, because the duties of the two were somewhat different. For instant, on takeoff the pilot concentrated on using the flight controls and throttles. The co-pilot was responsible for adjusting the mixture controls and raising the landing gear and flaps on the pilot's command. He also was responsible for monitoring the engine instruments, radio and clearing outside the aircraft on the right side. During flight the C-P mostly just rode along and watched the instruments and his side of the plane. On landing he lowered the gear and flaps on the pilot's command and stood ready to take over if the pilot needed him to. This never happened in training, but may have on occasion in combat.

After about six hours we were soloed, and after then our solo and dual time was about evenly divided. We no longer did any aerobatics, but we did begin to get more instrument time, both on the ground and in the air. There was also some night flying and cross country, both day and night. The world takes on a whole new aspect after the sun goes down. The old familiar landmarks disappear and are replaced with new ones in the form of lights on the ground. You have to be able to translate what you see in the form of light patterns into what you know to be on the ground. This sounds like it may be difficult, but it is not so bad. You learn to rely on your instruments and radio more at night than you had been accustomed to in daylight. Around the base you very quickly learned to determine your whereabouts by the ground lights. Cross-country required more attention to time, distance, ground speed and direction, and less to landmarks along the way.

I got along pretty well except for one incident on a night flight. We were shooting touch and go landings, and on my first landing I forgot to lower my landing gear on approach. The instructor just let me go ahead and line up, and when I cut the throttle the warning horn about blasted me out of the cockpit. Between that scare and the chewing out my instructor gave me, I never overlooked the gear again.

There was a simple minded little routine check that was designed to prevent what I had done. It was called the **GUMP** check. **G** – gas tank selector to fullest tank; **U** – undercarriage down; **M** – mixture control to full rich; **P** – props in full low pitch. I had failed to do my **GUMP** check.

The instructor said that mistake could have washed me out if I had not been doing so well in everything else. That may have been to take the sting out of the asinine mistake I had just made. He assured me that another similar screw up and I was gone. The fact that I made it testifies to how well I learned my lesson.

Multi-engines means that occasionally one or more of them are going to fail and the flight crew must know how to handle the aircraft. Most combat planes with two or more engines will fly safely with one out, and even climb is the load is lightened sufficiently. This fact made it necessary to practice single engine procedures. The UC-78, with fixed pitch props flew very poorly with one out because the prop could not be feathered and stopped. It just sat there and wind milled and caused drag. For this reason, we never completely shut one down, just went through the procedure as though we could feather. I seriously doubt that the plane would have held altitude even if we could have feathered the prop. It was pretty under powered. We had to wait until we got in real combat planes with controllable pitch props to learn the single engine techniques well.

We began to learn the rudiments of radio range navigation in Basic. Our first exposure to this was in the Link trainer where we were familiarized with the shape of radio ranges and how to locate ourselves with respect to the transmitter using the radio.

The Civil Aeronautics Authority (CAA) had established a system of ranges all over the country for the use by airlines. The military had taken them over and added more and more until you could hardly be out of the range of one before you were within range of another anywhere in the continental U.S. This made cross-country navigation much simpler than flying the "iron compass", i.e., following a railroad.

Near each airport capable of landing an airliner, such as a DC-3, or C-47 in Army terminology; there was a range transmitter that broadcast four code signals at right angles to each other. These were the Morse Code A(._) and N(_.). Where these signals overlapped the A and N blended into a continuous sound that was called a beam. Each station had a unique call sign that was broadcast regularly so by referring to the appropriate chart you could learn what airport you were near.

A basic navigation problem in the Link consisted of being placed somewhere in the vicinity of a range station on a random heading. You were to fly straight level until you could identify the station call signal, all the time hearing in your headset either an A or an N. You would then take up a heading parallel to the nearest "bisector heading", a compass heading halfway between two beams. By flying this heading and listening for the signal to build or fade you could locate yourself in a particular quadrant flying toward or away from the station. Once that location was established, there was a procedure for flying toward the nearest beam. If you were flying away, you would do a 180-degree turn and fly until you intersected a beam. If you were flying toward the station you continued until a beam was intersected. At this point, you didn't know which beam, or leg, you had intersected, so you always made a left turn and flew along the leg, once again checking for a build or fade. Once you knew where you were with respect to the station, you either turned or continued on the leg until you crossed the "cone of silence" which put you right over the transmitter. From there you should know where the field was. I really liked to fly radio range problems, both in the Link and in the air, and usually did it very well. Except once in Advanced, but that is another story.

As I look back up the pages, I realize that this is becoming a text on how to do instrument navigation. Perhaps I should not bore the reader(s) with this but to tell you that we were taught blind flying using state of the art procedures and equipment for 1944. I know it all seems very primitive to my son-in-law, Lt. Co. Bert Adams (ret.) who has roughly ten times the number of flying hours that I had, and in highly sophisticated equipment. I hasten to assure you that thousands of young men safely flew millions of miles with the same equipment and training that I got.

We were required at each phase of our training to get in a certain number of cross-country missions to test our dead reckoning navigation and pilotage skills. I described the one I had in Primary, and I had to do a similar one in Basic. The idea was to test our ability to navigate from one place to another and it didn't much matter what kind of plane we flew. Near the end of our time in Basic, we were assigned a cross country mission much like the one in Primary, but over different country, naturally.

As I told you earlier, many of the civilian Primary schools were being closed and there were scads of primary trainers around not being used. An area of Minter Field was being used a storage depot for these excess trainers until they could be scrapped or sold as surplus. Because of the abundance of PT-17's and the shortage of BT-13's and UC-78's, many of us flew our Basic cross-country in the PT's.

This was quite a thrill. Having now flown two more advanced planes, it made me feel like a real aviator to be told to go get in a PT-17 and do a cross-country. It felt exciting and a little overwhelming to taxi out among the bigger planes, get my clearance and take off, just like I knew what I was doing.

I had been given my charts, told the points to which to fly and with my plotting board, E6B, pencil and straight edge, had laid out and planned my mission. I don't recall any particular apprehension or doubt. Although, in retrospect, they were asking mere kids to do things we would never expect of our children and grandchildren today. If my parents had known what I was doing as a matter course, they would never have believed it. I find it now a bit difficult to believe that I did all those things without so much as a second thought.

Along about the middle of May, our time at Minter came to an end and we graduated from Basic. My last flight was 19 May. We had been told that we were to be the first group of cadets in the WFTC to fly combat type aircraft in Advanced training. It was to be sort of an experiment to see if our training could be speeded up, because of the need that then existed for replacement flight crews overseas. We were to train in the TB-25, which was a stripped down B-25. This seemed to me to be a rather large step, considering the few hours we had in the UC-78. The 78 was not even the biggest, most powerful twin-engine trainer in the inventory, and they expected us to handle a plane with two 1450 hp engines and a proven war record? Somebody was on dope! The prospect of going into a real bomber with no more time than we had should have scared the pants off of us, but with the sublime confidence of youth, we were all a bunch of eager beavers who just couldn't wait to show the brass that we had what it took. So, off we went to Mather Field at Sacramento, where we would be introduced to a <u>real</u> airplane.

Chapter VIII

ADVANCED FLIGHT TRAINING

While we cadets were shipped off to Mather Field by troop train; the wives, including Laverda, packed up and made their way the best they could to Sacramento. It will always be a source of amazement to me how the wives were able to cope with the conditions under which they chose to live. Most of them were hundreds, maybe thousands of miles from home, among total strangers in what must have been to them, completely alien surroundings. Somehow they managed to find their way to the next base, get a place to live and show up at the post gate at visiting hours looking as beautiful as brides. All I can say is, they must have loved their husbands totally to have endured the hardships that kind of life imposed on them.

As I have said before, the whole country was into this war and wherever we went, with few exceptions, the population around a military base did its best to accommodate the families of the servicemen. Sure, there was some gouging of the dependants in some of the larger cities, and there were some who were not as pleasant to them and the servicemen as one would like. But, by and large, people tried to make the best of things without seeming to take undue advantage.

Very soon, Laverda had found a place to stay where she was comfortable and safe while I was on post, and where we could be together in the hours I could get away. There was also some time most every evening on post when we could visit in a day room for a couple of hours. Buses ran regularly so she could get to the post and back. The only trouble was the walk from the bus stop to her rooming house. It was through a residential neighborhood that was not as well lighted as one would like, and she admits to being pretty scared a few times, going in after dark. She was followed by a man one night who appeared to have no good in mind, so she ran all the way to the house. She didn't tell me about this until we were getting ready to leave Sacramento for fear of distracting me from my training. You can be sure that I would have been distracted, all right. I'm not sure what I would have done about it, probably not much but worry. Short of making her go home, which she would not have done, there wasn't much else I could have done.

Mather Field was an old, established Army Air Corps installation, having had an aviation presence there since the 1920's. At the time we arrived there was a contingent of night fighter trainees, all officers, flying the B-25's. Once they had transitioned into the 25, they did all their flying at night, leaving the day flying to us. This meant that the planes were in use most all the time. These planes were meant to be flown. It made sense to keep them in the air as much as possible, and although they were war-weary, they were still very serviceable and reliable.

I keep calling these planes war-weary, because many of them had actually been to war. They had come from the Aleutian Islands where they had flown in some of the most absolutely horrible weather conditions you can imagine. After several months of fog, rain, snow, sleet, wind and mud, these old ladies deserved to live out their days in the sunshine of California. I'm not sure they deserved to be flown by a group of ham handed cadets with no appreciation for their finer qualities, but they bore up nicely, thank you.

The planes had been flown back as newer models replaced them. All combat aircraft were constantly undergoing changes and modifications as technology developed and the shortcomings of the current models were revealed. As far as I know, no fighting plane ever goes to war in a configuration that remains static. There are always modifications on the drawing board or in the mind of engineer or flying man that will ultimately make it on the plane.

Perhaps a short discourse on how the Army designated its aircraft and identified the various models would be in order. This may be a boring subject to the reader, but I'm having fun.

Prefixed letters were used to identify the types of planes, and numbers were assigned sequentially. For instance, The "B" meant bomber and "25" meant this was the 25th bomber design accepted by the Army since this system of identification was adopted. The first design accepted was identified by XB, meaning experimental, followed by YB to indicate a model being tested for acceptance. Once accepted, the X and Y were dropped. As major modifications were made, letter suffixes were added beginning with A. Minor changes resulted in number suffixes to the letter suffix. Just what constituted a change major enough to rate a letter is a mystery. I suppose in the archives of Wright Field there must be a manual defining all the parameters of identifying aircraft, if one were curious enough to look for it.

In response to the Army request for a fast, light attack bomber, the North American Aviation Corp. submitted a design they called the NA-40. It first flew in January, 1939. It was underpowered and not as fast as hoped, but it had many other desirable qualities. The design was so good that with some changes in wing profile and location and the addition of 1350 hp Wright engines the Army accepted it and called the XB-25. I'm sure there was a YB in there somewhere, but it didn't figure in the development much. The next step produced the B-25A, of which 40 were built. These were used for testing and training while bugs were being worked out and new modifications were being applied.

The first B-25 to go to war was the B model and this was the famous Mitchell that Doolittle took over Japan in his Tokyo raid. The first B-25 to go into real mass production was the C/D model. The only difference in the two was the serial number plate on the instrument panel. The C was made in Englewood, CA, and the D was made in Kansas City. The planes we flew at Mather were C/D's that had been stripped of their guns, armor plate and command radio. This was the large radio used by the radioman/gunner and was a pretty heavy piece of merchandise. Losing all this weight made our trainers a going piece of plunder. Flat out they would top 320 mph!

Class 44G at Minter Field graduated 171 pilots rated in twin engines. There must have been some washouts and I know two were killed, so there must have been close to 200 at the beginning. Two hundred barely trained young men about to assume command of a bona fide, highly advanced fighting machine before they even had their wings and pilots rating. This was to be a daunting experience and it's a good thing the B-25 was such a forgiving airplane.

WOW! Do I get to fly that?

Orientation was very brief since we were pretty much used to the training school regimen, and training at all levels bore great similarity. Our first trip to the flight line was memorable. They took us in trucks out to the field and set us down to inspect our new steeds. Wow! Those things looked big!! On the ground the B-25 is a fairly ugly airplane, with its droopy wings, drippy engines and ungainly landing gear. But to us, it was just about the most beautiful piece of machinery we had ever seen, and we couldn't wait to get in and try her out.

As we toured along the line we came up on a 25 with the nose compartment all broken out and leaves scattered about in the bombardier's position. The story was that one of the night fighter students had been doing a little buzz job at the end of his flight period, about sunup, and had flown through the top of an oak tree. He brought back about 25 feet of oak limb sticking out of the front of his plane. Other than the loss of some Plexiglas, the plane was all right. I expect the pilot was at that time actively pursuing some other line of work.

There was a certain level of trauma associated with each change of station. We usually knew very little about the field other than hearsay, which most times turned to be just that, hearsay, with little substance. Each post had its own character, or characters, as the case may be. Mather, by virtue of being an Advanced Flight training base, had more the feel of permanent Air Corps base. The cadets were treated more like officers, since we were only about nine weeks away from being officers. Even the permanent party enlisted men seemed a bit more respectful. There was a good chance that some of us would be stationed at Mather when we were commissioned, and might encounter some of the EM when the rank situation was different. It behooved them to bear that in mind when they encountered a cadet on post.

The significant trauma associated with Mather Field came in the person of Maj. Carter C. Speed, Commandant of Cadets. Maj. Speed was a big man, in all dimensions. He was one of those unfortunates with a weight problem that was exacerbated by the fact that he had a desk job, consequently he got very little exercise. Usually associated with such bulk as his is a decided aversion to exercise and an equal attraction to the dinner table, and the breakfast table, and the lunch counter. Maj. Speed was simply *fat*. He could put on a freshly laundered and pressed tailored uniform and it immediately looked like he had slept in it. He was red headed and of florid complexion. He looked very much like Gert Frobe, who played Goldfinger, in the James Bond movie of the same name. (This, of course, is said in retrospect, since no one had ever heard of James Bond in 1944.)

Maj. Speed tried hard to be a military man, but somehow, just could not pull it off. Suffice it to say, he had the position and the rank to exercise all the authority necessary, but his comical appearance and demeanor earned him little respect. We were never openly disrespectful to the man, we just made fun of him behind his back.

He got off to a bad start with us when he decreed that we would all have to get a haircut, and get it cut like his. He had what today is called a buzz cut. Most of us had what we felt was a sufficiently military cut, and had no interest in a new style. No one had long hair like we went into the Army with, and it had taken some doing to get our hair so it looked good when we took our caps off. Any hair over a quarter inch long was excessive according to Maj. Speed. So, off to the barber we went and discovered that the civilian barbers in California were just as sadistic as those in Georgia, or Texas, or Illinois, or any other induction post where we were first shorn to Army specifications. Once again, uniformity of hair length had set in. None of us had to get more than a trim for the rest of our cadet lives.

Actually, Maj. Speed had a minimal effect on our lives beyond the haircut. Some of his orders of the day seemed a little nonsensical and childish, but they didn't have much impact. We were entirely too busy flying and going to ground school to be much bothered. We were more bemused by him than anything else. We did wonder, at first, how he got to be a major and Commandant of Cadets of what was supposed to be "spit and polish" outfit. It turned out that he was the son-in-law of Col. Pyle, the bird colonel post commander, who, himself, seemed to be in his dotage. I have often wondered if he might not have been a "retread." (Retread: A reservist called back in to fill a post of limited importance.)

Co. Pyle seemed to be more or less a figurehead. The staff actually ran the post and Col. Pyle officiated at reviews and other official functions, but seemed to have little to do with the day to day running of the post. That was pretty much the way things were at all training posts, as nearly as I could tell. Smart cadets tried to have little to do with rank much higher than that of his immediate instructors and check pilots.

One last word about Maj. Speed, who, by the way, became Lt. Col. Speed before we graduated. In civilian life, I have a feeling he would have been nice guy to get to know. He just wasn't cut out to be a soldier.

Mather Field, being an established post of pre-war times, had all the amenities of such a post. There were excellent athletic fields and gymnasiums, a large post theater where first run movies were shown, wonderful chow halls with excellent food, paved streets and sidewalks, well equipped day rooms and canteens. A canteen was just across the street from our barracks area, and we spent a great deal of our off duty hours there at the soda fountain. It was more like a real drugstore than a military post facility.

One of my buddies was Clarence C. Cotten, from Memphis. Clarence, being a good old Southern boy, had grown up on buttermilk, which most of the Army seemed never to have heard of. For some reason the canteen near our barracks served good Bulgarian buttermilk at the fountain, and Clarence could be found there every evening, drinking buttermilk like many of the guys would drink beer at a bar. He took a lot of good-natured ribbing from the Californians in the outfit, because most of them thought buttermilk was what you fed the hogs after you extracted the butter. I pretty much feel the same way about buttermilk, but I could identify with Clarence's homesickness for something uniquely familiar and came to his defense; verbally, not gustatorially.

Once again, our daily lives were divided into flying periods and ground school periods. I don't remember much about ground school that was unique to Advanced training. There was the usual navigation, weather, armament, PT, etc. One new wrinkle was added. We began to learn the intricacies of being an officer. For the past fifteen months we had slowly progressed up the ladder of respect from the lowest form of life in the Army, a buck private; to advanced Aviation Cadet, not quite an officer and a step above an enlisted man. As I noted earlier, by Army regulations we rated, but seldom got, a salute from an EM. This never seemed to matter to any of us, and when it happened, we were sure the EM had mistaken our insignia for some weird kind of officer's badge. This was very likely true, and the EM was taking no chances. It was better to waste a salute on us than to take a chance.

It was just a little bit scary to think that we were about to become more of an individual than just one of a group that moved from place to place as a unit. Very little thinking was required of us while in training regarding getting to a new post. We just fell out when the CO told us to, marched to the troop conveyance and were transported en masse to our next post. There we were marched to our barracks area, still in our own group. Everything we did, everywhere we went, except on pass, we did as a group. We never saw our orders. They were handled by an officer or non-com in charge of getting us where we were supposed to be. Very soon, we were going to have our commission or warrant and our wings, and be handed a set of orders and told to report to a certain post by a certain date, ground transportation authorized. From there on, it was our responsibility to show up where we were supposed to be and do it on our own.

To prepare us for this drastic new life, we had courses on how to act as an officer. We automatically became a gentleman by act of Congress as soon as we received that commission; at least, that was the assumption. I had been raised to be a gentleman, as had most of the other cadets, but being a civilian gentleman and being an officer gentleman were not quite the same. The same basic qualities were desired in both environments, but the uniform was supposed to impose certain expectations not a part of civilian gentlemanliness. There was a certain standard of conduct that went with the uniform that was supposed to set us apart from the rest of society. Most of us took that responsibility seriously and tried to live up to the Officer's Code, but there were a few bad apples that were just plain slobs, especially when they got liquored up.

My Advanced instructor was Lt. Erickson, a very unlikely looking pilot. He was slightly built with a severely weak chin and a deprecating manner, but he could fly the wings off a B-25. He was one of those instructors who took it personally if one of his cadets did poorly, and he worked very hard with us to make sure we all flew well enough to pass all our check rides with "flying" colors. I grew to like him immensely. There were a few instructors that thought their mission was to wash out as many cadets as possible. I really felt sorry for the cadets that got someone like that. The more responsible instructors watched out for people like that and they didn't last long in the instructor field. There were a few of those knot heads at every level. Fortunately, I never got one of them, except as a check pilot.

Although the B-25 was a true combat type aircraft, it was easier to fly than the UC-78. It was heavy on the controls and took some muscle to fly but could be trimmed up to fly along, very nicely hands off. It was also extremely noisy. The wings were attached mid way up the fuselage, right at the bomb bay, and all the noise and fumes from those massive radial engines wafted right into the fuselage.

All of the flying in Advanced was done from Mather. I don't remember there being any auxiliary fields like we had in Primary and Basic. This meant there was quite a bit of traffic there like we would encounter in combat transition stateside and in combat overseas. This was good training in the use of radio and in air discipline. You had to be always on the alert for other planes, both in the air and on the ground. There was a continual potential for accidents, especially on the ground. At the beginning of a flight period, it must have looked like a Chinese fire drill from the air. Planes were taxiing around all over the place. We had to pay strict attention to the tower and do exactly what we were told by the controller.

Taxiing was done using both brakes and engines, the nose wheel not being steerable. The main gear brakes were very reliable and effective. I was told they were made by Bendix and operated like bicycle brakes, alternating plates of steel, one set attached to the axle and one set locked to the wheel hub. When you applied the brakes the plates were squeezed together hydraulically. I never did it, but I was told that you could completely lock the wheels at landing speed. In all likelihood, if a pilot ever had to do that, the nose wheel would collapse and the plane would go skidding down the runway on its nose, and its flying days would be over, as well as those of the pilot.

The plane was very maneuverable on the ground, and having a tricycle gear, the pilots had excellent visibility. No more of this weaving from side to side like in a tail dragger. There was nothing out in front of you but the bombardier's compartment, and it sloped down. You could actually see the ground just under the nose, and if you wanted to hang out the side window, you could see the nose wheel.

The Wright engines on the 25 had a very unique sound when idling or running at low speed while taxiing. There was staccato pop-pop-pop to the exhaust that was sort of a signature. We all got so we could tell when a 25 started up anywhere within earshot. I recall being at an airshow in Tullahoma, TN, back about 25 years ago when a 25 cranked up. I was in a hangar talking to a man restoring a BT-13, completely out of sight of the flight line. There was that instant start of recognition that took me back to my war years and my heart began to pump a little faster. I practically ran outside to where I could see the plane getting ready to taxi to another part of the field.

Take off in a 25 was simplicity itself. You taxied into position, rolled forward just a little to straighten out the nose wheel, dropped the specified degree of flaps and with the props in full low pitch, advanced the throttles to the stops. Almost immediately you had some rudder control because of the twin rudders directly behind the engines. You picked up speed pretty fast with each engine putting out 1700 hp at 2400 rpm, and at 75 mph you eased back on the controls to raise the nose wheel. As it passed through 100 mph, she started to try to fly. A little more back pressure and you were airborne! When you were well aloft, the gear came up and your speed noticeably began to climb. With the gear up, the co-pilot eased the flaps up and away you went. The engines were throttled back on climb out and the prop pitch increased to adjust the rpm to about 2300.

As I said earlier, every take off in every airplane was a thrill, but the maximum take off rush of all was the first time I flew the left seat as first pilot and heard those big old Wright R-2600s thundering away out there on those bent wings and felt my back being pushed back against the seat as we accelerated down the runway. The most beautiful feeling of all was that I really felt like I was in total control. There was no tendency to yaw or wander. You just kept the nose wheel on the runway centerline and rolled. **WOW!!**

The ready room at Mather was a long, low wooden building with a covered porch its full length. There were benches to lounge on and watch the traffic. There was also one of the first Coke vending machines I had ever seen. It was always loaded with the old classic green bottle Coke, since there was no other kind in 1944, and they went for a nickel. It was a pretty primitive affair and was not always reliable. It would frequently take your nickel and give you no Coke. For that bit of perversity, it was considerably maltreated. Occasionally, it would give down with more than one drink, so we didn't abuse it too much. One very hot afternoon, a plane taxied in and a cadet jumped out and ran over to the machine to get Cokes for the instructor and the two cadets. When he put his nickel in, Cokes began to fall out of the machine, one after another, faster than he could pick them up. He gathered as many as he could carry and ran back out to the plane. Always the opportunists, the cadets at the ready room were right there to keep the stream of little green bottles going. It finally quit giving up Cokes when it emptied itself. Needless to say, that machine found its way to the repair shop when the franchiser found his take that day seriously out of balance with his Coke input.

Single engine performance was one of the strong points of the B-25. It would easily hold altitude with one engine out and the prop fully feathered. The ones we flew, with all the extraneous weight stripped out, would actually climb fairly well on one engine. My first experience with a really dead engine came the first time Lt. Erickson demonstrated the engine out procedure. He pulled the throttle back on the right engine, cut the ignition, hit the feathering button and the engine wound to a stop. He put the plane through its paces on one engine to show us what it would do, even turned into the dead engine, which is generally a no-no. When he tried to start the engine by unfeathering the prop, the engine refused to start. Even the electric starter would not make that engine go again. Also, he couldn't re-feather the prop, so there we were with a true emergency, on one engine with a wind milling prop that gave a drag about like a barn door. Fortunately, we weren't very far from the field, so we called in our troubles and requested the field be cleared and we be cleared for a straight in approach. Clearance was immediately granted, and everything looked to be under control until a B-25 taxied out and lined up to take off on the runway we were cleared to land on. Some instructor was so busy instructing his cadets over the intercom that he failed to monitor the tower frequency, or call for takeoff clearance. There he was, about to begin his takeoff roll when we sailed in over his head and landed right in front of him. He turned the air blue giving us hell for landing over him. This tirade was interrupted by the tower controller with a tirade of his own, informing this Dilbert that his taxi and takeoff procedures stunk, and that he had better monitor the tower frequency a little more closely, next time.

There was no such thing as a true solo flight in a twin engine plane, since there had to be two pilots aboard at all times. Much of the instruction involved two cadets in the pilot's seats with the instructor squatting between them. Each of us learned, pretty much simultaneously, the duties of both pilot and co-pilot.

The pilot was in command of the airplane and the co-pilot, second in command. We each had specific duties, especially on takeoff and landing. The pilot actually taxied, took off and flew the plane while the co-pilot handled the communications with the tower, lowered the flaps, monitored the engine instruments and handled the props and fuel mixture. On the ground, the props were always in full low pitch and the mixture full rich.

The co-pilot made sure the fuel tank selector was set on the fullest tank, and made the proper switch between tanks as the flight progressed. The pilot did the pre-flight checks and engine run-up and magneto checks before lining up for the takeoff.

When we were cleared to roll, the pilot advanced the throttles all the way while the co-pilot watched and called out the manifold pressure and engine rpms. On the roll, the co-pilot called out the air speed so the pilot would have some idea when to lift off. Once airborne, the pilot signaled "gear up" by a thumbs up. He also gave the signal when he wanted the flaps to come up. These were the co-pilot's responsibility. As the pilot pulled back the throttles to climb out setting, the co-pilot adjusted the prop pitch to get the proper engine speed. He also needed to synchronize the props so there was no harmonic throb.

Each airplane had its own peculiarities, so there was no setting the rpms the same and expecting the props to be synchronized. You had to do that by ear. Fortunately, the 25 was easy to synchronize, because the engines pretty much stayed at whatever speed you set them. The German Ju-88 was impossible to synchronize, so they say, so you could always identify one in the air, even at night when you couldn't see it. The B-36, which came along after the war, with its six engines, was also impossible to synchronize, and you could tell it as far as you could hear it. It must have driven the co-pilot crazy.

During a normal flight, about all the co-pilot had to do was ride along and keep an eye on the engine instruments and fuel gauges and keep a look out to the right side of the plane. We all learned how to fly from the right seat because there would be many times when the pilot would need to be spelled. Flight and engine controls were handled with different hands, depending on which seat you were in.

On returning to the field, the co-pilot took his directions from the pilot as to when to put the gear and flaps down and when to go full low and full rich with props and fuel mixture. The pilot did all the flying at that point. The co-pilot never got to make a landing from the right seat.

Instructors usually had four students per flight period, and usually the same two students flew together, so they knew each other's techniques and habits. When we "soloed", the instructor turned it over to us with a set of instructions on what to do and got out and we "soloed." Later, our sessions consisted of certain prescribed procedure missions, which we would carry out both as pilot and co-pilot. We had some cross-country exercises and also some night flying, both with and without instructors.

Some of the cadets were more adventuresome than others and tried some rather risky things. Out in the Sierra Nevada's there were a number of canyons that seemed to act as magnets for some. They liked to get down below the rims and fly. Not in our class, but earlier, we heard about the cadets that got down too low in a canyon that turned out to be a box canyon. Imagine their surprise when they made that last turn and all they had before them was canyon wall. More than once, B-25's were flown into a wall by pilots with lousy judgment.

As I said earlier, our planes would really go and it was not unusual to be able to cruise one at about 250, or better. One day a pair of our cadets were coming down the San Joaquin Valley on a cross country, when they saw a P-61 going their way. Smart alecks that they were, they overhauled it and went sailing by waving as they passed. They felt pretty smug. They had passed a fighter plane. Before long, the P-61 went zooming by like they were parked and the pilot gave them the finger. To add insult to injury, the 61 had one prop feathered. Two more chastened and awe struck cadets you never saw. They had just tangled with the plane the Air force termed the fastest, most maneuverable in the inventory, and it was almost as big as the B-25.

A good deal of our time was spent in instrument flying under a hood and in the Link trainer. We flew a lot of radio range problems and, I must say, I wasn't doing badly. The B-25 is such a sweet flying, stable aircraft instrument flying was a breeze. It was a breeze until I took my last instrument check ride before graduation. I got a real jackass for my check ride. He must have hated all cadets and want to wash them out. It started out badly on the ground when he gave me my flight instructions. He didn't use the intercom like you would think he should. He reached over and pulled my headphone out and yelled them directly in my ear. He proceeded to tell me everything he expected me to do from taxi out, to take off, to the radio range and beyond. The instructions came in such rapid fire no one could keep them straight, although I thought I had them until he yelled, "Savvy?" and let the headphone go POW! right in my ear. That pretty much drove all he had said out the other ear. I was totally rattled by then.

I managed the takeoff without running off the runway, although I need some help from the instructor. That seemed to make him all the more fractious. We got out to the range and started into the problem. I checked the range signal, listened for my sector ID, and headed out on my bisector heading. I usually had no trouble picking up the build or fade, but that day I flew and flew and couldn't seem to pick it up. I finally guessed and guessed right. When I intersected a beam, I made my procedure turn correctly and once more tried to detect a build or fade. Once again, I had trouble, but finally managed to locate myself and flew in toward the cone of silence. From there I had to fly over the field and indicate when we were over it. By this time everything had gone so wrong that I was almost a basket case, but I did locate the field, by the expedient of seeing it through a small gap under the hood. The instructor caught me. He took over and flew us in while I sat there and watched my entire Air Corps life pass in front of my eyes as he gave me such a chewing out as you never heard. He flunked me, big time.

When Lt. Erickson found out about my check failure and read the instructor's write up, he said he wasn't sure he had flown the right cadet. He said that of all his cadets, he would have least expected me to fail. He did say that that instructor had a bad reputation and seemed to like to fail cadets. At this point, regulations said that before I could graduate I had to pass a check by the head of the Instrument School, Lt. Copenhaver. If I failed that one, I was gone. Before that final check ride I went back up with Lt. Erickson and flew the same problem perfectly. He gave me some reassurance.

Came the day of my final check ride with Lt. Copenhaver and I was, needless to say, a bit tense. Copenhaver turned out to be a very large, easygoing man with a very reassuring air. We went up, flew the problem, and once again, I flew it perfectly. There was never a problem detecting the build or fade, and I hit the airport right on the nose without peeking. Copenhaver was such a quiet, gentle man that he inspired confidence. Back on the ground, he was very effusive in complimenting my performance. He said he didn't see how the first check ride could have been such a disaster. He gave me about the best evaluation I ever got on a check ride, and most of my rides were good. That was the only one I ever failed.

In analyzing it later and putting some things together that I had seen but dismissed, I came to the conclusion that the reason I couldn't detect a build or fade was that the SOB instructor was turning the volume control on his side of the plane. It was in a position alongside his right hand and he could turn it without my knowledge if I wasn't looking for it, and I wasn't. If that was what happened, that was about the dirtiest trick a man could pull on a cadet. Nobody should have to go through the agony that I went through that day. I knew I wasn't as lousy an instrument pilot as that ride made me seem.

Although Lt. Erickson was our regularly assigned instructor, there were times that we flew with different officers. I remember one in particular, a Lt. Knox. We were to have him for a cross-country mission one Monday morning. He showed up on time, but was obviously hung over, big time. He gave us our flying instructions, which were to take off, climb to 7,000 ft. and fly about 25 minutes on a heading of about 85 degrees. With that, he slumped over against the co-pilots window and went to sleep. After the specified time, we woke him up. He breathed some pure oxygen from the plane's system to clear his head and took over the controls. It turned out that we were over Lake Tahoe where his girl friend was a cocktail waitress in the hotel. He proceeded to give the lake and the town a real buzz job. I don't think he ever got over 50 ft. until we left to go home. That's the lowest and fastest I had ever flown up to that time. I'm not sure, but I suspect there was more than one broken window in that hotel that day. The other cadet flew over and I flew back with Knox again asleep in the co-pilot's seat. That was the extent of our cross-country training on that flight. I guess you might say that we did gain some valuable insight that day. One was that it doesn't pay to stay out boozing all weekend and try to fly a serious mission the next day. We also learned just what a good pilot could do with a B-25 at low level, even with a hangover.

When the war started, many of the movie stars joined up, among them, Jimmy Stewart, Clark Gable, Robert Montgomery, and others. We had our resident movie hero in one Robert Sterling. He had joined just after Pearl Harbor and had gone through pilot training. He must have been pretty good, because he was a flight instructor in the night fighter school at Mather. At the time he volunteered, he was just getting into his career, so he put it on hold for the duration. He was married to Ann Sothern, and more than once we saw them together at the movie theater. In person, she was a real slob. Her hair was an unnatural red and looked like a straw stack. Her face was mottled like she drank too much, and I suspect that she did. She was really fat and would never have been mistaken for a movie star. There were dozens of cadet wives that were far prettier than she was, especially my wife. Presented side by side, Laverda would have been chosen as more beautiful, 100 percent of the time.

At the time we were at Mather, Ann Sothern was a bigger star than Sterling. He was one of the young, handsome, up and coming stars, of whom a great deal was expected. Sothern was already an established star, and on the screen was quite a looker. It was a real disappointment to see her in the flesh. She and Sterling later broke up, like most of those Hollywood marriages did, and their careers went their separate ways. Sothern played in a number of movies, but never became a real blockbuster like Bette Davis, Loretta Young, Olivia DeHavilland and others. She starred in a couple of TV series in the fifties and sixties. Sterling came back to a rather undistinguished movie career. His main claim to fame was to father Tish Sterling, a young actress of today.

As graduation neared, we began to have to be concerned about some things other than flying. We were about to become officers in the U. S. Army Air Force, and had to think about buying all new uniforms. The old olive drab and brown enlisted man's duds could no longer be worn. Although the pay of a cadet was quite a bit more than most EM's, it was not enough to begin to buy the necessary officer threads. The Army provided a uniform allowance for all new officers, and also brought contract clothiers in to fit us for our clothing. There were minimum requirements that, if bought, would be more than adequate for the limited stateside duty most of us expected to see. The Army was more than generous and many of us were able to completely outfit ourselves and have considerable money left over. If we bought from the contract clothiers the quality would not quite be up to what a civilian tailor would provide, but there was nothing wrong with it. Some of the single guys, with outside resources, went to a civilian and had their uniforms tailored. I couldn't see that they looked much better than we cheapskates did. I had enough left over to buy Laverda's train ticket back to Rutherford.

Finally, all the flight training was over, the last washout had left and the graduation list was published. Not all of the cadets graduated as 2nd Lts. Some of them were made Flight Officers, which was equivalent to Warrant Officer. I never really knew what criteria were used to decide whether a man would be 2nd Lt. or a Flight Officer. It was rumored to be a matter of the Army's perception of whether a man had the qualities to command or not. In any event, there was a bit of an implied stigma attached to being a Flight Officer. Apparently, it had nothing to do with the persons flying ability, because I knew some of the Flight Officers were equally as good flyers as the Lts. Some of the men who were made Flight Officers were, in appearance, not quite as sharp as others, nor as forceful in personality. It was still a big mystery and the Lts. tried very hard not to notice their friend's rank, but I know it still hurt down deep inside.

On graduation day, 4 Aug 44, we all marched into the large post theater and were treated to a real graduation ceremony, with a band and lots of brass. We each marched across the stage where Lt. Col. Carter C.

Speed handed us our diploma, discharge, re-induction orders and wings. We shook hands with Col. Pyle and floated off the stage. We were dressed in our brand new "pinks and greens", sans insignia. When the graduation was over, we were dismissed and allowed to pin on our wings and bars, or as in my case, Laverda pinned them on me. Many other cadets had their wives and family there and it was sort of a ritual for someone of the opposite sex to do the honors, wife, sweetheart, or mother.

Another ritual throughout the Army was for the brand new officer to give a dollar to the first enlisted man to salute him. You can be sure the EM knew what was going on and many of them made a point to be outside when the graduation ended. Some of the lucky ones made enough for quite a few beers at the non-com club.

That night there was a graduation dance where we erstwhile cadets could now mingle with the instructors on more or less equal footing. It is hard to explain, but there was a definite difference in the relationship between us, now. There seemed to be a more comradely feeling and it seemed to be coming from the instructors to the new officers. It was as though we had just passed our trials and earned the right to join their ranks. I guess that was really the way it was. I think most of the instructors had a good feeling to see that their cadets had made it. Some of them envied us because most of us were going to be in combat in a very few weeks, which is where many of them would have preferred to be.

Lt. Erickson and I had been friendly enough, in fact, I thought he was a real nice guy. We had never talked about any personal thing, just flying. He didn't know I was married until he met Laverda at the dance. He said he would have put me in for instructor school if he had known that. I told him I was glad he didn't know it, that I didn't need any favors like that. From what I had seen of teaching cadets to fly it was more hazardous than combat.

My first orders after graduation assigned me to a holding Squadron at Mather Field, because they didn't have any place to put me and most of the others. The orders said I was assigned to be an instructor, after all, but that was only a mechanism to keep the paper work straight. The same orders also granted me a 15-day leave, in the public interest, which meant I could go home, if I could get there. I was told that I should get orders while on leave posting me to some Replacement Training Unit, RTU, or that I might have to come back to Mather. There is nothing like being sure of your future.

Speaking of the future, it appeared that our future was going to a bit different than our immediate past had been. From the beginning, Laverda and I had decided that we wanted a baby. We, like many other newly married service families, were fully aware that the serviceman had a finite chance of not surviving the war. There was a desire, an almost frantic desire on the part of many wives to have something of their husbands in case they did get killed. That is why there were so many children born during the war. To an interested outsider, this desire was beyond the realm of rationality. Why would any wife want the burden of a baby without a father? Families, especially, seemed perplexed at this. All I can say is, I would not expect anyone who had not been there to understand. It was all perfectly reasonable to us; therefore, **we were going to have a baby!**

Chapter IX

GRADUATION LEAVE

At this time, Laverda was just going into her morning sickness, and was miserable. Fortunately, we were able to get Pullman accommodations on the train from Sacramento to St. Louis, a four-day trip. I'm not sure she could have made a trip home like the one to California. As it was, she was not a well person. Thank goodness, for soda crackers. She lived on soda crackers and milk the whole trip.

Looking back on the trip in the light of the way most travel today, that train trip seems interminable. It took four days to come from Sacramento to Rutherford, but for that era it was not so long, after all. It must have seemed long to Laverda, though. She took it all like a trooper and I still have tremendous admiration for her. I know there were times she must have wondered why she ever got herself into such a situation. Was I really worth it? I thank God that she must have thought so.

There were several of my graduating class travelling back east on that train. I especially remember Clarence Cotten, of buttermilk fame, who became almost like an angel in disguise to a lady travelling with two little children. She had been in California with her husband and he had shipped out for the Pacific, leaving her to get herself and the children back home. The children were a babe in arms and a toddler, and they were a handful. They weren't bad, just energetic little kids, and they were wearing her out. You could see she was exhausted, so Clarence asked if he could play with the children for a while, explaining that he had some nieces and nephews about their ages. Although he was a total stranger, she was so in need of some kind of relief that she let him take them over for a time. Clarence was remarkable. He entertained those kids for hours, and seemed to thoroughly enjoy himself, and the kids loved him. Their mother just sort of leaned back against the side of the seat, smiled and dropped off to sleep. You don't see many single young men in any generation willing to do what Clarence did for that lady.

We knew that we were supposed to change trains in St. Louis, but were uncertain just how to go about it. The conductor was an old time trainman, who had a trainman's contempt for the travelling public. He was absolute monarch of his domain, which was that particular train. He didn't have time for foolish questions, like, "Where, when and how do we get on the right cars to change trains?"

We got to Kansas City where we luckily found out they were going to split the train and part of it was to continue to St. Louis, while the rest was to be picked up later and taken to Chicago. We didn't find it out from the conductor. He was particularly uncommunicative.

It turned out that we were on the part of the train to go to Chicago. Fortunately, the next car up was going to St. Louis, but the conductor told us we couldn't transfer up there because it was full. We would have to stay where we were. When we told him we had to go on to St. Louis, he told us we should have been on the other car, despite the fact that we had been on the same car from Sacramento and no one had told us we needed to be somewhere else. He had already closed that little expandable metal gate between the cars and when he did that, only God could open it again. He was the most exasperating old man I have ever seen. As soon as he was out of sight, I grabbed Laverda and our bags, opened the gate myself and boarded the other car, to Hell with that old goat. What was he going to do, force us back into the other car? I'm glad that he never saw us again, or that rail line would have been looking for another conductor. I wasn't about to be stuck in KC trying to figure out how to get to St. Louis. It was true that there were no empty seats, but we just sat ourselves down on our luggage and rode that way on to St. Louis. After all, Laverda had ridden all the way from St. Louis to Bakersfield sitting and sleeping on her luggage, and it's not very far from KC to St. Louis.

We made our connection in St. Louis all right and headed south. We got into Rutherford on the 11:30 PM train that we had always counted on hearing while we were dating. The whistle of that train was our signal to be getting Laverda home, since she had to be in by midnight. Both our families were there to meet us. There are three images that I retain from that homecoming. One was Mama running to meet us and hug us, Aunt Annie right behind her, and my going over to Mrs. King to hug her. That seemed a perfectly natural thing for me to do, because I was a part of her family, now. I don't know how she felt about it, but I came to love her like I was one of her own.

By the time we got home, four days of my fifteen were used up. If I had to go back to California, I had only seven days of leave time in Rutherford. That's only a week, and I had a lot of things to get done in those seven days. There was family to visit, friends to see, and places to go. Very shortly, I received orders to report to the 3rd Air Force Replacement Depot, Plant Park, Fla., for duty as co-pilot on B-25J aircraft. Reporting date, 31 Aug 44. That added twelve more days to my leave, which was welcome, indeed!

As soon as I got my orders, I began to try to find out where Plant Park, Fla., was, and how to get there. I went to the bus depot and the agent tried to find Plant Park, Fla. No luck. Same story at the train station. It appeared there was no such place as Plant Park, Fla. Now, this <u>was</u> a dilemma. How do you get to a place that doesn't seem to exist? I sent a wire to Mather Field explaining my predicament and asked for clarification. Shortly thereafter, I got another set of orders to report to Sqdn. R, 329th AAF Base Unit, Columbia Army Air Base, Columbia, SC, by 31 Aug 44. No explanation, not that I expected one. With an additional twelve days of leave, I felt a little less rushed, and could relax and enjoy being home again.

The next few days were a blur of coming and going and catching up with what had happened to my friends from high school. Most of the boys had gone into the service and were not around. My best friend, Quinton Boyette, had a farm deferment and was as deserving of one as anyone I knew. His father was not physically able to farm, and Quinton was the sole support of his parents. He felt a little awkward, being a civilian when all his peers were in the service, but I tried to disabuse him of any notion that he ought to try to get in. He and his girl friend, Norene Wheatly,

Making the best of the time we had.

who later became his wife, by the way, were around for us to pal around with. We had some good times, going around to all the places we used to haunt back in high school. That was actually only two years before, but so much had happened it seemed like a lifetime. I had gone from a callow, pimply faced youth to an officer in the U. S. Army Air Corps. A man with a man's responsibilities. A war to fight and a growing family to support. There was no certainty that I would ever get to see them again, but that was a serious concern that was never seriously addressed.

My leave soon drew to a close and I made arrangements to get to Columbia. As soon as I got settled at my new post, I planned to send for Laverda so we could be together for the next three months while I completed combat transition training. After that, who knew what lay in the future. The war was winding down in Europe and the end was in sight in the Pacific. There did appear to be considerable fighting yet to be done in both theaters and I had no idea where I was headed.

Chapter X

COMBAT TRANSITION, HERE I COME

With my orders in my pocket and my heart in my throat, I kissed Laverda and our families goodbye and boarded the bus for Middleton, TN, where I would board the train for the east. I was a true novice at traveling alone in the Army, but I pretended that it was an everyday occurrence, so no one would know just how terrified I was. I was an officer in the Army. I was supposed to know everything. If only the people back home had known just how little any of us knew and how apprehensive we were about our situations, they would have had serious misgivings about our ability to fight this war. We were all just kids, for crying out loud! Yet, here we were, not yet old enough to vote, and expected to drive these complicated, expensive machines of war and go out and save the world for our country. I'm glad that I didn't know then just what unlikely soldiers most of us were. Looking back, God must have been on our side all along, because we had to have divine assistance.

The route to Columbia took me through Atlanta, where I changed railroads. The whole trip was sort of a blur, and I don't remember much about it, except the car I rode on to Atlanta had to have been resurrected from the Frisco Line's bone yard. It had wicker seats and a coal fired stove in one end. Fortunately, it was summer and no additional heat was needed. I hope they only used it in the summer.

I reported in to the Columbia Army Air Base on time and was assigned to a BOQ (Bachelor Officer's Quarters). I had no specific assignment and could pretty much come and go as I pleased while I waited for new orders. I was told that I was not to stay at Columbia, but would get orders within a week.

It was at Columbia that I encountered a phenomenon that seemed to be unique to South Carolina. The place was infested with gnats. They swarmed around your head, in your eyes, ears and nose whenever you stood still. As long as you kept moving they moved along behind you head in a little black cloud. As soon as you stopped they just enveloped your head. It was sort of funny to see someone walking along with this cloud following along, sort of like Joe Btfsplk in Lil Abner, the little hard luck guy who had disaster following him like a cloud. Fortunately for us, they were only gnats, not disaster.

It was also in Columbia that I was introduced to grits and/or fried potatoes for breakfast. Since I was at loose ends for a week, I spent some of my time in town, and when I ordered my first breakfast in Columbia the waitress asked me if I wanted grits or potatoes with my bacon and eggs. Since I had never had grits, I opted for them, and I've been hooked ever since. I don't think I have ever had grits that came up to my first order. The next day, I ordered potatoes and they were good, too. Sometimes I would order both. They were part of the order, just like toast and jelly. Maybe it's just the enhancement of distant memory, but it seems like I've never had better restaurant breakfasts than I got in Columbia, SC.

Near the end of a week I got orders to report to the Greenville Army Air Base (GAAB) as part of a shipment of 87 1st and 2nd Lts. and Flight Officers. We were to be the input for 33 combat crews to enter replacement training. My orders were to leave Columbia on 8 Sept and report to Greenville the same day. That was easy because they are only about a hundred miles apart.

Greenville was my first semi-permanent post, so I had to go through the Army procedure of reporting in as specified by the Officer's Guide. It turned out that in wartime the time honored ritual of presenting of oneself to the CO, which involved marching into his presence, saluting smartly, and saying, "Second Lieutenant Crouse, reporting for duty, sir," had been replaced by a visit with the clerk and assignment of quarters. What a letdown!

I was assigned, along with all the others, to Squadron S, 330th AAF Base Unit, Replacement Training Unit (RTU) MB. It was there that I was to be introduced to the rest of my crew, with whom I would spend most of my time for the next 10 months. I was to be co-pilot to 2nd Lt. Ralph G.

Dromgoole from Nixon, TX. Ralph was a wiry little guy, a little shorter than I was and not much heavier. He had considerably more experience in a B-25 than I had, having been through instructor school and instructed for a while. Our bombardier was 2ⁿᵈ Lt. Charlie Harbeson, from Jersey City, NJ, fresh out of Bombardier school. The engineer/gunner was Sgt. Francis X. Flynn, from Quincy, MA. Flynn was a Sgt. because he had been in longer than the rest of the crew EM, and had worked on the line somewhere. He was a good engineer, although he generally looked like an unmade bed, sported a permanent "5 o'clock shadow," and seemed to be lazy. He wasn't. He just moved and talked slowly. The radio/gunner was Cpl. Roy E. Gaines, Jr. from Sanford, NC. Roy was just out of school and seemed to be a naïve kid who only had to shave once a week. He was slender and stood about six feet tall. He turned out to be sharp as a tack and a crackerjack radioman. The armorer/tail gunner was Cpl. Edward B. Ely from Shaw, MS. He, too, was just out of school, a superb gunner. He later shared in the only German fighter shot down by our squadron while we were in combat.

Greenville Army Air Base was strictly a wartime installation. Greenville had never had a military post and the people in the area had not become callused to the presence of uniforms. They treated us royally the whole time we were there, and I heard from others who had preceded us that they also were treated well. That was a far cry from the general attitude of the people on the left coast, who had always had the military with them.

The purpose of the training we were to get at Greenville was to prepare us for combat service; therefore, it was to simulate actual combat as much as possible. We flew most of our time as a crew. At this point, all of us were supposed to be relatively proficient at our respective jobs, so it was now time to integrate our skills into the crew concept so that we could operate as a unit. On each mission each of us had specific responsibilities that we were expected to attend to.

The training was designed so that about half of our flight time was as a crew, and the rest was spent concentrating on certain aspects of our specialties. For instance, the gunners would often fly with instructors on practice gunnery missions. They would fire at towed targets from their assigned positions, or, on occasion, would be subjected to fighter passes by P-39's. They didn't use the special frangible bullets that were used at some schools. Cameras replaced the guns and their accuracy graded by their performance on film. They made it as realistic as possible, but could only approximate the real thing. Each EM was given further intensive training, both on the ground and in the airplane in their non-gunnery specialty.

Both Dromgoole and I flew a good deal of instrument time with instructors and with each other. There was also a lot more time in the ubiquitous Link. I flew both left and right seat time with instructors, but was in the right, co-pilot, seat all the time with Dromgoole, since that was my MOS (Military Occupation Specialty) at the time. We got a fair amount of formation time in three ship elements, but that didn't begin to approximate what we later had to do in combat.

Many of our missions as crew were cross-country. There is where we came to appreciate Charlie Harbeson as a navigator. He was actually a Bombardier/Navigator, having gone through all the training of a navigator except celestial navigation. He did all the flight planning. It was up to him to lay out the course(s) with the headings, airspeed, elapsed times and ETA's. This was done, of course, in conjunction with the pilots, but he was responsible for all the calculations and pretty much had the last word about how we would do it. Once he had laid out the routes and we got under way he usually snuggled down behind my seat and read comic books or slept. If we encountered anything not in accordance with his plan we would wake him up and get his take on the situation. We soon began to function well as a team and developed confidence in each other.

On cross-country missions, the tail gunner was sort along as ballast and comic relief. Ely kept us entertained with jokes, stories and comments in his Mississippi delta drawl. Occasionally, it was necessary for him to make observations from his position in the tail turret, but his value from that position only became really apparent when we got into combat.

Flynn, the engineer/gunner pretty was just much along for the ride, his duties having been primarily done on the ground before takeoff. He had to make sure all mechanical systems were working properly and that the engines were preflighted and the fuel tanks properly topped off. He also looked over my shoulder from time to time to make sure I wasn't overlooking anything that might show up on the engine instruments. Otherwise, he read and slept, too.

I probably got more actual flying time from the right seat with Dromgoole than most co-pilots. Having been an instructor, he knew a proficient and happy co-pilot was one that got to fly the plane. He was meticulous in seeing that I was at the controls about half the time. On the really boring mission, like simulated searches, I expect I flew more than

50 percent of the time. He was a fidgety type, and liked to get out of his seat and roam about the plane.

Gaines, the radio/gunner, was responsible for long range communications with his big radio in the waist. Our sets in the cockpit did not have the range his command set did. He also could send and receive code, which the pilots couldn't. With the trailing antenna out and using code, he could reach out about a thousand miles. This was extremely comforting to know. He kept us abreast of weather conditions ahead of us and any other information coming in from a long distance.

Despite all these tools of communication and navigation, it turned out that we navigated in the States more with the radio compass that any other instrument. We tended to confirm all of Harbeson's headings by tuning in on a radio station at our next checkpoint and flying in on "the beam". If the destination happened to have a commercial station that played dance music, we tuned the directional antenna to that and flew the little airplane on the instrument panel straight toward it. This sometimes ticked Harbeson off after he had spent a good bit of time laying out our flight plan. He didn't take it too kindly that we flew the radio compass after all his hard work. It took a long time to convince him that we really did trust him. More than once, he roused up from his sleep to hear the sounds of music on his headset and knew that we were homing in on radio station instead of flying his plotted course. That usually resulted in some (expletives deleted) on the intercom.

All dressed up for a day at the office.

Some of our cross-countries were at night, and a favorite one was south to the Florida Gulf coast and back. This one was simple because there was a light line from our part of South Carolina straight down to the coast. This light line was a relic of the early days of airline travel. The government had set up strings of rotating light beacons sort of like highways in the sky. They were stationed about forty miles apart in straight lines between airports. In clear weather the airliners could fly along this line from place to place. Each light had an identifying code, usually a combination of letters and

127

numbers, and you could tell where you were by identifying the beacon you were flying over. It was a very reassuring sight to look out ahead of you and see this string of flashing lights stretching out along your course. The Civil Aviation Authority, now the FAA, was committed to maintaining these lights as long as they would work. I've been told that there are a few still working.

One night we were tooling along down the light line when we ran into some unanticipated cloud cover that obscured the lights for awhile. We had just about reached our turnaround time when we broke out in the clear. Instead of Florida piney woods, all we could see was water. We were over the Gulf of Mexico and we weren't supposed to be. We had no idea how long we had been over water or what direction we might have drifted, because we hadn't been paying as much attention as we should have. You can bet that our inattention suddenly dissolved into an adrenaline high as we executed the single most important maneuver a pilot can learn, the expeditious 180-degree turn. Our turn around point was supposed to be somewhere in the vicinity of Tallahassee, but we seemed to be out over the Gulf near Panama City. We assumed that we had drifted west so we corrected back to the east, and sure enough, we soon picked up the light line again. As we flew back north, we noticed that our heading was about ten degrees east of the light line, which we were exactly paralleling at the time. Harbeson calculated that we had a 40-mph northeast wind that we had not counted on, and it had drifted us west and increased our ground speed so that both our course and elapsed time were screwed up. It's things like that that get people lost out over the Bermuda Triangle.

Life at the Greenville Army Air Base soon settled into a comfortable pattern. As soon as I got settled, Laverda came over and we moved into a room with kitchen privileges in Greenville with a wonderful lady named Mrs. Homer Godbee. Her husband was in the Navy and she had a son about ten years old. She sort of took over as Laverda's surrogate mother. This was about as pleasant a time as we had had together, so far. It was more like being among home folks, because South Carolinians talk pretty much like we do and Laverda and Mrs. Godbee share the same values. Mrs. Godbee made us feel right at home. It was more like having a regular job than being in the Army. I was home every night, except when I had to fly, and even then I got the next day off if I flew very late. Although I was required to maintain a room in the BOQ, I never stayed in it the whole time I was there.

There wasn't much to do in Greenville, but we didn't want to do much but be with each other. We would catch a bus downtown and go to the drug store for sodas, or to the restaurant for dinner. The movies on post were newer than the ones in town, so we usually went there. There was a nice officers club where we could take our wives and where the bachelors took their girl friends. The food was good and plentiful and served cafeteria style. On special occasions like Thanksgiving, we ate banquet style on white tablecloths and china with silver flatware. It was nice.

We had just gotten settled when Laverda developed an abscessed tooth that really gave her a fit. It was one of the front ones and the old dentist we went to said it had to come out. Almost before she knew it, he had put her under with gas and yanked the tooth. She was in tears of mortification when she woke up and saw that gap in her face. He immediately made an impression and scheduled her to come in for fitting with a partial. I don't remember how long it took, but it wasn't long. Although the old dentist was brusque and businesslike, he was also compassionate. He had her fitted with a very natural looking tooth in just no time. You could hardly tell it from her natural tooth, and she kept it for a number of years. As I recall, she finally heaved it down the toilet when she was in morning sickness with Danny in 1948.

These were happy days.

Laverda's pregnancy was progressing satisfactorily. When she came to Greenville she was still in the throes of her morning sickness, living on soda crackers and milk. She probably should have not come over so soon, but there was no way anyone could talk her out of it. I don't recall whether or not she went to a doctor while we were there. I'm sure prenatal care was available on post, because there were pregnant wives everywhere. As I recall, Dromgoole's wife was also pregnant at that time.

She soon got over her nausea and began to eat everything in sight. We were so busy making the most of the little time we had left before I left for overseas, neither of us remembers much detail of those days.

In the fall of 1944, there was a late season hurricane in the Gulf that caused the evacuation of the military aviation facilities there. For some reason, the planes from the Pensacola Naval Air Station were sent up to Greenville. I was out with an instructor flying instrument problems when the F6F's began to come in and began to cause all kinds of complications. The Navy guys flew with total disregard for the pattern discipline of our field, if they ever knew it. I really think they were showing off in their hot little fighters for us truck drivers. They could plead ignorance if they were called on the carpet for screwing up our traffic pattern.

The first we knew they were anywhere around was when one cut through our flight path so close to us that the instructor took the controls from me and banked crazily off to the right. He immediately got on the radio to the tower and demanded to know what was going on. It was then that we were told that we had visitors from the Navy, and to be on our guard. A few more near misses and the instructor called it a day with several choice words for the Navy hot shots.

I'm sure that the air discipline around the Naval Air Station was about the same as at our base, but the Navy pilots were away from home and had a gut need to show off for the Army. They approached our field like they were coming in to a carrier out in the Pacific and needed to get down as quickly as possible. They formed a landing circle and showed us how the Navy did it. This consisted of dropping down to about fifty feet, and with the gear and flaps down, props in low pitch and dragging it in under power right on the tree tops. They racked their planes around in very steep banks and plopped down as near the end of the runway as possible. Their landings violated every tenet in the Army manual of how to land an airplane. Just as they leveled out over the runway, they cut the power and just sort of fell out of the air. Fortunately, those Grumman's were pretty tough machines, and took that kind of mistreatment in stride.

The Navy not only took over the air around the Greenville Army Air Base for a while they also took over the Officer's Club for a couple of nights. There was always a cadre of females that showed up at the club at night to dance with the bachelor officers. The Navy took over the women, as well. The Army guys just sat around and groused about the visitors. The Army sort of got the last laugh, though, because it had already begun to get cool at night and we were in our winter uniforms. A short coat felt good after dark. The Navy was still in summer khakis and flight jackets and they got well chilled when they went outside. They complained the whole time they were there, but didn't get much sympathy from the Army.

The Army felt like there should be a measure of interchangeability within a combat aircrew, so it required that the co-pilot on bombers be able to operate the top turret guns in case the gunner was hurt or killed. To get a little training in this, they incorporated a session for us on a low-level air to ground gunnery mission. There was gunnery range over at the Myrtle Beach Army Air Base with targets set up along an undeveloped stretch of beach. The whole mission was to be at low level. There was an instructor in the right seat, because it was primarily for the benefit of the pilot and gunners that the mission was flown. I was just along for the ride and a turn in the top turret.

The mission was fairly long and would carry over the lunch hour, so box lunches were provided for us. To get me out of the way, I had to ride in the radio compartment with Gaines and Ely. That was the first time I had ridden in that part of the airplane, and I learned that there was an entirely different set of motions, noises and smells back there. I wasn't feeling real great when we started out because I had missed breakfast for some reason.

We took off and as soon as we were airborne and flying clean, Dromgoole took it down almost to ground level. It was then he demonstrated his prowess with the B-25. I do believe he was below the tops of the cotton, sometimes. I know for sure that he had to climb to get over the trees around the fields. He twisted and turned, climbed and dove all across South Carolina. He was having a ball, while I was getting airsick in the back. It was obvious to the guys in the back with me that I was turning green, and they loved every minute of my discomfort. When it came time to eat, Ely broke out the greasy old baloney sandwiches and, with an evil grin, offered me one. I was too sick to even cuss him out.

Things didn't improve when we got to the gunnery range. We made pass after pass at low level so all the gunners could get their turn at the targets. Add to the smell of engine exhaust the smell of cordite and the contortions Dromgoole was putting us through, and I just got sicker and sicker. When it came my turn in the turret, I couldn't see straight. I was lucky to even see the targets. I just pointed the guns in the general direction of the ground and blazed away. I had a certain number of rounds to fire and I was in a hurry to get them away before I heaved all over Flynn's guns. I have never been so miserable in all my life, and if had had the strength, I would have brained Ely.

Fortunately, the return to base was at a reasonable altitude, so I was beginning to feel like I might live by the time we got back. I was still sick, but was not on the verge of throwing up. Amazingly, the moment my feet touched solid ground my nausea left me and I have never been airsick again. I also have never again ridden in the back of a B-25.

The daily routine of training went on with each man getting more and more proficient in the duties required of members of a B-25 combat crew. Sometimes we flew as a crew and sometimes as members of a special instructor led mission to sharpen those individual skills. There were attempts to incorporate the kind of flying we might encounter in any theater. Numbered among the permanent party flying officers were men who had flown in all theaters. We even had at least two men who had been on the Doolittle raid on Tokyo. I don't recall that they contributed anything special to our training except to regale us with their stories of the raid. These tales were entertaining, but of little instructional value. As I recall, the Doolittle raiders were sort of like icons that didn't do much but sit around for we greenhorns to look up to. They actually seemed a little embarrassed by any attention, because they knew that they were not really special. They just happened to be the guys with the most time in B-25's when the call went out for crews for the mission. To them, the Tokyo raid was just another mission, and not an especially successful one at that. They lost all their airplanes and did precious little damage to their targets. With the passage of time, analysis of historical records has lent an aura of heroism to what they did that they seemed not to appreciate at the time I knew them.

We learned from the combat veterans that the B-25 was used in a variety of different ways, depending upon the demands of the particular theater. The 5th Air Force operating in the Southwest Pacific, did a lot of low level work, strafing, skip bombing, parafrag drops, as well as medium altitude precision bombing. They also flew mostly over water and operated against shipping. Their modus operandi seemed to most of us to be the most desirable of all combat worlds. Any time one of us expressed such a sentiment to a veteran from there he threatened to have us up for a Section 8 for being crazy. Although their flying seemed to us to be just the ticket, they hastened to tell us about the miserable living conditions they had to endure, and the constant moving about from one island to another. The way they told it, going up to be shot at by the Japs was far better than being on the ground at the base. It was pretty hard to imagine life being as miserable as they painted it for us.

We knew little about the China-Burma-India (CBI) theater except that conditions there were decidedly primitive. Veterans from there were unanimous in their dislike for the operating conditions, the Chinese High Command, the British and the terrain. All supplies, especially gasoline, were flown in over the Hump, so they never had enough of anything but time, which hung very heavy on their hands. These were guys from the 10th and 14th Air Forces.

Strangely enough, I don't remember encountering men from the 12th Air Force, so we were not especially aware that medium bombers were much used in that theater. Most of us were sure that we would be sent to the Far East, because that seemed to be where the B-25 was the primary medium bomber.

The only war story I remember coming out of the Mediterranean Theater was from a P-40 pilot back from his tour of duty and sent around to training bases to boost the morale of the cadets and fire up our fighting spirit. He told of his first encounter with the German Bf-109 over North Africa. It seems he was on patrol pretty much by himself when he caught the German by surprise from above and behind. Before he could get in range the German pilot spotted him and immediately half-rolled and split-S'ed into a dive. This made him a sitting duck, because all the P-40 guy had to do was half roll and split-S and he had him. When he told his tale back at his base the reason for the apparent stupidity of the German was explained. It seemed that the P-40 was so new in the theater that not many Germans had seen one. The only Allied fighters with in-line engines that they were familiar with were the Spitfire and Hurricane. Their engines had float bowl carburetors and a distressing habit of cutting out when rolled. Knowing this, all the Germans had to do to escape them was half roll and split-S. The Brits couldn't follow them and they would get away. The P-40 engine ran just as well upside down as right side up, so they were able to follow the 109 through this maneuver and shoot them down. I expect the Germans took a crash course in aircraft recognition after losing several planes this way.

In the ongoing effort to prepare us for whatever assignment we got, our training included at least one long range, over water search mission. This mission was memorable only for its length and monotony. We were assigned to fly out over the Atlantic off the Carolina coast and look for stuff. Just what we were expected to find was never revealed to us. Patrol flights generally don't have a specific target to find, but are designed to cover areas in a systematic manner and report whatever is there.

We flew about 50 miles out and began a rectangular search pattern. I don't remember the dimensions of the pattern, but we were to cover thoroughly a specific area of ocean. We flew at about 1500 feet at the most economical cruise settings until we had just enough gas to get back home. The B-25 at economy cruise and an auxiliary tank will fly all day. Time dims my memory a bit, but it seems to me that we were in the air almost 10 hours. I sat in my seat the whole time and ended up with a numb rear end that lasted two days. The only excitement of the day was when we saw a coastal freighter plowing her way up the coast. We went down to deck level and flashed the call letters of the day, just like we were supposed to, and the freighter ignored us. We duly reported its position and went on our way. It could have been a U-boat tender and we couldn't have done more than that. We didn't even have tomato can we could throw at her. I'm sure our report saved the East Coast from serious depredation. At least, it would make a good story that way.

By the end of November our crew was beginning to function quite well. We all seemed to be compatible and liked each other. There were no personality conflicts, and we each were proficient in our performance. We were ready! Apparently the Army thought all the new crews were ready, because we were all alerted for shipment early in December. All our proficiency checks were satisfactory and we had checked in all the equipment we had been issued for training. Orders were cut and we were told to report for shipment to Hunter Field in Savannah, GA.

It was strange how the longer we trained together the more tightly focused we became on just our crew. We were aware of other crews taking the same training regimen, and we fraternized with most of them in off-hours. We kept cursory tabs on some of the men we had been with in cadet training, but they were just other units doing the same things we were. There was only surface camaraderie, not the deeper identification that went along with our fellow crewmen. Looking back, I can visualize our crew's activities and association, but all the others that I know were there, are sort of shadowy figures milling all around us. There was no particular interest in whether other crews were going where we were, or whether we would be separated. Uppermost in our thoughts was where would we (Dromgoole's crew) be going and what it would be like when we got there? This was a very strange feeling. It was almost as though by some strange metaphysical mechanism we had become a single entity. (I think I'm getting in over my head.)

Although we both knew all along that sooner or later we would have to part, neither Laverda nor I were quite prepared for it when the time came. There was precious little we could do to prepare ourselves, so we just lived each day like we had a million more together. There was little to say or do that would make the leaving any easier. It seemed better for me to just say goodbye like I would be back that night than to make it a dramatic farewell. So that is what I did. I had to go to the base early, so I got up, dressed, kissed her goodbye and left my very pregnant wife in bed. I know both of us shed some tears when out of sight of the other, but that was the way it was in wartime. You did what you had to do, and prayed God would somehow keep each of you safe until you could be together again.

Laverda had made arrangements for her sister Grace to come over to Greenville to make the trip back to Rutherford with her. That must have been an experience for Grace. It was the first time she had ever been that far from West Tennessee, and she had to do it on her own. I will forever be grateful to her for that. Knowing that Laverda would not have to get back home alone gave me a modicum of peace of mind. If I had known just how scared Grace was I might have felt more apprehension. But they made it all right, two frightened little country girls travelling alone in a world where frightened little country girls were travelling alone every day. I wish someone would write a book about the millions of wives that endured the loneliness and heartache of travelling around the country after their husbands during the war. I think that is a story that needs to be told. They were just as scared and heroic as any of the men who went to war.

Chapter XI

OFF TO WAR I GO

The troop train ride to Hunter Field was pretty much like all troop train rides, boring. There was a heightened feeling of anticipation, however, that made this one a little different. We had been in training for 1 – 2 years for the next step – combat! None of us knew just what we were getting into, but we were sure we were as ready as we were going to be. We knew our airplane, we knew our crew members, and thought we pretty much knew ourselves. All that was left was to get on with it.

The time at Hunter was spent drawing equipment, getting lectures on how to conduct ourselves should we get shot down and imprisoned or in the hands of partisans, settling personal affairs; such as, making a will, sending home personal effects we wouldn't need overseas and making sure all pay and allowances were in order. It all had a ring of finality about it. We all knew, of course, that we were coming back and some of the stuff was a waste of time. Our opinion was not asked and we were given no option. We all did the things required to cover the eventuality of not coming back.

The ID picture I carried in my wallet

We all drew new fleece lined flying clothes; jacket, pants, boots, helmet and gloves. We also got a new A-2 jacket and lightweight gloves; two pairs, one nylon and one pigskin. The idea was to wear the nylon gloves under the leather ones for added warmth. The AAF was covering all possible temperature conditions. The thing that brought home to me the reality of going into combat was when I was issued a sidearm, Colt .45 caliber automatic w/holster, and fifty rounds of ammo. Somebody must have thought I might have to shoot someone. **SonavaGUN!!**

The most important thing we were to get at Hunter was a brand new B-25 to take overseas. They were expecting a shipment in any day, and as soon as they came in we would be assigned one and sent on our way. After we were processed, which took about three days, we were on our own until our plane arrived. It was getting near Christmas, 1944, and it was cold, damp and miserable in Savannah, so there was not much to do but loaf around the base and go into town occasionally.

Hunter Field was a typical Army Air Force base with the typical facilities. The mess halls and officer's club were adequate and the movie theaters carried first run movies. I believe it was there that I first saw "Thirty Seconds over Tokyo", Ted Lawson's account of the B-25 raid on Japan in April, 1942. The movie was sort of hoked up with a big romance between Van Johnson, as Lawson, and Phyllis Thaxter as his wife. Most of the flying action was pretty authentic because they used real B-25 crews in the filming. I had met some of them in Greenville, not the real Tokyo raiders, but the flyers in the film. I had known some of the original raiders there, too, as I have said earlier. Flying for the film must have been fun, because the crews got to do all sorts of crazy low flying, like chasing coyotes in the desert and flying under the Golden Gate Bridge.

Once the processing was over, the waiting began. Each day we checked with the flight line to see if any B-25's had come in overnight. There was a lot of coming and going of all types of planes, and it was there that I saw my first B-29 up close. I had seen some parked at the air base in Denver as we passed by on the train to the east. There was nothing with which to compare them for size, so I was not particularly impressed. It was not until I got to actually get close and touch one that I realized what a monstrous bird it was. It made our little B-25 look like a primary trainer

In December, 1944, the 29 was the ultimate in long range bombers. They didn't call it the Superfort for nothing. To me it looked huge. We were allowed to climb all through it and marvel at the complexity of it. In addition to two pilots, it had a flight engineer that sat back of the pilots and monitored all the same instruments the pilots had and kept the four big engines properly functioning. He did a lot of what pilots on other planes did. There were so many systems to keep up with the pilots would not have time to tend to their pilotage without the flight engineer.

All compartments were fully pressurized and insulated so engine noise was minimized. There was a tunnel over the bomb bay connecting the front and rear compartments and crewmen moved through it on a little cart like a mechanic's creeper. The tunnel looked about a hundred yards long and you couldn't hear a shout through it, it was so well insulated. The whole nose was glass and the two pilots and the bombardier sat out there like they were on a sun porch. Visibility forward and back to the wings was unobstructed. I would think you would feel awfully exposed in the front of a 29.

When the engines were idling you could almost count the revolutions the props made, they turned so slowly. With 2000 horsepower in each engine nacelle, you can imagine what a racket they made on takeoff. I don't think I would have liked to pilot a B-29. Those that did thought they were just about the cream of the crop, and never missed an opportunity to remind you that they were highly trained aviation specialists, and we lowly pilots of only two engines owed them some respect. They were highly trained and usually had a bit more rank than most, but the plane they drove was a truck. All you had to do was sit and steer for hours on end and end up being a sitting duck for any interceptor that could get to them. They couldn't get out of their own way.

I guess I shouldn't look down my nose at them anymore than they should at me. We all had our special thing to do in a war that exploited all the skill and ingenuity mankind could muster and no one plane or weapons system won the war single-handedly. In fact, Gen. Eisenhower was said to have commented that without the Jeep and the C-47, we would not have won at all. That should put us all in our places.

Our wait extended through Christmas, and I don't know that I have spent a lonelier, bleaker Christmas in my life. I think I missed being with Laverda that Christmas more than the previous one. Somehow, Christmas in Southern California didn't seem as much like Christmas as Christmas back in the South. Combine being among people that talked like me, with the bone chilling cold of winter in South Georgia, and the dreary nights necessitated by the dim-out and you get a very lonely time. I couldn't find much joy in the streets of Savannah, so I stayed in my room at Hunter and re-read the story of Christmas in Luke. That helped some, but it was hard to believe that Christ came to save a crazy world like the one we were living in.

On the night of December 26, I heard the beautiful sound of B-25 engines pop-pop-popping their way to the flight line. Our ships had literally, come in. The next morning, when we went to the flight line, there were several brand, spanking new shiny Mitchell's, fresh from the assembly line in Kansas City, just waiting for us to take them to war. Sure enough, one of them was ours. We were told to take it out for a check to make sure all systems were functioning properly and that everything was where it ought to be. One of the things we had to do that was supremely important was to make sure the magnetic compass was properly calibrated. We first checked it out on the compass rose that was a part of every Air Force base, and then took it up and flew a known course. This course turned out to be a railroad that ran a straight as an arrow north and south through South Georgia. When we established that all navigation instruments were right, we were told to load up our gear and head for our port of debarkation, West Palm Beach, FL. It would be there that we would get our final orders, take on some cargo and head out to who knew where.

We left Savannah in the wintertime and reached West Palm Beach in the spring, or that's what it seemed like. The weather was very balmy and pleasant. It's amazing how much difference a few hundred miles south can make in the temperature. We weren't going to have much time to enjoy the pleasures of South Florida, though. We were to go through our final checks, get our orders and head out.

The route we were to follow was known as the Southern ATC Route. That was a series of airfields down across the Caribbean, through South America, across the Atlantic to Africa. From Africa we could go to the Mediterranean, Middle East, India, China or Burma. It was possible, I suppose to even island hop down to Australia or the Southwest Pacific. At the point of receiving our orders, we only knew that we would be starting out on that route, destination unknown.

As I recall, we were only to be at West Palm for a couple of days. I don't even remember what sort of activities we engaged in. I just remember that we were told that the airplane we were flying was ours until we got to our destination, and we were responsible for its safety. They required that one of the crew, armed, be in or near the plane during the night. That seemed a little strange because the base was patrolled by armed MP's who looked perfectly capable of protecting our property. Nevertheless, we mounted a guard and operated in shifts of four hours each, alternating officers and EM's. The weather was so nice that we couldn't get Flynn to go to the barracks when his tour was up. He was from Massachusetts and cold natured. The weather in Florida seemed like heaven to him, so he slept in the plane.

The Army had adopted the tactic of using all planes going overseas as transports to the limit of their carrying ability. Medium bombers were made to deliver one thing, bombs, so there was not much cargo space on a B-25. Ours was equipped with a Tokyo tank, which was an auxiliary gas tank mounted in the top of the bomb bay. This had been developed for the Doolittle raiders, hence, the name Tokyo tank. That left some space between the tank and bomb bay doors and it was filled with stuff. Every cubic foot of space not needed for crew and crew cargo was stuffed with stuff, even the bombardier's compartment and the tunnel to it held a bunch of K Rations. They knew the bombardier would not be aiming any bombs and would have no need to go into the nose, so his office was cargo space for this run.

Looking back over the years with the advantage of experience and maturity, my mind boggles at the very idea that six "kids" were being entrusted with a $125,000 weapon of war, equipped with primitive, by today's standards, navigational aids, pointed south and told to go. There was no reason under the sun that we should have been expected to be able, with our limited training, to fly of out sight of land safely, much less fly 10,000 miles and not get lost, except that young men all over the world, with no more training than we had, were doing it every day, through some of the most horrid weather and over some of the most forbidding terrain on earth. The enormity of what we were about to commence never occurred to us. It was all in a day's work. It's just as well we didn't know that we were not supposed to be able to do things like that. We knew that if others were doing it, we could too. We were just as good, or better, than they were. Ah, the foolishness and superb confidence of youth. It's plain to me, in retrospect, that war is a young man's game. Only kids would be foolish enough to do the things we took for granted.

The officers of the crews leaving together met with the base navigation officer for a briefing on our first leg, which was to be from West Palm Beach to Borinquen Field in Puerto Rico. Although we knew we were travelling the Southern ATC Route, we didn't know just what each leg's destination was and how far it was between stations. It seems we were shown the route on a map of the Western Hemisphere, but it showed all of the ATC routes, so we couldn't get much of a handle on where we might be going. We would be given maps and pertinent navigation data at each stop, so we wouldn't have so much paper around in the plane to get messed up and lost.

Our bombardier/navigator was responsible for plotting our course and determining our time en route and generally keeping us from getting lost. Charlie was good at his job and the crew had all confidence in him. It was just as well that we did, because he was what we had. Each day, he would carefully gather all his maps and plot his course, calculate our ETA's and relay that information to Little Joe and me.

After we took off and got on course he usually hunkered down behind my seat and read comic books or slept, with an occasional look over my shoulder at the compass and clock to see if we were doing things right.

I notice that I automatically called my pilot "Little Joe". This nickname came about early in our time together as a crew. Ralph was from Texas and was about 5ft., 7in. tall and slender. Charlie was about 6ft. and pretty husky, so Ralph looked small to him. There was a country/western song popular about that time called "Little Joe, The Wrangler", and Charlie immediately hung that name on Ralph. It stuck, and from then on, he was known as Little Joe or just Joe. Many of our squadron mates overseas didn't know he had any other name.

The morning of 31 Dec 1944, we were handed our orders and told to take off, and not to open the orders until we were 200 miles out to sea. With no one to check up on us, surely they didn't expect us to obey such a nonsensical order. As soon as the gear and flaps were up and we were climbing on course, Little Joe told me, who was holding the orders, to find out where we were going. The orders were to proceed via the Southern ATC Route to the Replacement Depot (Repl. Depl., in Gi-ese) at Caserta, Italy, there to release the airplane and await assignment as replacement crews in the 12th Air Force, Mediterranean Theater of Operations. We were somewhat perplexed; because we were sure we were destined for India, Burma, China or the Pacific. We were hardly aware that the 12th Air force existed. We were to later learn that medium bombers were the heart of the 12th, and had been from its beginning.

The weather that day was as nearly perfect as one could ask for. We could see the Gulf Stream as plain as if it was a blue green river flowing through dark blue farm land. I had heard that that was so, but had to fly over it to be convinced. At that time, no one had heard of the "Bermuda Triangle", so we felt no apprehension at all about flying over that part of the ocean.

Our course lay roughly parallel to the chain of islands known as the Bahamas, running in a string to the southeast toward Cuba, Haiti and the Dominican Republic. Puerto Rico is a little chunk of volcanic material just east of the Dominican Republic.

The Bahamas looked like a string of pearls strung out in the middle of the Gulf Stream. There seemed to be no end to them, and then, suddenly, there was, and we had nothing but open, featureless ocean before us. I think that then we all began to realize that we were well and truly on our way. The anticipation of what unknown thing lay ahead and trepidation about what we were leaving, sort of overwhelmed us, but left us eager to get on with our grand adventure.

After many monotonous hours we finally spotted Puerto Rico right where Charlie said it would be at the time he said it would be there. We were cleared to land at Borinquen Field and were told by the tower to land long because B-29's landing there had broken up the first hundred feet of the runway. Apparently, the runway builders never contemplated handling planes as big and heavy as the B-29, and built too lightly. Fortunately, there was plenty of runway for us since it was 10,000 feet long - nearly two miles! It was also very wide, said to be wide enough for Piper Cubs to take off across it.

The base was a very modern facility, having been in operation since before the war. It was there that we encountered our first "Follow Me" Jeep. At all ATC bases there was white Jeep with a big sign across the back that said "FOLLOW ME". Since most traffic into these bases was transient, someone needed to direct incoming planes to their parking area. Some bright Pfc. probably thought the idea up and was rewarded with a weekend pass while the base engineering officer took credit for it. After about two more stops on our way with a Follow Me Jeep to meet us, our tail gunner, Ely, observed, "Man, that must be some kind of fast Jeep. He beats us in to every base."

We were in the tropics now, and the weather was balmy and nice, even on January 1, 1945. The base transient quarters at Borinquen were luxurious by comparison to anything any of us had encountered before. The food at the O-Club was excellent and the place was generally pleasant. The club sat on a cliff overlooking the Caribbean. It was the sort of place at which everyone hoped to be stationed for their overseas duty. But, we were scheduled to only be there overnight.

Although we pretty much made that leg on our own, there were other crews going the same way, with takeoff times staggered so that we arrived

15 mins. to a half hour apart. No particular effort was made to keep us all together, although we would occasionally see another 25 near us along the way.

The next morning, we collected our navigation information, plotted our next leg, which was to take us to Georgetown, British Guiana, in South America, cranked up and taxied out to take off. When Little Joe ran up the engines to check the magnetos, one of them failed the check. It was dead. That scrubbed our scheduled take off until we could get a new magneto installed. Although, B-25's by the dozens went through there every month, there was no magneto for our Wright engines on the island. The replacement had to come from the states by courier. We had to lay over in that tropical paradise until our bird was once again airworthy. Gee, what a letdown, said he, with a smirk on his face.

We were there a total of four days, during which time we explored as much of the island as we were allowed to. One trip took us down the coast to the little town of Aguadilla, where we found a little bit of the U.S.A. with a Spanish accent. There were drug stores where we could actually get a chocolate soda. We found a lot of things that were non-existent in the stores stateside. I don't know if they were black market or legit, and I didn't ask.

I had gotten away from home with nothing to write letters with, so I bought a first class Schaefer fountain pen and a bottle of ink. I used that pen and ink the whole time I was overseas. I also found some film for my Kodak Brownie camera that I had gotten for my high school graduation. Back home I could only get one roll at a time, when I could find the 616 size. There in the drug store, were cases and cases of all sizes. I got a case of 24 eight-exposure rolls. That turned out to be a real find. I would never have been able to get even one roll where we were going. It was also on that excursion that Little Joe got drunk from too much Puerto Rican rum and nearly got us all in trouble. We had managed to find a bar open in the local hotel, and for some reason he drank too much. In fact, I think that may have been one of the few times in his life he ever drank anything intoxicating. I never saw him take a drink again in the time we were together. He was the only one that imbibed too heavily. Most of us didn't drink anything.

It was getting dark and we were on our way to the bus station with Little Joe reeling along and acting a fool, when some little kids began to pester us for money, or chocolate, or anything else they could think of. Joe kept telling them to beat it and leave us alone, but they persisted, as do beggars everywhere. One of them grabbed him and tried to get into his pocket. That did it, and he put his foot in the kids stomach and shoved him a way. It was not quite a kick, but it sent the kid reeling. That got them off of us and drew some very hostile stares from the natives in the street.

The sober ones of us grabbed him and hustled him away to the bus station as fast as we could. I had visions of us lying in an alley somewhere with our throats slit. Even Little Joe must have had some sobering thoughts about what he had done, because he quieted down and went along peaceably. I was pretty sore at him and let him know in no uncertain terms how I felt about his actions and drunks in general. I didn't talk to him all the way back to the base. I later heard him tell someone that he thought his co-pilot was mad at him. He was right!

The next day our plane was ready with its new magneto and we took it out for a test flight. Everything checked out OK and we were ready to go on south, pretty much alone this time, because the others had gone already.

We updated our flight plan and took off for Georgetown. This was a fairly short flight, mostly over water, and we made it into Georgetown right on time. Charlie's navigation was looking better and better.

The base at Georgetown had been hacked out of a tropical rain forest out of town. Facilities were on the primitive side, but adequate, and the food was not bad. The weather was hot and muggy and it rained a lot. After all, we were pretty close to the equator where there is no winter or summer, just dry seasons and wet seasons. It was nearing the wet season there, so everything was damp all the time. Not a pleasant place.

This time the Follow me Jeep was driven by a local civilian employee of the army, a black man, a very black man with a cultured English accent. This was a shock to the ears of those of us from the South, especially Ely, who was from Mississippi. He had never heard a black man speak with an English accent. He was used to, "Yassuh, boss." To his credit he treated the man with the greatest of respect and carried on a long conversation with him just to hear him speak. He was enthralled with him, not at all like the Mississippi redneck he claimed to be.

Nothing of memorable import happened at this stop that I can remember. There were a couple of minor things that come to mind. I had set my musette bag down on the ground in front of the plane's nose wheel while we were doing the ground check prior to take off, when a tug came by to tow us out of the parking hardstand. The driver ran over the bag and ground a hole in the cover flap and flattened my mess kit. Needless to say, I was more than a little put out, but there was not much I could say, because I really should have put it in the plane. I still have the bag with the hole in it, somewhere in the basement.

Also, during that same check out, Little Joe ducked under the nose of the plane and cut his eyelid on one of the radio antennae. It was a fine wire between two terminals and ran parallel to the fuselage about four inches down for about three feet. All of us had made that short cut many times, but that time Joe just didn't duck enough. He bled profusely for a few minutes. I examined the eyelid and could see that the skin had been barely broken, and he was not about to go to the dispensary and be grounded, so we doctored it on the spot. We broke out the first aid kit and put some iodine on the cut. Fortunately, we didn't get any in his eye or we might have blinded him. He jumped around and cursed for a little bit, but soon go over it. The real excitement of that day was yet to come.

The weather at Georgetown, when we got ready to take off for Belem was marginal, at best. The ceiling was about 500 feet and the visibility maybe a mile. Reports from the weather planes said the overcast did not extend south of us for more than 150 miles before it cleared up, and stayed CAVU (ceiling and visibility, unlimited) on in to Belem. Since Joe and I were both fully instrument rated, we were allowed to take off.

Belem, Brazil is located at the mouth of the Amazon River and lies about 900 miles east-southeast from Georgetown. The course took us over the rain forests of British Guiana, Suriname, French Guiana and Brazil. This area was largely unsettled, except by scattered Indian tribes, and many planes had gone down in that jungle, never to be seen or heard of again. It was not the most hospitable terrain you could fly over, but at least it was more or less solid and not salty. Our attitude was that we were not going to go down, but if we did, we would rather go down in the jungle than in the ocean. In retrospect, we probably would have been easier found in the water, provided we managed to survive a water landing.

We took off, circled the field to get on course and immediately went on instruments as we climbed on course to our assigned flight altitude of 9,000 feet. The plane was performing perfectly, and Joe was settled in comfortably flying on instruments. Since all the flight instruments are in front of the pilot, it was his place to fly as long as we had to be on instruments. I could, in a pinch, take over from the right seat, but it was a little awkward.

I don't think either of us had ever been in such a dense cloud. You could barely see the wing tips, about thirty feet away. We had been told that the overcast was only about 6,000 feet thick, and we kept thinking we would break out on top any minute. Instead of thinning out to blue sky, the cover just kept getting thicker.

At 9,000 feet we leveled off and set up our specified cruise speed and settled down for some classic instrument flying. After about thirty minutes, the air began to get a bit turbulent. Some alarm began to set in and the adrenaline began to pump. What were we getting into? Pretty soon it became obvious what was happening. We were flying into a thunderstorm. Since we couldn't see, there was no way to avoid the weather ahead of us. The best course was to remain on course as best we could and just bust our way through.

Almost before we knew it, we had gone from mild turbulence to a most vicious roller coaster. It began to rain torrents. Lightning flashed and roared and the plane bucked like the wildest rodeo bull you can imagine. One instant we would be going down at 3,000 feet/min. with the wheel back in our laps. Next, we would be going up at 3,000 feet/min. with the wheel full forward. By this time, I was on the wheel with Joe, and we were both fighting it with all our strength and wits. We weren't so much flying the plane as hanging on and trying to keep it upright. Mother Nature had our little B-25 in her teeth and was shaking us like a terrier shakes a rat. I think I can truthfully say that that was the most frightened I ever was in an airplane. Not even in combat did I feel as helpless as I did then. In combat at least you could see the ground and see where the enemy was with a chance to maneuver, but in that storm there was no visibility and no way to get away from what had us.

I looked over at Joe and he had the wheel in a death grip with his eyes fastened on the instruments. None of the massive gyrations ever made him lose his concentration. He was flying on pure instinct at that point. He was a smart enough pilot to know not to fight the turbulence too much and risk breaking the plane. We had to pretty much just ride it out and hope the storm would get tired of us and spit us out.

I checked on Charlie and Flynn and they were holding on for dear life. For once, Charlie was not asleep. Flynn was belted in his seat by the upper turret base and had his arms wrapped around it like it was a tree trunk. He was white as a sheet.

After about thirty minutes of roller coastering across the Amazon jungle, we suddenly burst out in the clear into brilliant sunshine. We had survived!

Once clear and sure that everything was intact, we turned and looked back at what we had just come out of. There was a line of thunderstorms that stretched from horizon to horizon and up to 50,000 feet. They were so continuous that had we been able to see them ahead of us, we probably could not have found a course through them. It's probably just as well that we blundered in with no time to get scared. Apparently, this squall line had formed after our last weather report, and the ATC didn't have time to warn us. Very likely, we would not have heard them, because in the storm the radio static was so bad we couldn't transmit or receive.

Joe was wringing wet with sweat and shaking like a leaf when the relief reaction set in. He pushed the seat back and motioned for me to take over while he sat there and shook. I flew while Charlie checked our position as best as he could, and he reported that we had come out of the storm pretty much on course and on time. Amazing!!

After that harrowing experience was behind us and the weather looked peaceful enough ahead, we began to look around at the terrain we were flying over. It was green, very green as far as you could see. There was an unbroken green carpet that seemed to stretch out to eternity. This was the famous Amazon basin rain forest, some of the last unexplored wilderness in the world, and at the moment, my exploring gene was completely dormant. All I wanted was to see some kind of evidence of civilization, a house, a road, a clearing, anything. From 9,000 feet, if you've seen one rain forest you've pretty much seen them all.

When we were about an hour out of Belem, we discovered that we could see the Atlantic Ocean off our port (left) wing. Knowing that Belem was on the Amazon, near its mouth, we let our course drift a little east until we could see the ocean plainly. We could fly that course into Belem and see the Amazon, which we had heard was quite a sight. It turns out that the river mouth is well over a hundred miles wide and is more like a huge bay than a river mouth. There is such a tremendous volume of water flowing into the ocean that fresh water has been reported in the ocean as much as two hundred miles out to sea. Flying over it was like flying over the ocean, except the water was brown, not blue.

Needless to say, we were glad to find Belem just where it was supposed to be, and we got on the ground with a profound sense of relief. There was that little Follow Me Jeep, again, leading us into our assigned parking place. Once out of the plane, we all gave it a good going over to see if there was any damage from the storm we had flown through. There had been reports of planes flying into thunderstorms and being broken into little pieces, so we wanted to see if we had any pieces missing. Not so much as a popped rivet or cracked plexiglass. North American sure made those B-25's tough. We were becoming more and more attached to our bird.

There was nothing notable about Belem. It was just a convenient place to have an airfield halfway between Georgetown and Natal, our jumping off place to cross the Atlantic. I remember nothing about the base, so it must have been adequate. No room service in the barracks or gourmet food in the mess hall, nothing to leave a lasting impression. I expect all we wanted to do was stay planted on solid ground for a few hours and forget about the day's events.

Suddenly, a glimmer of a memory does come back. It was there that I bought a pair of short boots, commonly called in the Air Force, Karachi boots. As we encountered other crews on the ATC route, we noticed that many of the ATC crewmen were wearing sharp looking boots that had tops about ten inches tall. They told us that style originated in Karachi, India, and were a favorite of the English. They were definitely non-regulation, but then, we flyer types were not regulation, either, or tried very hard to not be completely GI. You could get away with wearing these boots away from the states, because they looked like regulation shoes when you were standing at attention. They looked so good that even the generals wore them, which made it all right for the rest of us.

Although the boots were originally made in Karachi, they had spread all along the ATC routes all over the world and into all the combat zones. They were actually pretty hard to find and I was fortunate to find a pair my size in the PX in Belem. I can't remember what I paid for them, about $25, I think. I was really cool. Actually, cool had not come into the language in that context in 1945. I was really sharp.

Belem lies just below the Equator and in a perpetual state of summer time. That must be severely monotonous to transplants who have experienced the season changes of the temperate zones. The day we were there the climate was very pleasant due to the tempering effect of the nearby ocean, but it would not have been my idea of an ideal duty post.

Another impression comes to mind, now that I think back. It was there that I took one of the most memorable showers of my life. The water was very soft and the showerhead was large so the effect was like standing out in a warm tropical rain. The roof was thatched and there was a lot of open space above the walls. It was an altogether salubrious feeling. I also got one of the slickest shaves I had ever experienced. The post barber was a Brazilian and he honed his straight razor on a 2 x 2 piece of the whitest wood I ever saw. Uncle Willie T. (the town barber back in Rutherford) would have been envious.

Our next stop was Natal, Brazil, which, if you look at the globe, lies on the easternmost tip of South America. That is the part of the continent that is said to have once fit against Africa and drifted away due to tectonic plate shift. Since we were going to have to cross the Atlantic to get to Africa, one could wish that it hadn't drifted quite so far.

Because of its proximity (?) to Africa, Natal was as good a jumping off point as was available to the ATC. Just about every kind of multi-engine plane in the AAF inventory flew through there on the way to Africa, the Middle East, Europe and the Far East; B-29's, 17's, 24's, 25's, 26's, C-46's, 47's, 54's. They were all there on the field when we were.

Because the next two legs of our flight were long ones over water, we had a two-day lay over while our plane was thoroughly checked and determined to be airworthy enough to make the trip. Being a brand new plane and having survived a bout with a tropical thunderstorm, we were sure it could take us anywhere there was gas enough to reach. Our confidence was sky high. Fourteen hundred and seventy-five miles of water couldn't scare us. Those 1475 miles of ocean would take us to Ascension Island, a rock in the South Atlantic where the ATC had established an air base.

Ascension Island, the remains of a volcano, is an almost barren rock with an area of 34 square miles. As I remember, it is about 4 miles wide by 8.5 miles long. It was first discovered by the Portuguese in 1501, and remained uninhabited until the British took it over to establish a military garrison when Napoleon was exiled to St. Helena, about 700 miles to the south. I guess they thought that if Napoleon ever escaped he would head for Ascension as being the nearest island. That seems rather far-fetched, since he would be even worse off there than on St. Helena. I read somewhere that the whalers working the South Atlantic used it as a coaling station. When the war started, there was a population of 200, all living in Georgetown, the one town on the island.

The Army built a refueling base for the ATC by bulldozing out an 8,000-ft. runway right across the middle of the island and providing facilities for personnel to operate it. By having a base in the middle of the ocean, planes could carry more cargo by not having to carry a large fuel load.

After our plane was released, we were given our orders to proceed. Charlie gathered all the pertinent data, plotted our course, calculated our ETA (estimated time of arrival) and we were ready to go. It was pretty simple, really. All we had to do was take off, climb to 9,000 ft., heading

93 degrees, fly about 9 hours at 165 mph, and, voila! we were there. You know, we actually approached it with just that sort of blasé attitude. We could do anything. Looking back, it now makes a knot in my stomach just thinking about what we were expected to do. When you realize that a 1-degree error in flying our course would mean that we would never see the island, it does give one pause.

The weather was a little "iffy" when we were ready for takeoff. There was some rain ahead of us and the winds aloft were stronger than was safe. We didn't have enough gas to fly much beyond Ascension Island, and the Army wasn't taking unnecessary chances with us. It was at that time that we were made aware of what is called "the point of no return." That's the point in a flight at which you don't have enough fuel to return to your point of origin, and have no choice but to continue. It has an extremely fatalistic ring to it. We had never given much thought to the concept because we had never flown over that much water before. Always before, there had been alternate sites we could go to if it became certain we could not make our destination. Even over the Amazon, there was terra firma below us, even though there was lots of terror there was a lot more firma than over the South Atlantic. (That's a terrible pun.) The airfield commander scrubbed our take off and said we would try the next day.

With a good bit of relief, we went back to our billet and hit the sack, because we had gotten up pretty early that morning. I guess our exuberance got a little out of control because we got chewed out by a B-29 pilot of a next door for making so much noise. He let it be known that he was a *captain* and was *pilot* of a B-29 and that he had just flown all night and had to fly all night that night, and that we lowly lieutenants were disturbing his beauty sleep. The man *was* a *jackass*, but we were outranked, so we said, "Sorry, sir," and went to bed.

The next day, we updated our flight plan and tried again. This time the weather had improved greatly and there appeared to be no reason our flight shouldn't go smoothly. Weather over water could be fairly well predicted in those days, if observations could be made at various points, such as islands, ships at sea, and planes. Centuries of observation by sailors had helped meteorologists develop an understanding of ocean weather patterns, so if the weathermen told us the way should be clear all the way to Ascension Island, we felt like we could believe them.

Charlie gave us the course to fly, the ATC people assigned us an altitude, and we knew what our airspeed should be for economical cruising, so off we went. There was nothing to do for the next seven plus hours but maintain our heading, transfer our fuel when need be and listen to the radio. Once we got over the nerves associated with something so new, the trip became downright boring. At any given time only the pilot or co-pilot was doing anything very useful, and their activity was minimal. A B-25 can be trimmed to fly hands off as long as everyone stays put. The only attention needed is to make sure the heading doesn't change and the airspeed remains constant. That doesn't require constant attention.

As an aid to navigation, we were equipped with a radio compass that we used as a backup to the magnetic and gyro compasses. We could tune in to any radio station, AAF or commercial and determine the bearing toward that station. If the station was where we wanted to go, we just pointed the airplane in that direction and "homed in." As an interesting sidelight, the Japanese used the Honolulu all night music station to direct them to Pearl Harbor. A flight of B-17's coming in to Hickam Field on Dec. 7, 1941, used the same station, and arrived right in the middle of the attack.

This navaid was a comfort except when we thought of the stories we had been told about the Germans using a counterfeit signal from a submarine to lure planes away from Ascension. They would surface and transmit just far enough to either side of Ascension that a plane could home in on their signal and miss the island by fifty miles and never realize it until they were out of gas. We were assured that the sub menace was no longer a problem because they had been cleared out of that part of the ocean. We hoped so.

Our fuel load was sufficient to get us to Ascension with about 45 minutes reserve. This meant that our point of no return was just over half way, about 800 miles out. Charlie had determined this point before we left and as we approached it, all hands were notified. We all scanned the ocean very intently to see if we could spot it, but each wave pretty much looked like the last one. Needless to say, realizing we were irrevocably committed marvelously sharpened our will to fly that trip perfectly. Suddenly, each instrument began to stand out like it was etched by Currier and Ives. Each imagined hiccup of the engines sounded like a cannon report. We were tuned in on the Ascension Island frequency to the last micro-megacycle, and we listened so intently that our ears hurt.

Remember, we were up there alone. There were no other planes going our way that day that we could tag along with. Several had taken off for Ascension that morning about the same time we did, but, due to differences in cruising speed they were either out of sight ahead of us or behind us. I suppose that was about as alone as six people together could feel.

After a while, we began to return to our more normal selves, and continued the trip more or less like it was an everyday thing with us. The plane was performing flawlessly, the weather was beautiful, the radio reception was good, and Roy on the big command set was making all his checks right on time. Charlie was sound asleep behind my seat, Ely was sacked out in the radio compartment, Flynn was dozing in his seat, and Joe and I were taking turns flying. We both were monitoring the Ascension range frequency, listening for their call signal. The signal had the reputation of being one of the strongest in the world, although it didn't reach our point of no return. We had kept our radio compass tuned to the Natal station, and kept it directly behind us as long as we could hear it. There was a dead zone halfway between Natal and Ascension where we could hear nothing from anywhere. That was a spooky feeling, because in the States we were never out of range of some sort of signal. Roy could communicate by code on the command set, but we could hear nothing, not even an occasional plane or ship transmission. Talk about feeling alone!

We finally began to receive the Ascension signal and it sounded like the Heavenly Chorus. Our radio compass showed us to be right on course. Ascension Island was dead ahead. There was a bunch of miles yet to go, but we knew our next dry spot was right where Charlie said it would be.

As we approached the ETA Charlie had given us we began to scan the horizon very carefully. We raised the tower and gave them our inbound heading and approximate position and got cleared in. We began to gradually let down about 100 miles out until we leveled off at about 1500 feet, in sight of the island. With no point of reference and not realizing how small the rock is, we thought we had quite a way yet to go. We got Charlie to check and see if he wanted to change his ETA, and he thought we ought to add about fifteen minutes, which we did. When we touched down, it was within a minute of Charlie's first ETA. The island is so small we thought it was much farther away than it actually was. The tower people said that happened to most first time visitors.

Because of our changed ETA, we forgot to alert Roy, who was on the command set using the trailing antenna. This was a 75-foot wire with a 5-pound iron ball on the end. It was used when we wanted to send and receive over long distances, and was supposed to be reeled in before landing. As we came in over the cliff at the end of the runway, the ball hit the cliff and snapped off the antenna. We were told this happened a lot, because crews were not prepared for getting to the field as soon as they did, since they had overestimated the time to touch down. Needless to say, Roy got more than a little hacked off at us.

Ascension Island has to be one of the bleakest, most barren places in the entire world. It is the remains of the cinder cone of a prehistoric volcano. There was originally no place to land a plane, so the engineers blasted and bulldozed a runway through the center of the island. The runway was wide and 8,000 feet long with a hump in the middle. The hump was high enough that planes on opposite ends of the runway were invisible to each other. More than once, planes had taken off simultaneously from opposite ends. That created a unique situation that tested the flying ability of all concerned. Occasionally, a heavily loaded plane would top that rise at just below flying speed, and the pilot, thinking he was airborne, would pull back on the controls and stall out back into the ground. One hotshot, flying a B-26, raised his gear too soon and bellied back into the runway. The plane was still visible in the bone yard, the bone yard being the collection of plane carcasses from local crashes.

We discovered, as we traveled across the world, that fields with tricky landing characteristics tended to have bone yards prominently situated near the runways. This was not without purpose. The sight of wrecked planes of every type tended to get ones attention and suggest that maybe one ought to be somewhat more careful than usual. Everyone was warned about the hump at Ascension and given options for takeoff that should provide for safety, but there were always those that knew better than the locals. They were those that contributed to the growing bone yard.

Ascension Island was one of the most interesting places we visited, in the short term, at least. It was totally barren, no trees, grass, bushes, and very little wildlife. There were a few seagulls and shore birds and maybe a lizard or two, otherwise, it was lifeless. If you wonder why I call it interesting, it is because of its very lifelessness. We had never seen anything like it before. It was as much like the surface of the moon as any place on the planet. Since we were there less than twenty-four hours, we didn't get the full flavor of the desolate environment. Permanent party said it was easy to go crazy there. In fact, there were reports of more than one suicide because of the deadly boredom.

Being only about 8 degrees south of the Equator, the temperature seldom varied. The sun burned down all day and the nights were always warm. Fortunately, there seemed to always be a wind that made the evenings relatively pleasant. There were few of the amenities that one found at even the newest, most primitive bases. Most of the housing facilities were tents, since all building materials had to be shipped or flown in. Some of the maintenance work was done out in the open because there was very little rain and bad weather to contend with. There was no town to take leave in, and rotation back to the states was unheard of. Occasional rest leaves were granted back to Natal, but these also were scarce. There were men there who had not left the island in two years. They were the ones that adapted or went bonkers.

I think all of the personnel who were stationed on Ascension Island did or will go to heaven when they die. They have already had their turn in Hell. To put young virile American males on a rock like that, 1450 miles from the nearest woman, deprive him of booze, make him work in searing heat, sleep in tents and eat C rations is to consign him to purgatory, at best.

We had two meals there, dinner and breakfast. Dinner was C rations and hardtack and Kool Aid. Breakfast was powdered eggs, powdered milk, dry cereal, Spam and coffee. All the water for the island was brought in by tanker, like oil tankers. That meant showers were at a premium and were only for permanent party. Transients had to wait until they got to the mainland of Africa. The permanent party said that sometimes the water tasted like they hadn't rinsed out the tanker well.

We did a little exploring before dark by going down to the shore, or as close to the water as we could safely get. There was no beach. The surf rose suddenly about fifty yards from the island and crashed against the cliffs where we stood. As the sun went down it shown through the waves as they leapt up out of the ocean, and you could see the fish swimming in them like in an aquarium. Since the island rose out of the ocean so steeply, the waves were just large swells until they got close in when they rose, that night, to about twenty feet and smashed into the island. It was quite a sight to this old country boy, who, before basic training, had never seen a wave higher than the one you got when you threw a brick into the pond.

That night we saw a movie in the outside theater. That was the primary entertainment vehicle for the base, and there was, they told us, a great air of anticipation any time a new movie came in from the states. I don't remember what the show was, so it must not have been one of your star-studded attractions. It did give us something to do with our time before hitting the sack.

Our next destination was Roberts Field in Liberia. Our course was almost due north and the distance was about 950 miles. Since the distance was less than our last leg, we were able to cruise at a higher speed, about 180-mph. At 165, our last leg speed, we felt like we were just dragging along and not getting anywhere much. Although it was only 15 mph faster, it psychologically gave us a little boost in spirits. The fact that we would be getting over land again also helped.

There was nothing unusual about the take off except we opted to start our roll near the middle of the field so we would be over the hump in the runway before we got anywhere near our take off speed. A fully loaded B-25 doesn't need but about 5,000 ft. to get airborne, and besides, we would be going slightly down hill, giving us a little better acceleration. Not that there was ever any doubt, but we made the take off with lots of runway to spare and were on our way.

After 5 hrs. 20 mins. of uneventful flight we were on the ground at Roberts Field, and once again, Charlie's navigation was right on. Of course, we checked his fight plan with the radio compass and found that we were right on course all the way. He had gotten over minding that we used the radio to double check his navigation, but seemed to get a secret delight when he was always right.

Roberts Field was hacked out of the rain forest of Liberia, right on the bank of a river that emptied into the Atlantic. We were a few miles inland because the ground was too swampy to support a field on the ocean. The town of Robertsport was several miles away, and there was not much in the way of transportation, even if we had wanted to go there. We were to only be there overnight, anyway.

As far as facilities go, they were fairly primitive, though not as much as Ascension Island. There were wooden buildings and maintenance shops and some pretty substantial hangars. I believe the base might have been a Pan Am stop before the war, because the runway was all weather and long enough to handle anything the AAF inventory at that time. Living quarters had wood floors and canvas sides with screens, and mosquito netting around the cots. It was impossible to eliminate all the mosquitoes along the coast, although the Engineers did a pretty good job. The last thing we did before turning in the tropics was to spray inside our netting with a pyrethrum bomb.

Roberts Field was about 8 degrees <u>above</u> the Equator, so it was summer all the time there, too. We were cautioned not to go out in the sun without a hat in midday, or preferably, not go out at all. We were told that sunstroke was almost assured if we ignored their warnings. So, it came as sort of a shock to see the civilian employees on the base squat down against a building in the noonday sun and take a nap. Of course, they were all Africans and appeared to be immune to the heat, anyway.

Malaria has always been the scourge of the tropics, and was a concern to Americans at the bases where the Anopheles mosquito thrived. When the Japanese took the East Indies, the supply of quinine, the preferred drug for malaria, effectively dried up. To function in the malaria zones, there had to be found an effective substitute. The Germans had developed one called atabrine, an aniline derivative, aniline being a yellow dye made from coal. It was too costly to supplant quinine, so it was not extensively produced. When there was no quinine, atabrine had to be substituted, regardless of its cost. When white men went into the tropics, they either protected themselves with atabrine, or they sickened and died from malaria.

In South America and in Africa, atabrine tablets were on all the mess hall tables along with salt tablets. We had instructions to take atabrine with every meal. This applied especially to the permanent party, and you could tell who was permanent party by their jaundiced appearance. The longer they had been there the more yellow they were from the atabrine. By the time we got out of the tropics and away from the malaria belt, we were beginning to show a little yellow.

In addition to being told to take atabrine to avoid malaria, we were admonished not to fraternize with the natives. Transients like us didn't need any such warnings because the natives were all still black to us. It was said that they became remarkably light skinned the longer you were away from women of your own kind.

There was a small village on the opposite bank of the river bordering the field, and you could see the natives going about their daily chores, whatever they were. There was a fence around the field as much to keep the GI's in as to keep the natives out. They told the story of the young corporal that had been away from female company for far too long, and his hormones finally overpowered him. He skipped his atabrine, skipped over the fence, swam the river and bartered for the village chief's guaranteed sixteen year old virgin daughter. As a result of his escapade, he came down with malaria, gonorrhea, and a type of syphilis invariably fatal to white men. His body was shipped home, a casualty of war.

Roberts Field was memorable for the oppressive heat, atabrine tablets, and the equatorial natives who were so black they had a blue sheen to their skin. The food was ordinary, but better than on Ascension Island. I expect grocery deliveries were better there than in the middle of the South Atlantic.

Our next stop was Dakar, the capital of French West Africa, later Senegal, on the coast. It was a relatively short hop, taking only 3 hrs., 50 min. The base there was originally an airline field established in 1941 as the closest point to Natal, Brazil. Some of the long range planes like the C-54 and the four-engine bombers could fly directly from Natal to Dakar, nonstop. We went by way of Ascension Island and Roberts Field because our range was too short to make that hop.

The one thing I remember about Dakar was the presence of the Senegalese soldiers guarding the base. The French had taken the warrior class of natives in the area and trained them in the French army. They all wore spotless, brilliant white uniforms with the typical pillbox shaped billed cap with the little neck cape. They were all slender and tall, and ramrod straight. Their skin was jet black but their facial features were fairly angular. They were obviously a proud race, and had the reputation of being fearless, fearsome fighters. They, along with the Sikhs and Punjabi from India and the Philippine Scouts, were some of the scariest fighting men in the world, according to some of my infantry buddies.

Overnight in Dakar and then on our way to Marrakech in French Morocco. We were getting closer to the war every day.

Passing a B-24 off to war like us. 15th AF, I guess.

We had to fly inland over Mauritania to avoid Spanish Sahara which we couldn't fly over, since Spain was officially neutral, but with sympathies toward Germany. That considerably lengthened our trip. Mauritania is mostly desert, and on that day was experiencing a terrific dust storm. We flew at 9,000 ft. and were safely out of the dust, but we couldn't see the ground and the horizon was indistinguishable. Because there were no visual references, we were on instruments even though we were in the sunshine. It was a very strange sensation. We were also bucking something of a head wind, which cut our ground speed down some.

We finally got over the dust storm and could see the ground once more. Not that it was much help. As far as you could see were sand and rocks and little else. No trees, grass or even cacti. But at least there was now a horizon and we could keep our wings level visually.

When we were safely past Spanish territory, we began to bear west toward Marrakech. Our head wind must have been stronger than we thought because when we established where we were, it became obvious that we didn't have enough gas to get to Marrakech. A quick check of our maps showed us there was an auxiliary field at Agadir, on the coast. It had been a French fighter field, but was large enough for us to get in and out of safely. Our information said there were refueling facilities there. We radioed Marrakech our condition and informed them we would be a little late.

As we circled the field and tried to raise someone on the radio, it seemed that the tower personnel had taken off for a siesta. No one answered, so we came on in without clearance. We taxied in to what seemed to be refueling facilities and were met by a thoroughly perplexed and somewhat hostile native soldier. He spoke no English and we spoke no whatever he spoke, French, I think. Finally, a more official looking personage who spoke a little English drove up in a jeep. He had a little trouble with Joe's Texas accent, but understood what our problem was, and authorized the purchase of enough gas to get us to Marrakech. We didn't actually buy it, but signed off on some kind of paper that I'm sure got altered to reflect more gas that we could have possibly gotten off the ground with. Anyway, we got airborne again and Joe gave them a good buzz job in appreciation.

Our destination was a former French Foreign Legion post outside the sizeable city of Marrakech. It had one long, east-west concrete runway, paralleled by a narrow taxiway. The tower informed us that there were some French pilots training in the area and to be on the alert, looking out for C-47's. The warning stood us in good stead and came at just the right time. As we were on our approach to the east, lo and behold, there was a C-47 also on his approach, to the west. No amount of screaming on the radio by the tower or me could get the guy's attention. He was sure he was right and with true Gallic stubbornness, he'd be damned if he was going to give way to any Yankee. At the last moment, Joe skidded to the left and landed on the taxi way as the Frenchman made a touch and go on the runway. Fortunately, the taxi strip was plenty wide and as long as the runway, so we made it all right.

Apparently, what the Frenchman was doing was shooting touch and go's by landing, taking off, flying out far enough to turn around and land going in the other direction. This is not the recommended way of doing touch and go's. You are supposed to fly a normal pattern and land the same way all the time. He must have been in a hurry to get in his prescribed number of landings and take offs that day, so he figured this way he could get done sooner and back to his girl friend in town. That was a hair-raising end to an unusual trip that day.

This post had a look of permanence about it that was lacking in the previous two stops. It looked very much like the setting of "Beau Geste", starring Gary Cooper. The buildings were all stone and mud with sandy colored stucco covering everything. All the compounds were surrounded by low walls studded with broken wine bottles. This was supposed to discourage trespassers of the Arab persuasion. I'm not sure just how effective they were, but it did lend an air of romance and mystery to the place.

As it did everywhere it set up camp, the AAF employed a lot of local civilian labor to keep the place picked up and repaired, so there were quite a few Arabs, or A-rabs as Ely called them, about. They were dressed in their native costume, which seemed to consist of mattress covers wrapped around them covering the strategic areas. The men wore extremely baggy pants. The local PRO (public relations officer) told us that, according to Moslem tradition, the Prophet Mohammed would return someday to be born of a man. Each Moslem male thought he might be the chosen one, so he wore these pants to make sure The Prophet didn't get away. So help me! That's what he told us.

When we were coming in to Marrakech, we could see the weather building up in the east. That first night it began to rain, and the weather was miserable for the next eight days. We were grounded. A couple of days off would have been welcome because we had been flying pretty hard since 31 Dec 44, and this was 11 Jan 45, but not eight days. There was not much to do but lie around the billet and sleep or read, and eat when chow time came. There was the requisite movie theater and officers club, since this was a major stop on the southern ATC route to the Mediterranean, Middle and Far East. The food was passable. The O club had places to read and write letters, and a piano. All O clubs had a piano, and there was usually someone around to play it. Those attractions palled pretty quickly, even for transients. Permanent party were free to go into Marrakech in their time off but it took a lot of doing for transients to go there. We never even tried to go. That was probably a mistake, but we were not what you would call comfortable in such an alien setting. So, we just lay around and groused and wished for the weather to clear.

The billet Joe and Charlie and I were in was a small apartment that had been occupied by a French officer when it was an active Legion post. It was comfortable enough, except there was no glass in the windows. They were covered by ill-fitting wooden shutters, which kept out the light but not the cold, and there was no heat in the place. One thinks of Africa as being all tropical and hot, either dry or humid. I'm here to tell you, that ain't so. It gets miserably cold in North Africa in the winter, and the mud must be the stickiest in the world. Days were not too bad, but night was <u>cold</u>.

We had our own bathroom that included an odd little device that looked like an oval toilet with no lid or seat. Besides that, it flushed straight up! Since there was a conventional toilet, also, we were mystified by it. In one of our orientation sessions, the kindly PRO explained that it was a bidet, or "little horse", and was designed by the practical minded French with the female in mind. In GI parlance it was a douche bowl. I was sure it would never catch on in puritanical America. Time has proven me wrong. It is now included in some of the more upscale homes being built these days.

This same PRO was the one who told us if we should get a chance to go into town, to beware of the fresh fruit and produce. Although it looked great, it might just make you very sick to eat it. Their fields were fertilized with "night soil", human excrement, and those people were infested with and survived parasites that would destroy a westerner. He also warned us against eating their watermelons. It seems that they were sold by the pound, and it was the native custom to soak their melons in the sewer ditch over night before bringing them to market. He said we would wonder about the nice, salty taste.

My flight logbook shows a 50-min. flight on 14 Jan 45, but I can't remember why we took it. A vague image in my mind seems to say there was some small malfunction of an instrument that showed up early in the flight out that caused us to turn back. Or, it may have been rapidly deteriorating weather, because we next flew on 19 Jan 45. Anyway, it must have been of little import, because my normally razor sharp memory tells me nothing.

Our next stop was Tunis on the Tunisian coast opposite Sicily. Our route took us over some of the most fiercely fought over real estate in North Africa. Looking down on it from 9,000 ft., it was hard to see just why anyone would want it. It was all rock and sand with a few olive groves scattered about. At that altitude one could not see the evidences of war and the blood that was spilled by both sides, thank goodness.

Tunis is on a natural harbor and has been fought over for centuries. It was first the site of the ancient city of Carthage, the ruins of which are still visible on the edge of the city. It became a French protectorate in 1883, and with the fall of France in 1940, the Germans took it over. When the Allies booted the Germans out in 1943, they assumed authority, but pretty much turned civil control back to the French. It was a major center for military administration of the Mediterranean Theater.

We were allowed to go into the city the one night we were there. I remember it as being relatively modern in character, with well lit, clean streets with not many Arab civilians visible. Most of the people I saw were military with a few French North Africans about. Most of the shops were closed in the early evening, so there was not much in the souvenir line available. We were able to get a pretty good steak dinner in the headquarters hotel there, which made the trip worthwhile. We were told there was a native quarter, which was off limits to GIs. It was called the Kasbah. I'm not sure whether it was the Kasbah of the movies. I think all North African cities had a Kasbah, which was the area into which westerners went in peril of their lives. I'm sure they were not like the romantic haunts of Pepe Lomoko, played by Charles Boyer of "Come weeth me to ze Kasbah," fame.

The final stop on this tour of the Western Hemisphere was Naples, Italy. This was where we were to turn in our plane and await assignment to a combat unit.

Our course took us by Sicily, another well fought over chunk of rock. We deviated slightly west of our assigned course just to see this place. It also looked not worth fighting for, but we marveled at the ruggedness of the coastline and wondered how anyone could have gotten safely ashore against even half-hearted opposition. Not in my wildest imaginings could I picture what it must have been like.

Our destination was the replacement depot at Caserta, a suburb of Naples. I think the airstrip must have been the Naples International airport before the war, because the runway was all concrete and short. It was plenty long enough for the airliners of the thirty's, but came somewhat short of what was needed for bombers like the B-17 and 24. Everything in the inventory flew in there because it was a major depot for all of Italy.

As we usually did when coming into a strange field, we over flew it and sized up the runway. It sat on the top or a hill overlooking the Bay of Naples on one side and overlooked by Mt. Vesuvius on the other, which, incidentally, was still smoking from the eruption in 1943. Imagine our dismay to see a well-stocked bone yard at the end of the runway. There seemed to be carcasses of all kinds there. The instructions from the tower were to land short and stop soon. We had already surmised that there might be a problem. Nevertheless, it was disconcerting to see the fire engines and crash wagons racing alongside us as we landed. It turned out that they did that with every landing so they could be quickly on hand when a plane ran off the end of the runway. There was very little room at the end of the runway before the ground dropped away into a deep valley, so most pilots would ground loop and wash out before going over the cliff. That accounted for the well-stocked bone yard.

Our landing was uneventful because Joe touched down about ten feet from the beginning of the concrete, and we completed our roll out well short of the other end. I think the problem must have been that pilots were tired after long hours in the air and having had very long runways at all other stops, were careless in their touchdown. Many pilots, especially ones without very many hours, were loathe to go around once they were on the ground. They seemed to feel that overshooting made them look incompetent, so they would just show everybody and make that landing. It's sort of like speeding a car through a foggy night. If you make it you have bragging rights. If you don't, you'll probably kill yourself and won't have to listen to people tell you what a damn fool you are. Never could understand that mindset.

As soon as we landed and reported in, Joe signed over our faithful steed to the depot and we never saw her again. We were told that after some modification there, such as taking off the package guns, stripping off some of the armor and removing the Tokyo tank, the plane would be sent to a combat unit and put into service. The reason for the removal of the guns and armor was because in the Mediterranean, at that time, B-25's only operated at medium altitude, never at low level. Our J model had all the modifications that had been made so it could bomb from medium altitude and then come down to the deck and operate as a strafer, like they did in the Southwest Pacific and the China-Burma-India (CBI) theaters. The MTO modifications made the plane a little faster and faster was always better in combat.

It came as a little bit of a letdown to find that they were not exactly waiting for us with open arms when we landed. Here we were, come to get this war over with and obviously were just what the 12th Air Force needed at the moment and nobody seemed excited to see us. Just a little jocularity there.

We checked in at the depot headquarters and were told that we were to be assigned to the 379th Bomb Squadron, 310th Bomb Group (M) in

Corsica. We would have to be billeted at the depot for a few days, until some other crews showed up and we would be flown to our new units.

The transient facilities consisted of a collection of pyramidal tents arranged along gravel streets. Apparently, since we were not expected to be in residence long, the AAF didn't feel it necessary to provide the amenities of a permanent camp. The only things in the tents were six army cots, each with one GI blanket. The floor was dirt and there was no way to heat the things. We had our own sleeping bags and all the rest of our gear, so we picked one of the better looking tents and moved in as a crew. This was the first time I had lived in a tent since my trips to Tent City in Miami Beach in Basic Training. I thought my rank and station in life entitled me to better than this, but apparently the AAF didn't necessarily agree with me.

We had no responsibilities except to check in with the depot headquarters every day to see if we had transportation to our units. The rest of the time was ours to occupy as we could. There were mess halls where the food was fairly good, and recreation rooms where we could read and relax. We were confined to post, not that there was much we could see or get into in Caserta. We pretty much just lounged around the place and waited.

The first night in our tent at the Caserta Hilton, it rained, a cooold rain. We could hear it pounding on our tent most of the night, but we were so tired we didn't pay much attention. Sometime after midnight, I heard Charlie let out a string of curses as he sat up in bed. He had about a dishpan worth of water trapped on his sleeping bag. The tent had leaked. Charlie's outburst had waked up everyone else and they too began to curse. Everyone in the tent was wet but me. Somehow, I had managed to select the only place in the tent that wasn't under a hole. That pretty much spoiled the rest of the night, and when it began to be daylight we could see the holes. It looked like someone had laid inside and shot the tent with a shotgun. Fortunately, the sun came out that day and we were able to move our bedding outside and dry it out.

As soon as we could, we began to survey the other empty tents around us, of which there were many. When we found one that had no visible holes, we moved in. It was no better than the one we had left, except it did seem to have an intact roof. It was still unheated and extraordinarily primitive, but the dirt floor was dry.

Late in the day, the second day, there was a weather change. It went from a rather pleasant, balmy Italian day to a snowstorm. The second night it didn't rain, it snowed. Morning came with about ¾ in. of snow on the ground. We were lucky this tent didn't collapse in on us.

I believe that night was the most miserable night I have ever spent, anywhere. The night before, I had slept in my GI long johns and was fairly comfortable. This night, I went to bed in my clothes, and was still cold. Before I could get warm enough to get to sleep, I had added my winter flying suit over my clothes. My body was warm enough, but my feet were like two blocks of ice, and I can never get to sleep until my feet are warm. Finally, about 1 AM, I put on my fleece lined flying boots, zipped up in my sleeping bag, covered with my one blanket and, then and only then, did I get my feet warm enough to go to sleep. I couldn't turn over, but I was warm, at last. I had always heard about "Sunny Italy." I didn't experience it during my stay at Caserta. Looking at the world globe, you find that Naples is almost exactly the same north latitude as New York City, and you know what kind of winters they can have in New York. Naples wasn't quite that bad, but it does get cold there in the winter, to that I can attest from personal experience.

Chapter XII

COMBAT – NEXT STOP

After about three days, we were loaded onto a C-47 for the flight to Corsica. The pilot detoured over the Anzio beachhead so we could see where the ground forces had gone ashore to relieve the pressure on the stalemate at Cassino. How anyone ever survived that invasion is difficult to comprehend. From our altitude you could see that every square foot of beach had at one time or another been hit by a shell. There seemed to be nowhere to hide. It gave me chill bumps to think about what those GIs must have gone through. It made me glad I was in the air force with my moving foxhole.

The 310th Bomb group was stationed at Ghisonnacia, Corsica, which is on a plain along the east coast. There were other medium groups on the island, scattered all along the coast. As I recall, there were three or four more B-25 groups and one group of B-26's, comprising the 57th Medium Bombardment Wing of the 12th Air Force. The 12th also had fighter groups, troop carriers, reconnaissance and some light bombardment (A-20's) groups. It was a self-contained tactical air force, capable of operating independently of all other air support.

There were four squadrons in the 310th; the 379th, 380th, 381st, and the 428th. We were assigned to the 379th, as I have indicated before, and one crew we had trained with was assigned to the 380th. I have no idea where any of the other crews from Greenville ended up. Our focus tended to be on our crew first, squadron second and group third. I was only vaguely aware that there were other groups flying out of Corsica, because we seldom operated cooperatively. Our combat actions were generally group efforts, because the targets were too small to accommodate a lot of planes at once. But, I'm getting ahead of myself.

The first order of business when we arrived at the 379th was to get assigned to our billet. The 379th squadron area seemed to be near the center of a little village, or just a collection of stone buildings. Most of the officers had quarters in the permanent buildings and the EM in pyramidal tents set up in an olive grove nearby. Squadron headquarters was just across the street from our house. Actually, everything in the squadron area was very close.

Joe and I were assigned to the second floor of a substantial stone house with either four or six other guys. At the moment, I can't remember for sure. I seem to recall there were a total of four double decker bunks and a large table in the room. Each of us had adequate storage for all our gear and we were not crowded. Charlie was assigned across the hall to a smaller room with just room for one double bunk. Anyway, the accommodations were not bad.

Our room seemed to be sort of a gathering place for some of the officer personnel. It was large. It had this huge table in the center of the room where there always seemed to be a collection of goodies; nuts, candies, cookies, crackers, canned meats, cheese. These were things that the guys received from home and brought to our room to share. It doubled as mini-recreation lounge, when the officers club got boring. The new guys were made to feel at home and were initiated into the daily life of the squadron.

There was also a fireplace. This was an amenity that was lacking in most of the other billets. There was a scarcity of wood because the Corsicans had pretty much harvested it all for themselves. To supplement what little burnable material we could scrounge up, they had rigged up a device to drip diesel fuel onto the wood to make it burn better. There was a five-gallon bucket on a stand beside the grate with a shut off valve and an aluminum tube to direct the fuel into the fireplace. All in all, this was extremely dangerous and required judicious attention to prevent the place from going up in smoke. I was a little nervous about it, but I was assured that the system had worked for over a year without mishap. I wonder why that didn't reassure me?

Winter nights in Corsica could get more than a little chilly, so that fireplace was one of the reasons our billet attracted visitors. I found the guys living in the room and the ones who were most often visiting to be quite a convivial bunch. I'm sure there were some that you wouldn't want to introduce to your sister or bring home for dinner, but most of them were like me, there because they had to be and wanting to get on with the war and get back to some sort of normal life.

My introduction to the life of a combat flyer had to wait a few days for us to go through some sort of orientation. This consisted mainly of meeting the ground adjutant, a Capt. Phil Canale, from Memphis, who showed us around the base. We visited the supply room, dispensary, mess hall, officer's club and flight line. Phil was a very nice guy, well liked by the whole squadron. The name Canale was familiar to me because there was a grocery wholesaler in Memphis named D. Canale, who advertised in The Commercial Appeal and on the radio. It turned that Phil was his nephew. Right away, we established a bit of rapport because we were practically neighbors. Hearing a West Tennessee accent made being 6,000 miles from home a little easier.

While we were out at the engineering office, which was in a tent alongside the runway, the group returned from the mission of the day. They must have known there were new guys on the base, because we thought the show was just for us. We heard B-25's in the vicinity and the Engineering Officer said, "Let's go out and watch them come in."

The 310th coming home

Just as we stepped out of the tent six B-25's in echelon to the right came roaring in over the field with the lead ship about 25 feet off the ground. It seemed like they were headed right for us. About the middle of the field the lead ship whipped up into a steep climbing turn to the left with each ship in trail following in turn. As the lead ship's speed bled off, the gear and flaps went down and without ever leveling off, continued its turn, rolled out on the approach and landed. I had never seen a B-25 get on the ground so fast. This maneuver put each ship in the landing circle, one after another, spaced properly for landing without anyone crowding the ship in front. It was beautiful!

As we stood there with our mouths gaped open, we were told that that landing method was developed in the desert when the fields were subject to German air raids. It was a favorite trick for the Jerries to try to catch a flight bunched up for landing, flying slow and at a disadvantage. This way, all the planes got on the ground and in their revetments and the crews in their foxholes as fast as possible. The 310th had the reputation of getting their planes on the ground faster than any of the other medium outfits, or so they told us. Besides, it was a helluva lot of fun to land that way. It was something you were never allowed to do away from combat.

New crews were split up for the first several missions and flew as fill ins. This was true of all crewmembers. I don't think I flew on the same crew with any of my training crew until we were all rejoined as a unit. Little Joe even flew as co-pilot until we all got back together. This was to thoroughly indoctrinate us into the ways of combat. With

On the way to a target

plenty of replacements coming in, this made for much better operations than had been possible in the early days. New crews were thrown into the fray as units in the North Africa days, and often lasted only one mission.

I much preferred the way I did it. I think part of the reason for new guys to be put in with seasoned fliers was to begin our education as combat crew. We were regaled at every turn about "the way it is done in the 310th.

We saw a lot of scenery like this

Much of what I heard in the bull sessions in our room was put to good use when I started flying.

By early 1945, the air war over Italy, as far as the 310th was concerned, had become one of trying to interdict as much of the German traffic in and out of the country as possible. This was done by bombing the road and rail system through the mountains on a daily basis, if possible. There were only a few passes through the Alps into Austria, so all traffic flowed through them. The strategy was to try to keep those passes impassable. The major pass through the mountains was the Brenner, which began at just about Verona and went more or less straight north to Innsbruck, Austria, following the Adige River. As roads do, when following a river, it was occasionally necessary to cross the river. It was these bridges that became our primary targets in the Brenner.

All of the bridges in the Brenner Pass were heavily defended by anti-aircraft guns, usually the infamous 88. The number of guns defending it gauged the difficulty of the target. There was also the size of the target to be considered. Bridges are not very wide and about the only way to have your best chance of hitting one was to come in at about a thirty-degree angle to its length and lay a string of bomb across it. Sounds easy, but with four to sixteen guns shooting at you, the pilot all over the sky in evasive action, and the target all but invisible, the poor bombardiers had a tough job. The bridges were of very sturdy construction and the German engineers were highly skilled people who could quickly repair bomb damage, so we had to keep going back to the same targets a lot.

The war in Italy had been stalemated through a good part of 1944, with the front running across the very narrowest part of the boot, through the Apennine Mountains. The line was anchored on the Mediterranean at Via Reggio and at Rimini on the Adriatic. The rail and road system that fanned out through the Po Valley gave us plenty of targets.

We were told that we had very little to worry about from fighters, since we had total air superiority in that theater. Most of the Germans had been pulled back to defend the Fatherland, leaving mostly Italians led by Germans to defend Italy. They seldom came up at all because there were always Allied fighters on the prowl, from sunup to sundown. Things were so quiet, fighter wise, that we had only area cover. If we should happen to get jumped, a call on the fighter frequency would have an escort in just minutes. I didn't see an enemy fighter in all my 31 missions. The only time our squadron got jumped while I was there, I happened to not be flying, for one reason or another. I think maybe we had an assigned escort twice during my tour. Occasionally, we would see some of our fighters in the area, and they would come over and look us over, but usually they just said hello and went off looking for targets of opportunity.

Our basic combat formation consisted of six ships flying in two V's of three each. Three ships were called an element and six ships a box. A squadron usually put up 18 to 24 ships on a mission. This was 3 to 4 boxes, flying loosely V's of boxes. The squadron leader went in first with each box trailing along in its assigned position.   Squadrons were usually spaced 500 ft. apart, vertically, with the low squadron going in first and the high squadron in last. Actually, It was unusual for more than one squadron to hit a target because they were small; rail or road bridges, marshalling yard choke points, railroad fills, and ferry landings.

Our normal bomb load was eight 500 lb., GP (general-purpose) bombs. Depending on the type of target, we might carry four thousand pounders. They obviously made a bigger bang, so they were used on the sturdier targets. It didn't much matter to the crew, because the different bomb loads made no difference in our tactics.

My first mission was flown on 31 Jan 45, as co-pilot for Capt. Fitzsimmons. I was to fly with him for my first five missions. Fitz was a box leader, whose regular co-pilot had just gotten his own crew. As I remember him, Fitz was a big man, quiet spoken and highly competent. He had to be to be promoted to box leader, because on occasion, he might be called on to lead the squadron. I felt somewhat honored to be chosen to be the co-pilot for a box leader. In looking back on it, it might not have been such an honor, after all. Flying box lead was a breeze compared to flying wing. All the box lead had to do was fly more or less straight and follow the lead box. Wingmen were constantly jockeying the throttle and controls to stay in position on the lead ship.

Everything went just like a practice mission back in South Carolina. The co-pilot's duties in a B-25 were pretty much the same, no matter who was flying the left seat. I was responsible for flap settings, mixture controls, raising and lowering the landing gear, and some of the radio calls. Most pilots liked to obtain the taxi and take off clearances themselves until they had flown with a particular co-pilot for a while. I knew what I was doing in the right seat, so Fitz and I got along just fine. Once we formed up and began to climb out on course, Fitz let me fly the plane. To and from the target, I probably flew a little more than he did, because it was his job to take us over the target.

Each plane had a bombardier, but each plane did not have a bombsight. This may seem like an inconsistency, but Norden bombsights were still highly classified and scarce, so only the lead ship in a box and the element lead had sights. The bombardier in the lead ship would make the run and all ships in the box would toggle off their bombs when they saw the lead drop. The element lead might have to take over the lead if something happened to the box lead, so that is the reason there was sight in that ship. That never happened during my tour.

As I recall, each box had a navigator, but the squadron lead navigator navigated the mission, with the box navigators backing him up. Although it didn't happen during my tour, it had happened that the lead ship went down or the lead navigator got killed and one of the other navigators had to take over and get the mission back.

Our target for that day was a rail bridge at a tiny town in the Dolomite Alps in northeastern Italy, not far from the Yugoslavia border. My mission log calls it Chuisaforte. The area was undefended, that is, there were no anti-aircraft guns guarding it. We flew in, dropped our bombs and came home; elapsed time: 4hrs, 40 min. It was, I was told, a milk run.

The next mission was also a milk run. Mission three was not. It was what was called an anti-flak, or flak suppression mission. Early on in the war, someone got the bright idea that it might be possible to cut the losses by first putting the flak batteries defending a target out of action. They suggested sending in a small formation of three to six ships just ahead of the main formation, in sight of it, actually. The Germans, seeing the larger formation might wait for it and allow the small one to drop and get away. The anti-flak formation would be loaded with fragmentation and white phosphorous bombs, the idea being to smother the gun emplacement and put it out of action. The first time it was tried it worked to perfection. The group was able to bomb without loss a target that had been a real killer before. After this worked a couple of times, the Germans got wise and began to try to shoot up the anti-flak ships. They were no dummies.

Mission three was to a target in the Brenner Pass, which was heavily defended, as most of them in the pass were. That day I saw and heard and felt my first flak. They saw us coming and knew what that little bunch of six planes meant and they opened up well before we got in range. Flak gunners were not used to being the target, because their emplacements were usually not in the target area of the bridge. When they saw us, they knew they were the target this time and had better defend themselves with vigor.

The first thing I saw was some puffs of oily, black smoke appearing ahead of us. At first, they were way ahead and above us, but as we got nearer the target they got closer. They were firing into the area over the target that they knew we would have to fly through. I guess the hope was that the barrage would distract us and it might spoil our bombardier's aim. From the time we turned on the IP (initial point) to start our bomb run,

Fitz began to take evasive action. He climbed and dived, swerved and turned to try to throw the gunners off. At some point however he had to level out at the proper altitude and course so the bombardier could make his run. He hoped to make it a short as possible, so the Germans would not be able to get the range before we dropped and broke off the target. A good pilot/bombardier team could some times pull of a successful run of less than 20 seconds. That was usually enough to minimize the amount of flak we might get on target.

Typical target area

Experienced flak gunners at a given bomb target, could pretty well know at what altitude and course we would have to use, so would fill that area with bursts that we just had to fly on through. The actual bomb run was the time we were the most vulnerable. We were, more or less, like sitting ducks. There was nothing to do but fly straight in until we dropped our bombs.

When they got our range, I began to hear the "whump, whump" sound, typical of the 88, and see the flash of the explosion. A few flak pieces began to rattle off and through the plane. They sounded like hail on a tin roof. Some close bursts actually rocked the plane without hitting us with flak pieces. Apparently, the pattern of a burst sent the pieces of shell casing flying mostly horizontally, and if one went off right under us, we felt the concussion, but got no hits.

We made a good run and shut down the battery so the

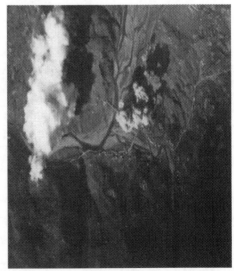

White smoke-flak guns. Dark smoke, target

172

main formation was not shot at much. We got back home intact with only three small holes in the plane.

The purpose of flak suppression was to put the flak battery out of action by destroying both the guns and the gunners. The weapons we used were particularly vicious. The fragmentation bombs were about twenty-five pounds of RDX packed into small cans and wrapped with spring steel, and were dropped by the hundreds per airplane. When they exploded the steel was shattered into hundreds of jagged, irregular bits of red hot metal flying out with the speed of a rifle bullet. They ripped through flesh and bone and made horrible wounds. The white phosphorous bombs spewed burning phosphorous in all directions, and stuck to whatever it hit, and burned. If that happened to be a human the results can only be imagined. In retrospect, that was a particularly inhuman thing to do. Thinking back on it turns my stomach.

One could not then, and should not now, allow oneself to think at length about the horrid things men do to each other in wartime. There is so little that an individual can do. If we had allowed ourselves to consider that we were destroying entities just like ourselves, with the same hopes, the same dreams, with wives, children, mothers and fathers; with bone, flesh, muscles, feelings, intellect and loved by the same God, we would have refused to get off the ground. I guess, however, that until all men, at all times and at all places come to that realization, we will continue to kill each other in wars.

In wartime, you have to take the callous attitude that your duty is to kill your enemy before he kills you, because that is what he is doing. In the case of air force people, we were fortunate to never look into the eyes of our enemy, so they never became people to us. We thought in terms of inanimate objects such as bridges, trains, ferries and roads. You never allowed yourself to even think that there were human beings in the vicinity of your bombs that just might get killed. Your duty was to destroy transportation so they could not get materiel with which to continue the war. In that way, war became an impersonal thing that you did because your country asked you to. The enemy was the enemy, not flesh and blood people.

Of the five missions I flew with Fitzsimmons, three were milk runs in which we saw no flak at all. We saw a little flak on my fourth mission against Dogna Town Bridge, but we were not hit. I noticed that the bursts this time were not black, but were a dirty gray. I was told that they were from 105-mm guns, not 88's, for whatever that is worth. On the subject of flak, we were requested to report the occurrence in terms of intensity and accuracy. It was a totally subjective evaluation, consisting of "scant, moderate, intense, very intense" and "inaccurate, accurate, very accurate." My log doesn't record much about the flak in those terms, just whether there was any and how close it got to me.

One more thing about Fitz's crew before I leave him. As I said, Fitz and his bombardier worked well together, but the bombardier had a routine he used every mission. As soon as he dropped, he would scream at Fitz over the intercom, "Bombsawaydoorsclosedlet'sgetthehellouttahere!" like it was all one word. It didn't matter if there was flak or not. He wanted to be away from the vicinity just in case the Jerries got mad and starting shooting.

Mission six was again as box leader co-pilot, but this time with a Capt. Jones. His co-pilot was away for some reason so I flew with him. Jonesy was one of those neat, clean-cut, meticulous young guys that PR types would choose to represent the best in Army aviation. He had the reputation of being one of the best pilots in the squadron and destined for greater things if the war kept on. He had led the group on a number of occasions. He had one idiosyncrasy. He always flew wearing the brown nylon gloves we had been issued. He wore them only, not with the pigskin over gloves. It was almost like he didn't want to get his hands dirty. I never liked to wear gloves at all, unless it was so cold I had to.

The mission was to the Solarno railroad division, and was a milk run, no flak. A railroad division is the "Y" where two lines come together. The theory was that by taking out the junction, we could take out two lines simultaneously. Conversely, it was much easier to repair two lines at the junction than at widely separated points, making the whole thing sort of an exercise in futility. Good targets were getting hard to find.

My next two missions were flown on the wing with Noah T. Shirley. I have no idea why I remember this pilot's full name when I don't most of the others. It may be because Shirley was unique. He was a "flak magnet". This was the term used for a pilot that seemed to have a special affinity for flak. If one ship out six was holed, it was Shirley's. If all the ships in a box were holed, Shirley's got most of them. This had happened so many times that even Shirley thought he was jinxed. It affected his flying. Though normally a more than competent pilot, when the formation approached the target, Shirley began to have trouble staying in tight formation. He would unconsciously begin to drift out, as though he was thinking about going home. Very quickly, he would move back, only to once again begin to drift away. The net effect was a constant rocking back and forth, in and out. Finally, he would end up going over the target with a wing tilted toward the formation, but holding opposite rudder wanting to go away. It seemed like his hands and feet wanted to do different things.

Our two missions together were to the Ora railroad fill, which, for some reason, was very heavily defended. These missions were on 9 Mar and 10 Mar, and we encountered heavy accurate flak both days. We got one hole on the 9th and none on the 10th. I guess I must have been Shirley's good luck charm. We were part of a group effort, and the other squadrons got hit more heavily than we did. Overall, three planes were shot down, with 19 crewmen missing. I don't remember any from our squadron being lost. I did find out many years after the war that a classmate from Mather was killed on that mission. His name was Stanley Caniglio.

I had been alerted as to Shirley's situation, so I watched him pretty closely. As I said, he was good pilot as long as we were not near the target, but as we approached, he began to get more and more agitated. He began to fight the controls to keep his fear of flak from making him a coward. He wanted desperately to turn back, but had no mechanical reason to do so. The plane betrayed him by performing perfectly. To his credit, he overcame his desire to be somewhere else and flew out the mission, albeit, a bit erratically. He knew he had problems, but he was determined not to let them stop him from completing his tour. I admired him for that.

I heard that the mission analysts claimed they could identify Shirley's bomb strikes, because they would be outside the target zone due to his weaving in and out. All strikes could be in the zone and there would be a string of six outside. Those would be Shirley's. That was a little unfair, I thought.

My next mission was also unusual in that I was co-pilot for Lt. Col. Royal B. Allison, group air exec. It was required that all qualified airmen fly four hours a month to keep their flight pay, so, once a month the flying brass would go out on a mission that was four hours long. This was the mission and I was tapped to be Col. Allison's co-pilot. Along on this mission, in Col. Allison's plane, we had the group gunnery officer, the group bombardier and the group navigator, all Majors. I was not completely outranked, however. We had a couple of EM gunners along.

A word about Col. Allison. He had the reputation of being an iron-assed, truly hot pilot. He had been in the war since the invasion of North Africa in '42. He had come over in A-20's, flown two tours, transferred to the 310th and flown a 50-mission tour there. Somewhere along the line, he had met and married an Army nurse, who was stationed in Cairo. This gave him incentive to stay in the war. With his record, he didn't need to be flying combat. He could have gotten his hours other ways, but, true to his reputation, he chose to get in his hours by going in harm's way.

Allison was a very composed, elegant, and somewhat withdrawn; with second lieutenants, at least, officer. He was not arrogant, just aloof. He told me just what he expected of me, which was nothing more than any pilot expected of his co-pilot. I found him to be a good man to fly with. It was obvious from the get-go that he knew how to fly.

Our target was some kind of munitions plant across the Adriatic Sea on the coast of Yugoslavia, near a town named Posthumia. As befits the second in command of a group, Allison was leading the group.

On the way out, the Col. was constantly checking the rest of the group to make sure they were forming up properly. He was a strict air disciplinarian. He stayed on the radio a lot while I flew the plane. All I had to do was climb on course, and even second lieutenants can do that. He was a little aggravated at the other boxes because they weren't shaping up just the way he wanted them to, and he let them know it. All this time the group gunnery officer was in the top turret interrupting him on the intercom. The last straw was when he asked Allison if he could swing the turret forward so he could see where we were going. The Col. responded, "I don't (expletive deleted) if you twist the (expletive deleted) turret out of the (expletive deleted) airplane." We heard no more from the Major.

The group navigator did his job right. We hit the target right on the nose. The group bombardier had a little more trouble. On a bomb run, the bombsight is connected to an instrument on the pilot's panel called the pilot's directional indicator (PDI). It was a pilot's job to keep a needle centered and the altitude correct during the run in or the bombs would not come near the target. As the bombardier made small corrections the needle would swing and the pilot had to maneuver the plane to bring it back to center. Normally, these corrections were small and the pilot could follow them. On our run, I noticed that the Col. was fighting the PDI. It was all over the place, and he was getting livid and swearing under his breath. We finally dropped, but it was obvious we were flinging bombs all over that part of Yugoslavia. We got nowhere near the target. Later, some wag said we had hit a nearby spaghetti factory because he saw some come up past his plane.

After we got off the target and started home, the Col. chewed on the bombardier for a while and found out what had happened. It seems that on the Norden sight, there are two course controls mounted coaxially.

The one next to the sight is a coarse control and the outboard one is the fine control. When the bombardier was supposed to be turning only the fine control, he, in his rustiness, was turning both of them, making for a very erratic bomb run. It took the Col. until we got almost home before he cooled down.

To top off the day, as we let down our landing gear, the radioman called the Col. and told him we had a big blister on one of the main gear tires. We had to abort the landing and circle the field until all the group was on the ground and then make our landing. Here was where the Col. showed his considerable flying skills. He came in one wing high and put down on one wheel. He held the suspect wheel off the ground until the plane wouldn't fly any more. We rolled along on one main and the nose wheel it seemed like forever. When we finally touched the second wheel down, it was like the kiss of a butterfly. You could hardly feel it. The tire held and we were home free. I could do without that kind of excitement. A blowout on a B-25 at 75 mph could do all sorts of bad things to a wheel on a pierced steel plank runway. I had visions of us spinning around like a top. That was the last time I had the dubious pleasure of accompanying group brass on their obligatory monthly mission, thank goodness.

Chapter XIII

BETWEEN MISSSIONS

Our missions from briefing to debriefing lasted from 5 to 7 hours, with a maximum of 5 hours in the air. Considering that I didn't fly every day that left me with a lot of spare time. I began to appreciate the description of bomber aviation as being "days of boredom punctuated by moments of abject terror." There was a lot of idle time. We were there to fly, so we were not assigned any onerous ground duties. That was the lot of the "paddlefeet," or ground troops.

When we didn't fly, many of the officers spent the day, from the time the bar opened at the Officer's Club, getting blotto, or in the running poker game. The poker game apparently had started about when the group had been organized and had been going on for the better part of three years. The faces changed from time to time, but the game went on. On payday the number of players swelled and the "game" broke up in to smaller groups, but by the end of the month it was back down to the same four or five players that ended the previous month, and they had all the money. The personnel changed as guys finished their tours, but there were always new sharks in the pool. Since I neither drank nor gambled, I had to find other pursuits to occupy my free time.

Corsica is an ancient island, as far as having been settled. The first settlers were the Ionian Greeks in about 550 BC. Over the centuries, it had been controlled by the Romans, Vandals, Lombards, Moors, Genoese Italians, French, British and Germans. France was the owner in 1945, and although the people spoke both French and Italian with equal fluency, they had a bit of problem with American, so communication with them was limited.

It is an island just made for exploring, and that was what I did a bit of. The terrain was very rugged and rocky and covered with scrub cork trees. In fact, cork harvesting and export was a major industry, pre-war. There seemed to be an abundance of goats and donkeys roaming around the landscape, and I suppose they belonged to someone. I never got near enough to any of them to know if they had any identification, or not.

One of my favorite pastimes was to draw some ammo for my .45 and go target shooting down along the creek that ran behind the squadron area. We used old 55-gallon drums that had been dumped there. I got so I could pretty well hit what I aimed at from 25 yards. Those were the only times I even carried my sidearm. We were advised to leave it at home on a mission. The rationale was that if we got shot down, the Germans would capture us and take it away from us. If the Italian partisans picked us up, they would, too. It didn't happen while I was in combat, but it was said that a man's .45 was the first thing to disappear if he was reported missing. His A-2 jacket was next, if he happened to not be wearing it.

Landscape just back of our squadron area

You remember I told about the Karachi boots I got in South America? They were the footwear of choice among us hotshots. Knowing that most of the flying officers wore these boots the brass informed us that they were not to be worn in combat. The rationale was that in case we had to bail out the boots would likely come off when the chute opened, and walking around in Northern Italy barefoot was not recommended. Combat boots were to be worn because they could be laced tightly on our feet. Made sense to me.

The Red Cross had a presence at each group in the person of women volunteers. They operated the service clubs and handed out coffee and doughnuts after each mission. Some of them had rather shady reputations as being there for the pleasure of high-ranking officers. They lived in a rather palatial house, by Corsican standards, just down the street from our billet. I'm sure the reputation was undeserved by some, but was obviously deserved by others. The only time I had any contact with any of them was occasionally at the service club and at coffee and doughnut time. They were pleasant enough, but I wasn't looking for female companionship, so I can't say more than that from personal experience.

The service club was distinct from the Officer's Club, in that, no liquor was served. It was the custom of the Army Air Force, to serve a medicinal shot of liquor at the end of a mission, if anyone wanted it. The liquor was the property of the flight surgeon, and he had long before made a deal with the command structure to use the official mission liquor to supply the O Club bar. No post mission shot for our squadron.

At the service club, you could read paperbacks, old magazines and current issues of Yank, the Army newspaper; and Stars and Stripes. There was a piano, and ping-pong tables, writing desks and a small canteen; where, on occasion, you could get juice, cokes, and cookies, which you had to pay for. Occasionally, there were other items of a sundry nature you could buy. It turned out that many of the items we had to pay for were donated to the Red Cross by the folks back home. This left a distinctly bitter taste in our mouths, and it was hard to find a veteran after the war that had much good to say about the Red Cross. This seemed to be the modus operandi of the Red Cross all over the world. The story was told about the GI in Alaska that paid a Red Cross volunteer $5 for nice, hand knit scarf only to find a note wrapped up in it from the lady who knitted it, saying she was doing it to be given to some needy soldier. Apocryphal or not, it was assumed to be true by those of us who had experienced similar things at the hands of the Red Cross.

Being in a combat zone meant there was a scarcity of the amenities normally found on a stateside base. There was no PX, for example. Periodically, we were treated to the availability of cigarettes, candy, cokes, beer, shaving stuff, toothpaste, soap and similar sundries. The luxury items(c,c,c & b) were rationed, and I don't remember just what quantities were allowed, but there was a lively bartering session on PX day. Non smokers traded cigarettes for candy and cokes, beer drinkers gave up their cokes and candy for an increase in their alcoholic libation. By the end of the day, everyone had acquired a surplus of stuff they liked by giving up stuff they didn't like. It was great fun and livened up our otherwise dull days.

Mail service was pretty good, now that the group base was fairly stable. I heard stories about months without a mail call in the desert in '43. Since the combat fronts were pretty fluid in those days, the group seemed to be constantly on the move from one base to another. It took the mail a while to catch up and packages of goodies seldom made it.

Due to the poor quality of the food the Army was able to supply us, letters home often mentioned the desire for something different from C rations. Although there was rationing back home, certain luxury food items, such as canned boneless turkey, Vienna sausage, cheese, fancy crackers and other such non perishables were available and shipped over in what came to be known later as Care packages. We always seemed to have a supply of these goodies in our room. These things went a long way toward alleviating the boredom.

Keeping clean was a bit of a chore, since there was only a central bathhouse where there was sometimes a scarcity of hot water. It was not uncommon to only get a hot shower once a week; shades of life back on the farm when Saturday was bath day. Shaving was not a problem because we all had a steel helmet that we never wore, but which doubled as a wash basin very nicely. I learned that it is possible to get a passable shave in cold water if you wash your face thoroughly and use lots of shaving lather and a very sharp blade. It was easy to run out of new blades before the next PX days, so all of us had our own system of keeping a sharp blade.

The razor of choice in those days was the Gillette double edge. There were two choices of blades, the Thin and the Blue. The Blue was a little thicker and more expensive and was supposed to stay sharp longer. The Thin gave a better initial shave but was only good for 2 or 3 shaves. I didn't want to pay the extra for the Blue, being cheap like I was, so I always bought the Thin and sharpened it as long as I could. I had a sharpener that was the envy of the billet. I had it from my civilian days, and by being careful, could make a Thin blade last for 10 or more shaves. Admittedly, the last shaves left my face looking like a cat had scratched it, but we never had inspections, so the quality of my shave was not of much concern.

Keeping our clothes clean was another problem. Khakis and underwear were washable, as were our summer flight suits. The EM had laundry facilities, but the officers had to find a local laundress who would do ours. That was easy enough, because all the Corsicans seemed to be bone poor and willing to work for the rich Yanks. A problem was encountered when we needed to clean our dress uniforms and winter olive drabs. They really needed to be dry cleaned, but the Corsicans had never heard of dry cleaning, and the Army didn't provide such luxuries for combat troops. We were left to our own devices. Someone found out early that 200-octane aviation gas did a credible job on woolens, and if you hung them out to dry long enough, the gasoline smell almost left them. This was a pretty risky business and had to be done outside, well away from any source of ignition. Fortunately, I seldom had occasion to wear my pinks and greens, so they stayed pretty clean. I'm not really sure why our dress uniform was called "pinks and greens." The blouse <u>was</u> a very dark green, but the trousers were a light gray. Perhaps it was because after a few cleanings in the aviation fuel the gray began to take on a distinctly pinkish hue from one of the chemicals in the gas. Then, maybe not. That terminology was used stateside, too. Most of us wore our woolens until they got pretty ripe before we cleaned them.

Spring comes early in the Mediterranean, so it was soon warm enough for the softball season to start. Teams sort of sprang up. Someone would yell, "Let's play ball," and all those interested would gather at the field and a pickup game would start. Once the pickup games got started, teams just seemed to come together and pretty soon there were enough to have a regular season. The Army supplied all the equipment and leagues were organized schedules published. The games were usually played in the afternoon after the mission for the day was over.

It has been so long ago that I don't remember much about the team I played on, except that we won more than we lost. Our pitcher was a big old bombardier from California named Johnson, called "Johnny." He had played fast pitch softball before getting in the Army and could really whiz the ball. He tended to be a bit lazy and was fatter than he needed to be and usually played in house slippers. This wasn't conducive to great foot speed, but he didn't need to be fast on his feet. He was so big and strong that when he batted he usually either struck out or hit the ball so far he could trot around the bases.

I never knew whether Johnny was just toying around with the opposition of if he was just haphazard. It was not uncommon for him to walk the bases full and then strike out the next three batters. It looked like he was a little careless until he realized he was in a pinch before he settled down and pitched the way he could. I hope he didn't bomb the same way. When he really put his mind to it, his pitches were very intimidating. I was always glad I was on his team.

I always had a pretty good batting eye and was a good judge of where the ball was going, so I played what was called "short center field." That put me between the infielders and the outfielders and allowed me to roam all over. I never had a real great arm, but I could occasionally cut off a grounder through the infield and throw out the runner. I was also death on pop-ups that would ordinarily fall in for hits. I had a great time.

I learned that it was not a good idea to play softball in shorts if you liked to slide into the bases, especially in Corsica, where the ground tended to be rather gravelly. I slid into second one day and skinned a place on my hip that resulted in a scar that I carried for years. In fact, it may still be there. I haven't looked lately.

There was in my billet the pilot of a special crew that was assigned to help develop a system of blind bombing using intersecting radio beams. His crew flew even less than I did, early on, so this pilot, Bob Clemence and his navigator, Leslie Dyson were always looking for some sort of diversion. Another of my roommates was a bombardier named Lewis D. (Buck) Starr who had become chummy with Clemence, so the four of us went out for a hike one day when we got bored, and on the way out of town, passed a school where the kids were out for recess. Each of us had brought along a box of hard candies, in case we saw any kids. We stopped to make a picture of them and pass out some candy. I got one picture, handed out some candy, and almost before I could get my camera rolled to the next frame, the crowd had tripled in size. In my picture collection, I still have these two pictures.

The kids were not beggars, like I saw in Naples, but they sure did enjoy that candy. It made us feel bad that we couldn't do more for them. I'm sure their parents didn't much care for us acquainting them with the type of luxuries they would never see again, once we left.

The food we were served was of somewhat uneven quality. The cooks did the best they could with what they had, and it was always palatable, to me, at least. Some of the more finicky eaters complained about it, but it sufficed. We had a lot of powdered eggs and powdered milk for breakfast, and occasionally would have some GI corned beef hash to go with our eggs. Pancakes were on the menu, occasionally, and that was one thing the Army cooks never learned to make edible. Drowning them in syrup and slathering them with the lardy tropical butter we had didn't help a lot, except one time before I got there.

The story goes that one morning the pancakes were exceptionally good. People were going back for seconds that never did before. Even non-breakfast eaters heard about the delicious pancakes and were coming in for breakfast. Everyone agreed that somehow the cooks had outdone themselves that morning. A mission was on for that day, but was stood down because of weather. About 10 o'clock, people began to report to the dispensary with severe gastro intestinal distress, bellyaches. These were not your run of the mill upset stomachs. These were totally incapacitating. The sufferers were doubled up in agony. Had the mission flown, they would have been just climbing out on course. Since this happened in the officer's mess, pilots, navigators and bombardiers were affected. It is likely that some crews would have been lost.

So many officers were sick that an investigation was launched to find the source of the illness. The trail led back to the pancakes and the discovery that somehow quicklime had gotten mixed in with the flour and thence into the batter. The quartermasters had provided the mess with lime to kill rats, of which there was an abundance. It was bagged pretty much the same way the flour was and had been left near the flour. In the dark of early morning, a cook had mistakenly dipped into the lime, thinking it was flour. They never found out how much lime was used, but no one suffered any lasting effects, and all recovered in a matter of hours. Needless to say, the Army's recipe for pancakes was not altered to include lime, even though it seemed to improve the flavor, considerably.

Someone with connections with the Navy base in Sicily worked a deal where we could get some rations to supplement our own. Every ten days, someone would take one of our war weary B-25's that had been stripped of all combat gear, down to Palermo, load it up with eggs, bacon, ham, pork chops, steaks, roasts, fresh vegetables, fruit and milk, and fly it back. They would pack every cubic inch not required for the pilots with these delectables. They could carry enough to let us feast for a week and then it was back to C rations until the next trip. For some reason, we could only do this every ten days.

Typical of the Navy, this base had all the comforts of a stateside base. The Navy really took care of its own, and the one thing they always had, even aboard ship, was good food and lots of it. Their idea of hardship was when the ice cream machine broke down. There must have been something we had that they coveted, because the Navy never did anything for the Army out of the goodness of their hearts. I never knew what we had to part with to get that food, but whatever it was, it was worth it.

For some reason, we had a crew of South Africans attached to our squadron. They flew missions right along with the rest of us and socialized with us just as part of the squadron. Their uniforms were British with a small patch on the shoulder identifying them as South Africans. It was easy to miss the patch and assume they were English. An easy way to get a tongue-lashing was to refer to them as English. I was informed by the bombardier that he was not a Limey, he was "a bloody, (expletive deleted) Boer." At that time I was woefully ignorant about South Africa, but I got a quick history lesson from him. Apparently, they were accustomed to this mistake, and since they liked Yanks better than they did Limeys, they tolerated our ignorance.

The two South Africans that visited in our billet were really interesting fellows. One, a pilot, was called "Tiny" because he was about 6', 4" and weighed about 16 stone (230 lbs.). He was not a Boer, but was of English ancestry, though born in South Africa. Before the war he had been an internationally ranked tennis player, and was a quiet, unassuming type who was very pleasant to talk to. The other was a massive Dutchman with flaming red hair and personality to match. He, also, was quite an affable fellow that never seemed to stop talking. When he got a little liquor in him, he liked to brag about how much he could lift with his teeth. His favorite trick was to grab the corner of a table in his teeth and lift all four legs off the floor. He demonstrated his prowess one night by lifting our table, which was about six feet long and made of rough sawn pine. The legs were solid chunks about six inches across, and the whole thing was a handful for two men to move. He squatted down, gripped the corner of the top in his teeth and with every muscle in his neck and shoulders bulging, leaned back and all four legs cleared the floor. That was an impressive demonstration!

Receiving the Air Medal from Gen. Knapp

Being in a combat zone, it was not often that we were required to wear our dress uniform. Usually, it was our olive drabs, or flight suits. The one time I can remember getting into my P & G's was for an awards presentation. The group had earned a battle streamer for participation in a raid on Benevento on 27 August 1943, and there were several medals to be handed out, as well.

On 16 February 1945, Maj. Gen. Cannon, from 12th AF Hdqs. came over with the battle streamers and a bushel basket of Distinguished Flying Crosses and Air Medals. We formed up on the parade ground, which was actually our softball field, and the general made his little speech and then personally pinned on the medals that were to be awarded. I happened to be in line for my first Air Medal, so I have in my archives, a picture of me shaking hands with Brig. Gen. Knapp, CO of the 57th Bomb Wing with my medal on my chest.

I must admit, I was a little dazed by the whole thing, because I couldn't remember a thing I had done to merit any kind of award. It turned out to have been for my second mission, a raid on a bridge at San Michele while I was flying with Capt. Fitzsimmons. According to my mission log, it was a milk run. All I did was ride along while Fitz flew the bomb run, and there wasn't even any flak. It was perhaps one of the least eventful missions I flew.

Early in the war, medals were not easy to come by. Each award has a description of the action that should take place to merit the medal, and the military pretty much stuck by the rules. For instance, it often took the extreme sacrifice to attain the Congressional Medal of Honor and many of them were awarded posthumously. The same was true of the Distinguished Service Cross and Silver Star. The Air Medal was one of the lowest ranked medals that could be awarded, and even it was not handed out, willy-nilly. As time went on, the requirements for the Air Medal became less and less rigorous until I got mine for just being there. The Air Force had cheapened the medals to the point that they had little meaning. I ended up with three clusters in 31 missions, which meant I got an Air Medal for every seven missions. That was about par for the course.

Based on the formula that seemed to be used, I should have gotten the DFC, as well. It was given for completing 25 missions, at the time I was over there. I really would have rather not had any medals, than to get one for just successfully completing a couple of missions. Most of us had essentially no pride in the medal. It was just another ribbon to wear.

Since there was so little significance attached to the Air Medal and DFC, none of us bragged much about our awards.

Fortunately, the highest ranked medals never were downgraded, and it took some excessively heroic actions to earn the Medal of Honor, DSC and Silver Star. Anyone who got one of those three definitely earned them, often at the expense of some sort of injury.

SCENES AROUND THE SQUADRON AREA

Primary means of transportation in and around Ghisonnacia

Look, Ma. No hands

School children lined up for pictures and treats.

Our billet in Ghisonnacia. Second floor right

Clemence, Dyson and Starr. We had been hiking

Joe in the donut line. I did not fly that day

Ely in the donut line after a mission.

Harrington was a better pilot than bike rider.
The O Club ins in the background

Little Joe and friends. Entertainment between missions

Chapter XIV

BACK TO THE WAR

After my trip with Lt. Col. Allison, I was assigned as co-pilot with Lt. Gordon Jacobs, who was an element leader. That put us in the number 4 spot, just under the box leader. The element leader was deputy box leader and might be called upon to take over the box if the leader got shot down or otherwise incapacitated. It also meant that he was in line for promotion to box leader and a captaincy. Men on the leadership track progressed this way, so Jake was leader material, and it was a privilege and pleasure to fly with him.

Jake was a big, easy going Midwesterner who could really fly a B-25. We seemed to get along fine, and I liked flying element lead better than box. I always preferred to be in close to the formation where I could follow the movements of the planes next to me. That's why I liked to fly formation. He let me fly most of the time to and from the target, just like Fitzsimmons had.

My first mission with Jake was to San Margherita, and we saw some flak that got pretty close, but we got no holes. The next mission, two days later, was to Campo North Town Bridge. This target was located at the south end of the Brenner Pass, where several roads and railroads came together to go through the pass. Because of its location the target was very heavily defended, and we got the poo shot out of us! They must have had some of the most experienced flak gunners in Italy at Campo, because they were very accurate and could put a tremendous volume of flak. It was like one pilot said, "You could let down your gear and taxi on it."

The sky literally turned black all around us and the bursts were close enough that I could see the fire of the explosion. Shrapnel was rattling off our plane like hail on a tin roof, and the concussion would actually bounce us around. That was the only time I remember hearing the explosions. On other missions where we encountered flak, the bursts were not that close. From that time on, I knew I was in a war. We made good bomb run, plastered the target and beat it for home. We knew we had been hit, because there were holes in the plexiglass of the cockpit and Jake had a small cut on his lip. I had shards of plexiglass in my lap. One burst had lifted our right wing up sharply, and the radioman could see torn aluminum out near the tip.

As soon as we cleared the target area we took stock and found that the airspeed indicator was out. All other instruments were functioning and the engines were purring along like normal. No one was hurt, except for Jake's small cut. All other ships in the formation reported some holes, but no one was hurt enough to fall out of formation. The trip home was uneventful, thank goodness. Those thirty or so seconds on the flak field was enough excitement for the day.

We declared a semi-emergency when we got back, because it is difficult to make a proper landing if you don't know what your airspeed is. We came in after the rest of our box had landed with one of our wingmen alongside, talking us down. Jake showed his mettle that day. The landing was picture perfect. This combat flying was beginning to get interesting.

Back home, we surveyed the ship and found that we had picked up 17 holes; the one in the wing was big enough to put your head in. It had missed the main spar, but had severed the line to the pitot tube, and that was why the airspeed indicator was out.

My next three missions with Jake were uneventful. One of them was what was called a "nickeling mission." How it got that name was never satisfactorily explained to me. What it consisted of was three planes loaded with propaganda leaflets, which we dumped out over German occupied territory in the Po River valley. They were supposed to encourage the Germans to give up because their cause was lost and their leaders were going to get them all killed for nothing. There was no record of any German in Italy using the leaflets as safe passage into our lines. More than likely, they were used for toilet paper or starting fires.

The mail from home had begun to settle into a fairly regular pattern. We didn't get mail call every day, but about four times a week. About the time I started flying with Jake, 14 Mar 45, was the time for our baby to be delivered, according to the doctor's best estimate. Being a quarter of the globe away from Rutherford, sort of removed me from the scene, but it didn't keep me from thinking about it and worrying that something had gone terribly wrong. Each day after 15 Mar, I kept expecting to hear something, but I didn't. Finally, on about 1 Apr., I got a cable announcing that we were the proud parents of a baby girl, named Betty Ann. That was the name we had chosen early in the pregnancy. There must have been a boy's name, too, but I don't remember what it was.

I had managed to find a box of old cigars somewhere and had tried, unsuccessfully, to keep them moist enough to smoke. I handed them out anyway and let the guys smoke them or chew them or throw them away, it mattered not to me. We had our baby and from all accounts, she was the prettiest baby ever delivered. This gave me added incentive to make it home safely. Being so remote from the birth, I couldn't really grasp the reality of being a father, and had to keep telling myself that I was and that my responsibilities had just increased dramatically. From that time on I thought of myself as a family man, not just a husband.

Sometime during the first two months of my time in Corsica, I learned that my brother-in-law, Dave Jackson, Dee's husband, was in a hospital near Naples. Since members of the squadron were often going to Naples for various reasons, I appealed to the Ground Adjutant, Phil Canale, for a pass to go to Naples to see if I could locate Dave. It was granted and pretty soon I was part of a party going to Naples to bring back an airplane from the depot at Caserta. There were four of us, Bob Clemence and his navigator were taking their plane to the depot to have some sort of Shoran equipment installed and another pilot and I were to pick up a new plane.

While the rest of the guys did their thing, I checked in with the Red Cross to see if they could locate Dave. They did some checking and discovered that, indeed, he had been stationed just outside of Naples, but he had become ambulatory and had been moved to a convalescent center up near Florence. That was too far away, and I had to forego a visit with him.

He had been wounded in the rump in Southern France, and was sent to Italy for treatment. The story goes that he had been crawling across a road when a German mortar round exploded near him and a piece of shrapnel hit him in the butt and drove him across the road into a ditch. It turned out that they had had mail call just that day and he had his mail in his hip pocket and the letters that Dee wrote were so thick and voluminous that they absorbed a lot of the jolt and probably saved his ass. Makes a good story even though Dee may not believe it.

That trip to Naples made a lasting impression on me in many ways. I saw what war can do to a town and a people. The town had been pretty hard hit by bombs and shells because the Germans defended it longer than was necessary. The harbor was full of scuttled ships that the Germans hoped would make it unusable for the Allies. All the U. S. Engineers did was lay piers on the hulks and use them for unloading ships. They didn't delay the use of the harbor at all.

Many of the buildings were just empty shells with no floors or windows. Others were usable but many of them had no glass in the windows. That was the case of the transient quarters where we were to be billeted over night. They had put rows of Army cots with a couple of blankets and a pillow each on the second floor of this burned out building, and that's where we were expected to sleep. There were lavatories where we could wash up and shave, but there were no shower facilities. Nothing was too good for our boys in the field. Needless to say, the permanent party in Naples were considerably better cared for.

The streets were dirty and full of ragged little kids begging for anything the rich American GI's would give them. What they would offer in return was their guaranteed virgin sister for the night. I heard that refrain everywhere I went. I felt sorry for them, but I didn't have anything to give them and I wasn't in the market for their virgin sister.

To while away the time, we went to an Allied Officer's Club, where those who drank could get a few drinks. There was an ongoing floorshow of "exotic" dancers and bar girls. They sat with the men and drank their own brand of watered down drinks. They were also for hire for the night to the highest bidder. There were English and American officers there, but the women always seemed to go with the Americans, because they had more money than the English. This seemed to not sit too well with the Limeys. The place closed at nine o'clock, I guess so the guys could get all they paid for.

Each of the guys I was with managed to procure a girl, but I was not the least interested. I had a wife I was being true to, which seemed to favorably impress the women, for whatever that is worth. I loaned one of the guys $20, and had a tough time getting it back later. In a way, I profited from the loan in that I got to use the blankets off of his cot, since he didn't use them. I needed them, too. It was cold in Naples that night. That was a decidedly unprofitable trip for me, except for getting to see how debauched grown men can be in war and away from home. The guy I loaned the money to was a married man, too. I hope he didn't take an unexpected present home to his wife.

During the time I was away, the squadron flew a mission in which enemy fighters jumped them, the only time it happened while I was in combat. One of our planes was damaged but managed to make it to a U.S. fighter field safely. I found out well after the war that the tail gunner was killed. One e.a. (enemy aircraft) was shot down with six tail gunners sharing credit. Ely, flying with another crew, was one of the six.

During the last several months of the war, our air forces had complete control of the air. Most of the time we flew with what was called area cover. That meant that there were American fighter planes in the air all over German held Italy, on sweeps to bomb and shoot up anything that looked German. If we needed them, we only had to put out a radio call and they would be on us in minutes. On occasion, we actually had fighters assigned to escort us to the target and back. It was reassuring to look out and see a formation of P-38's or 51's alongside or criss-crossing over us.

The 51's were identified by the markings on the vertical stabilizer. I don't know the number designations of the groups, but we called them the "Zebra Tails," red and white diagonal stripes; "Checker Tails," red and white checkerboard; or "Red Tails," solid red. I do know that the "Red Tails" were the all-black 49th, and they were good.

The fighter jocks preferred to escort the B-25's as opposed to the B-17's and 24's, because we flew enough faster than the heavies that they did not have to zig zag to keep from running away from us. There was usually some radio traffic between us, a lot of good-humored insults, because we all knew we would never see each other in person.

Since there was no opposition from the Germans, occasionally, in direct violation to standing orders, the fighters would make passes at us and the gunners would track them. There would be a lot of verbal machine gun noises on the air and outrageous claims, like, "I gotcha, you SOB. You're dead."

"Like h—l, you did. You couldn't hit bull in the (vulgarity deleted) with a bass fiddle. You're going down in flames."

All of this horseplay led to the situation recounted above when Germans jumped our squadron. The inexperienced gunners thought the incoming planes were ours, and withheld their fire until real bullets began to hit our planes. We were very lucky to not lose several planes in such a situation. The very next mission, the American fighters were back with their silly games. When a P-47, which looks, in head on silhouette, a lot like an FW-190; made a pass at a box of B-25's, all guns opened up on him. He went down smoking, but managed to make it back to his base. That ended the make believe until the end of the war.

Rumors had been flying around that our base was going to move to Italy, where we could be close to the front lines for the expected break out by the Allied armies. Around the end of March the rumor became fact and the base began to be dismantled and flown out. Combat activities continued like nothing was happening, but little by little the support personnel and facilities began to disappear. The last few days, we were down to eating K Rations and what edibles we had gotten from home, but the flying never let up.

Between 1 Apr and 5 Apr Dromgoole's crew was reconstituted as a unit and I flew my 15th mission back with the guys I had trained with. It was good to be back together again. That mission was to Steinach RR Bridge at the top of the Brenner Pass. It was a milk run, although a rather long milk run; 4hrs., 40min. We flew wing and it was good to be back flying formation, too.

While the group had been in Corsica, the men had shown great ingenuity in making their living quarters as comfortable as possible. There had been a lot of creative use of surplus material, such as, fuse boxes, ammo crates, scrap metal, fuel oil cans and anything cast off by the military. Since we could only take with us the things we had been issued, all these things had to be left. All of the pyramidal tents had been floored and walled against the weather, and some of them were almost palatial. Only the canvas could be taken with us.

The Corsicans were eagerly waiting for us to go so they could scavenge our leavings. Most of us were just as eager to let them have them, but some idiot barracks lawyer invoked the government regulation against unauthorized use of surplus material by civilians, and decreed that everything burnable must be burned. This was an almost criminal waste, and made most of us sore. We gave as much as we could to the locals before the brass found out about it and made us feed the bonfire.

Over in the EM area, where most of the good lumber was, they had a fire that would be the envy of any homecoming game. Some lame brain tossed some fifty caliber shells in the fire just liven up the party a little, and when they began to go off and ricochet around the area, the place was suddenly depopulated. No one was hurt, and it brought the wrath of the CO down on them, which broke up the party. The fire was put out and no more burning was allowed. I remember seeing the local people standing around the camp, just outside the firelight, almost in tears, seeing all that good building material going up in smoke. I will never understand the bureaucratic mind.

Just so the pressure would not let up on the Germans, we were scheduled to fly a mission from our base in Corsica and return to our new base in Italy. During form up after takeoff, it became obvious that the weather was not going to let us reach our target, so we were instructed to fly directly to Fano. The weather was a squall line running along the spine of the country and seemed to reach about twenty thousand feet. The service ceiling of a B-25 is about 23,000 ft, if the plane is new and in perfect condition and not carrying a load of bombs and fuel. Ours was old and loaded for a mission, which meant there was no way we were going to reach 23,000 ft.

We headed across the country and began to climb over the clouds. Having experienced a thunderstorm in the not too distant past, we were not about to fly through anything that even remotely resembled one. At 18,700 ft. our old plane was at its absolute maximum altitude, and was wallowing along just above stalling speed. Fortunately, that was just above the lowest cloud top and we went charging through.

At our altitude, a person can function for a while without oxygen, but after about ten minutes your lips begin to turn blue, your reflexes slow down, and you begin to act like a drunk. One should not be trying to fly an airplane under those conditions. Since most of our missions were flown around 9,000 to 15,000 ft. we seldom used oxygen, so our tanks turned out to be either empty or almost so.

There were three masks, two almost empty walk-around bottles and the low pressure system for the plane that was about empty, too. We hoped that if the rest of the crew, who didn't have anything to do but ride, would minimize their moving around, we could get by with the supply we had. Joe and I would take turns with the one mask in the cockpit, and the rest of the crew would share what was left. The pilot actively flying the plane would use oxygen and watch the other one for signs of anoxia, whereupon, he would give him the mask and let him fly. We had no idea how long we would be at altitude, so we were doing the best we could.

At one point, we heard Ely and Gaines in the rear compartment carrying on over the intercom like a couple of drunks. It turned out that their bottle was empty and they were beginning to be in trouble. I sent Charlie back there with his bottle to share with them. All this time, Flynn was draped around the upper turret base with his lips turning blue and a dopey look on his face. We had to revive him with our mask. Fortunately, several good whiffs of pure oxygen would snap us back to full operational potential, and we would then be good for another few minutes.

I don't remember just how long we had to fly at our maximum altitude, but it seemed like an eternity. As soon as we cleared the front, the cloud tops began to lower and we went with them. By the time we passed through 15,000 ft. going down we were out of danger and could get off the oxygen. Our experience, when reported to the squadron, prompted a change in procedure. All planes would have a fully functional oxygen system at all time with masks for all crewmen. From that time on, our orders were to go on oxygen any time we flew above 10,000ft. That was a little bit of overkill, but the brass wanted us to be at our sharpest at all times, and some people felt oxygen lack sooner than others.

The move from Ghisonnacia, Corsica, to Fano, Italy, was a move from a rural hamlet to a moderate sized resort town on the seacoast. Fano is on the eastern or Adriatic coast, about halfway between Ancona and Rimini. I'm sure that really locates it for most of my readers. At that time we were located less that 50 miles from the front lines, which had been static for the better part of a year. The Germans were far past being able to mount any kind of offensive in Italy, so that proximity was of little concern.

Prior to our arrival, there had been, first a British, then an American fighter base at Fano. We just took over the facilities, lengthened the runway some, enlarged the hard stands and revetments and were in business.

All our billets, officer and EM alike, were in the town. We, the Army, had taken over several apartment buildings and hotels and converted them into living quarters, offices, mess halls and all the other facilities needed to drive a combat unit. We were right in the middle of the city, with Italians living all around us. There was no particular fraternization between us, because some bad blood had developed between the towns people and the fighter group before us. The reason was never quite clear, but it had to do with the mistreatment of some of the young ladies of the town at a dance sponsored by the fighter jocks.

Many GI's allowed their baser instincts to rule their actions and attitudes when in the company of women in a party setting. They seemed to think that all members of the female persuasion were possessed of easy virtue, therefore, were there for their pleasure. The average Italian family was very close knit, and the daughters were protected and treasured. So when the parents allowed their daughters to attend a dance at the fighter base, they expected them to be treated as the ladies they were. When they were subjected to crude and vulgar behavior by the Americans, fathers and brothers took serious offence. Some said some rapes took place. Needless to say, that cooled the relations between the Americans and their co-belligerents, the Italians.

We were given strict orders to treat the Italians as allies, not conquered people. We were to be on our best behavior with them and act as guests in their town, not be patronizing or condescending. This strikes me as good policy for the military in any setting.

Since we were in closer contact with the Italians than we were the Corsicans, the language barrier became more acute. Few of the Americans could speak Italian, but we found a number of Italians fairly fluent in English. There was one man, I remember, who spoke English with a Mid-West accent. He had been a taxi driver in Detroit before the war and had been in Italy visiting relatives when the war broke out and was not allowed to return to the U.S. He seemed to be glad to see us.

There was actually little need for much interaction between us, unless one just wanted to socialize. Most of my contact with Italians was with an occasional tradesman, and by my very limited Italian and their very limited English, we managed to communicate somewhat satisfactorily.

One of the first things I needed to do when I got my billet assignment was to find some way to hang up my clothes. Our room was on the second floor of a hotel and consisted of two double decker bunks and no closets or even hooks in the wall. One might say, it was pretty Spartan. I was sharing the room with Charlie, a bombardier from California named Ning D. Lee, and Little Joe. We heard of a cabinet/carpenter shop down the street that had done some work for others, so we went to see what we could get done. By lots of hand waving, pencil drawing and our few words of Italian and English, we managed to get over what we needed, we hoped. Little Joe was a big help because he discovered there is a similarity between Italian and Spanish, so he could sort of transliterate between them and be better understood than most of us. We were told to come back in about three days. Three days later we picked up the neatest clothes rack you ever saw. It was very sturdy and strong and beautifully finished. The pole was not round, but was carefully octagonally shaped. The uprights had little decorative finials and the feet were carefully and gracefully shaped with all mortise and tenon joints. It was a work of art. I don't remember how much we paid for it but it was worth it. The man was a true craftsman.

Although we were in an old hotel, there were no bath facilities. Indoor plumbing had not become part of the Italian culture before the war, apparently, or all the pipes had been taken out to help with Mussolini's war effort. The building may have been built by the Romans, but they forgot to put in their famous baths. After about a week, most of us were beginning to be a little ripe. The grumbling got the ear of the brass and they arranged for us to go up to a British bathhouse in Pesaro, about 25 miles north of Fano. Pesaro was the headquarters for the British 8th Army and they had been there long enough to have proper facilities.

As I remember it, it was a communal shower room, which could accommodate at least fifty people. It was all pale green tile. There was plenty of good hot water and soap and clean washrags and towels. I don't remember ever feeling so dirty as when I went in, or so clean when I came out. Man, did it feel good!

From 1 Apr through 23 Apr, I flew 18 missions. That is almost one a day for the better part of a month. On 21 and 22 Apr I flew two missions each day and was scheduled for a third on one of those days when the weather closed in. We were briefed and waiting at the ship when we were stood down. That's a lot of flying.

An explanation for the above paragraph is in order. The war was winding down and the British Eighth Army and the American Tenth had started an all out push from their stalemated positions of the winter of 44, in an effort to push the Germans back to Germany, force them to quit or destroy them. The choice was theirs. Our job was to provide close support for the British and to keep the routes north closed as much as possible. As the Germans fled north, they came to a number of rivers where most of the bridges were out, and it caused a pile up of troops trying to cross. It was then that we began to drop fragmentation bombs on the concentrations. There is hardly any more devastating weapon on bunched up troops that frag bombs. I have never seen the results of an attack like that, but I can imagine that it is ghastly. My stomach knots up even now, when I think of it. This is the sort of thing you can't let yourself think about while you are doing it. It's war.

Our first frag mission was a fiasco! A group of three boxes would usually go in spaced vertically at 500-ft. intervals, no matter the load or target. No. 1 box would go in first at 9,000 ft., say, no. 2 at 9,500 ft., and no. 3 at 10,000. This was standard procedure. On this mission, some numbskull at headquarters set us up to go in just the reverse order, the high box went in first. Ordinary iron bombs, being heavy and streamlined, will drop pretty much straight down under the plane for the first few hundred feet before falling behind. Had we not been carrying frags, this screw up would not have caused any worry, unless the low boxes were too close in trail. Frags come out in clusters, and since they are fairly light and not very aerodynamic, they flutter back behind the plane like leaves. You can already see what was bound to happen. The high box dropped and the bombs came right down through the two low boxes. Almost before they knew what was happening, some of the middle box had been hit. Fortunately, we were in the lowest box and could see what was happening. Joe was flying, so his eyes were on the leader. I saw the bombs coming and yelled out at him just as our leader screamed out, "My God! They're dropping on us! Scatter!!"

Six airplanes went in six different directions. We had no earthly idea where our formation was, but there was a whole bunch of B-25's milling around up there trying to see what to do. We made a 360 and tacked on to another box with an empty slot and made the run, all the time looking up to see that there were no planes above us. That was about as exciting a time as I had the whole time I was in combat.

Only by the Grace of God was no one killed. One radioman in another plane was pretty badly chopped up when a frag hit the rear of the engine nacelle and exploded. The shrapnel blew a huge hole in the waist compartment right where the radioman was. It also shredded the main gear tire and the pilot had to make a belly landing. Another plane landed with a live bomb in his wing, and the pilot didn't know it. If he hadn't made a near perfect landing, it could have gone off and taken a goodly portion of the wing with it.

This seems like a good place to interject some comments about our Italian neighbors. Our field was open to the countryside. There were no fences. There hadn't been time to build any, consequently, the locals could get on the base about any time they wanted to. We had MP's to guard the vital areas, such as fuel and ammo dumps and our food supplies.

Before we stopped combat operations, the area around the runway, taxiways and hardstands grew up so much the grass had to be cut. The vegetation was pretty good hay, and the Army decided to let the Italians have it if they could get it without interfering with operations. We all watched in amazement as several couples showed up and began to rake the hay up into shocks. The men would then help the women load the shocks on their heads until you could see only their feet. They would point the women toward home and send them on their way while they, the men, went into town to have a little vino. It was hilarious to see these shocks of hay, apparently on their own, heading off across the base.

Our frag bombs came crated up in wooden crates about two feet square and six feet long. The wood was clear, finished pine, excellent building material. We were under such pressure to get the missions in that the armorers just dumped the boxes in a heap outside the bomb dump until they could clear them away. The Italians discovered them and three couples came in to help themselves. The men loaded their women up with all they could they could carry and started off. The MP's ran them down and demanded they take them back. After much arm waving and gesticulating, the women dumped the boxes in a heap and walked away. It took six GI's and a deuce and a half to cart them back to the dump.

Under ordinary circumstances, like earlier in the war, by the time I had 20 missions I would have had my own crew. We were flying so hard that my missions were piling up faster than headquarters could keep up with them. Joe knew it was time for me to get my own crew, so he arranged for me to fly a left seat mission with him as co-pilot. This was in the nature of a test flight to see how I would handle the responsibility of a first pilot.

The entire time I was in the Army, I only had one episode of tachycardia that I couldn't stop. This was it. Usually, if I was in a position to do so, I could get my heart to settle into a proper rhythm pretty quickly. Then I would have to pace myself and control my excitement and exertion. I had had so little trouble with my heart that I didn't anticipate this soon enough and before I could do anything, it was off and racing. Once the heart settled into its accelerated pace, I could function normally, although it was a little disconcerting. The episode started during briefing and didn't stop until after debriefing over three hours later. No one ever knew that I was having tachycardia.

The mission was to the San Ambrosio R.R. fill, and I was flying the no. 2 position on the wing of a box leader who was known for his wild breaks off the target. This day his break was to the left, which meant it was away from me. That is the easiest to fly because you just have to keep up, not get out of the way. The mission was normal in every way. Joe and I alternated flying and I took it over the target. I made no attempt to slow my heart down, because I knew there might be an adverse effect if I got it working right and it started up again. I just decided to wait it out and adjust it when I could relax and be away from people.

We made the run and on the break I stayed on this jokers wing like I was glued there. Joe later said I had flown a very good mission. The whole mission was a success, as far as I was concerned. I felt like a crew and a promotion were mine, if the war lasted long enough.

On 22 Apr we were up a before dawn take off to hit the Ficarolo ferry landing at sun up. Two more missions were scheduled that day. On the way home, the sun was just coming up and the air was as smooth as glass. We were all feeling pretty full of ourselves and flying good formation. The leader kept telling us to tuck it in closer, so Joe and the no. 2 man eased it in until our props were behind the leader's aileron and the wing tip was almost in the radio man's lap. He was going crazy, motioning us away. I would guess that there was no more than three feet between our nose and the leader's wingtip. That's really tight formation, and it's pretty stupid, if you think about it. Just a slight bump or sudden move by one of us would have wrapped six airplanes up into one big flaming ball. We didn't stay that way long, you pretty soon get jumpy with tension. If someone in authority had seen us, six crews would have been grounded.

We only had time to get debriefed, get something to eat and we were briefed for another close support mission to the Occhiobello ferry landing. Each of these missions was only about 1 ½ hr. long. This left us time for a third mission, which we were briefed for, but never flew, because the weather closed in. We were at the plane, just hanging out waiting for the weather to break, and it finally got too late in the day to fly. Our hardstand was next to an old bomb crater and the pierced steel planking hung out over it like a diving board. We had a great time springing up and down on it. We found out later that there was a live frag bomb lying on the hardstand and it was bouncing up and down while we were. That would have been to explain if we had been blown to smithereens while horsing around.

The next day we hit the Ostiglia ferry landing and that was it for our war in Italy. Mission #31.

Chapter XV

FINITO ETO, NEXT HIROHITO

As the war began to wind down in Italy, the British began to pull out of the line the troops that had been in combat the longest. Among them were the Coldstream Guards. This was an elite division that was known as the "Queen's Own." They had been in combat since they were sent to North Africa to become part of Montgomery's army in 1942. They, in concert with the Americans, had driven the Germans out of North Africa, Sicily and up the boot of Italy to the Po valley. They had seen some combat.

They were billeted in Fano, just down the street from us, and inevitably, our paths crossed. Most of them had been away from home for years, and all they knew about the American fliers was what they heard about the Eighth Air Force in England. What they heard was that they were "over paid, over-sexed and over here." Needless to say, they were less than overjoyed to find themselves encamped next door to a bunch of "fly boys." There was a certain level of tension between the two groups.

The Guards are a proud bunch, with an enviable combat record. It soon became evident that considerable restraint was advisable on our part when in the presence of Guardsmen. Restraint is not in the nature of many Americans, especially aviators, so ever so often MP's and the English equivalent had to be called out to break up brawls. This was usually for the purpose of rescuing the Americans, because they were not up to coping with the English troops. Not only were they tough and combat hardened, they were big. To be an enlisted man in the Coldstream Guards you had to be at least six feet tall. This requirement dated back to the formation of the Guard under Queen Elizabeth, and they were extremely proud to be able to meet that criterion.

The only people in the unit under six feet were the pipers and the officers. The officers were, for the most part, of the nobility and were little shrimps and haughty as hell. I think that must have been a product of inbreeding and the natural feeling of eliteness indigenous to the English upper class.

The Guards marched to the sound of bagpipes and the hammering of their hard, leather heels on the streets really turned heads. Anyone with a drop of Scotch blood in their veins had to be affected by that sight and sound. It would sort of make the hair of your neck stand up. They loved to parade through our area and show off. I must admit, I was impressed.

When the plans to celebrate VE Day were announced, the authorities, with admirable forethought, scheduled the two nationalities to celebrate on separate days, because there was bound to be copious consumption of the local vino, and there are few more belligerent individuals than liquored up Limeys. When the Guards celebrated, we were confined to our area, and vice versa when we celebrated. That way, both outfits were kept in shape to fight the Japs. It would not have been good policy or PR for a complete group of airmen to be invalided home with injuries suffered at the hands of their allies after the war was over.

Chapter XVI

PEACE COMES TO THE 310th

With surrender of the Germans and the end of the war in Europe, there came a period of aimlessness in the lives of those of us in combat with not enough points for rotation home. There seemed to be a feeling of confusion in the command structure. What do we do, now? Our objective had been to whip the Germans and Italians, and not much planning appeared to have been done for the time when we accomplished our goal. This, of course, was not exactly true, but it is pretty hard to suddenly change the direction of several million fighting men, half a world away from where the war was still going on.

Most of us with little time in combat were content for awhile to just relax and take it easy. We were in a foreign country where there were unusual sights and situations to explore, and there was time to check them out. Some of the old timers were busily adding up their points to see if they were going to get to go home. Basically, points were awarded for time overseas and actual time in combat. I don't remember just what contributed to a point score, but I knew I didn't have anywhere near enough to get away any time soon. Most of us who were still flying combat on VE Day felt that we would end up in the Pacific, if the war lasted long enough.

Once the celebrations were over, the mill began to crank out rumors at the rate of at least one a day. Some sadists would start a rumor in the morning just to see how it had changed by the time it got back to them in the evening. That was a sure sign that we didn't have enough to do.

Rather than just sit around and grouse about having nothing to do and wishing to go home, we set about making the area more comfortable and like the U.S. A group officers club was set up in a resort hotel down near the water front, where you could find card games, table tennis, magazines and books, a piano, and just a generally pleasant atmosphere. It was a good place to relax. Our officer's mess doubled as a squadron officers club, with similar facilities. Our cooks were Italians who took great pride in their work. Our food improved immensely once we were established in Fano. There are two things I remember about our mess, the delicious bread and the bowls of filberts on the table at every meal. As the weather moderated and the Italians were able to put in gardens and truck patches, we began to have fresh vegetables for lunch and dinner. We also began to have fresh eggs for breakfast on a regular basis.

Our softball teams continued their play in Italy just like we had in Corsica. There were games just about every day, usually after dinner, because the days were getting longer all the time. There were also trips to the beach as soon as the weather got warm enough. The beach at Fano was not up to the Florida and Carolina beaches in the States, but it was what we had. There seemed to be much less sand and more rocks in the Italian beaches.

Lest you get the idea that our life after hostilities was one long round of beach parties, ball games and eating, let me hasten to assure that the Army would never allow that to happen. We flew almost as much after the war as we did during the war. We were being kept sharp for the Japs. It was almost like being back in training. There were practice missions, formation flying, instrument flying and night flying. Night flying was particularly harrowing because of the shortage of navaids for nighttime. It only took one crash before the brass called off the night missions.

A peculiarity of that area was the mists that formed over the coast after sundown. They effectively obscured the horizon and made reliance on ones instruments absolutely essential at night. One crew took off one night and crashed in the sea just off the runway. The pilot had a lot of time, but it had been some time since he had flown instruments, and he apparently developed vertigo and stalled out just after takeoff. Only the engineer survived. You could see the plane in about twenty feet of water, with the life raft floating above it, still tethered to the plane. Seeing that plane in the water on every take off made us all just a bit more alert and careful. That's a pretty terrible price to pay for increased vigilance.

I still had not been assigned a permanent crew. I was flying as first pilot most of the time with whoever was assigned to me. For a time I flew with another Tennessean, Hoyt Payne, from Knoxville. Hoyt had come into the squadron earlier than I, having gotten there in November,'44. He had 44 missions as co-pilot but overall had less 25 time than I did. I was told I was to act as an instructor and get Hoyt ready for a crew. It turned out that he didn't need me to help him. He was ready for the left seat the first time we flew. He had one unfortunate habit that he had picked up from his first pilot. He had a tendency to drag the ship in on landing under too much power. If he had had an engine go out on the approach, he would likely have landed short of the runway, or rolled over on his back if he tried to go around. Your approach in a B-25, or any plane, for that matter, should be high enough, with enough airspeed to land, power off.

Hoyt sort of got us in a little trouble on one landing when he cut the throttles when we were too high. If you drag in under too much power, the engines are what are keeping you in the air. With them off, you tend to drop precipitously, resulting in not one, but several landings, if you are lucky. We did a fair amount of bouncing around that time, and must have looked like the rawest of cadets to those who might have been watching. I hope no one was. After I pointed out to him why we hit so hard, Hoyt stopped using so much power on landings.

I flew my last combat mission on 23 Apr and the very next day began practice missions. Over the next sixty days I flew fourteen more non-combat missions. Most of them were as first pilot, but they recombined Dromgoole's crew for some cross country, night and instrument flight. I guess they were getting us ready to fly back home. Every day a crew or two would get orders to head home. All aircrew were being allowed to take a plane back home, rather than being shipped by boat.

When a crew would leave, we would all go down to the field and bid them goodbye. It became the custom for the tower to allow them to make one final low level pass over the field. We saw some truly classic runs. It seemed to be the desire of every one to fly below the tower and blow over the engineering tent. Fortunately, no one "pranged his kite", as the British would say.

Between the end of the war and going home there was a lot of free time to be filled. Flying took only a few hours so there was a lot of time spent trying to find something to do. I would guess that bull sessions took up most of our idle hours. There was the group O Club that I have mentioned. As the weather warmed, there was the beach. It was at the beach that I encountered what must be a purely European custom, because I had never seen Americans perform this feat. There was a shortage of bathhouses, so the Italians and English demonstrated how to change clothes out in the open without compromising their modesty. This was not particularly difficult for men because they had only their lower half to conceal. For a female, it was another story, of course. They would show up fully clothed with their bathing suit and a large towel. They would wrap the towel around themselves, up to the armpits. Then slowly, one piece at a time, they would divest themselves of their outer clothes and their underwear and replace them with their bathing suit, all the while maintaining perfect decorum and exposing nothing. It was a sight to see, or actually, not to see.

Thinking back on the nom-combat time, I guess the daily routine was more or less unchanged from wartime, except there was certainly a more relaxed atmosphere. I was flying just about as much, now that the war was over, as I had when it was on. Gone were the daily anticipation of target assignments and the stress of knowing that you were going in harm's way. No one was shooting at us as we flew our missions. That reduced the adrenaline production considerably.

On 17 May 1945, I was promoted to 1st Lt. I had been recommended for promotion to first pilot and this increase in rank went with it. It was nice to know that the end of the war in Europe had not frozen promotions, but it also portended a reversion to combat status, unless the war ended before I could be shipped to the Far East. There was some talk that the group might be moved in toto to the China-Burma-India Theater, or on to the Southwest Pacific. I don't know what the logistics of such a move would have been, but it seemed to make more sense to send those with the least combat time out as replacements.

Immediately after cessation of hostilities, a couple of A-26's showed up at the base. All of us had heard of the A-26 and had seen a few of them fly over. From what we had seen and heard it was a machine to die for, not literally, of course. Everybody wanted to fly it, because it was really hot! It was some smaller than the 25, and much faster. It had only one pilot, a bombardier/navigator and one or two gunners, depending upon the configuration. At that time there were not many piston engined enemy fighters flat out faster than the 26. This made it seem to us like a fighter masquerading as a bomber, and, as I have said earlier, all pilots thought of themselves as fighter pilots under the skin. Rumor was that as many of as possible, would be checked out in it, because we would probably be retrained in it for the invasion of the Japanese home islands.

The designers of the A-26 had taken the lessons learned from the combat experience of the B-25 and A-20 and combined them in the A-26. It had two 2000 hp engines, dorsal and ventral turrets of two to four 50 cal. guns, four to eight fixed forward firing 50's, a bomb load of four thousand pounds and a range much greater than the 25. It was envisioned to operate somewhat like a fighter/bomber. It was to be used in close support, which most pilots thought they would be great at, even though it is the most dangerous kind of combat flying.

Naturally, the first to check out in the A-26 were the group brass, who very likely would not be flying combat, no matter what happened. But they were the ones doing the scheduling of the check outs, RHIP, don't you know. It didn't get down to the guys, the Capts. and Lts., who would actually be the ones taking them into combat.

After months of flying combat, it was difficult for most pilots to just cut it off and become ground bound and take it lightly. This was especially true for the fighter jocks. Since there were no Me-109s and FW-190s to chase nor anymore bridges to bust, the fighter pilots began to put on circuses among themselves. There was a natural rivalry between the P-51s and P-47s that usually erupted into a free for all dogfight, sans live ammo, any time they found themselves in the same airspace. In fact, that is what they did any time they took off. They went looking for each other. We got to see some really hairy melees around our base. They seemed to like to stage their shoot-outs near us, just to show off, I guess. Needless to say, it was entertaining until one P-47 flew into the ground. That put the quietus on that, for a while.

There were other show-offs in the area, too. Not far away was an American night fighter group flying the Mosquito. This was the British all-purpose fighter/bomber made of wood. It was a marvel of design and construction. It had a top speed of about 400 mph, a bomb capacity of over 4000 pounds and a range of 2000 miles. If you could keep the dry rot out and the termites away, it was a spectacular bird.

One afternoon, Charlie and I were walking back to the billet area from the field, when two of these Mosquito pilots came over and began to beat up the field. Each pass was a little lower and a little faster, and the pull-ups sharper and more violent. One of them was a bit more daring than the other, coming in lower and faster than his wingman. I guess he may have had more time or was just naturally crazier. As we stood and watched, they came screaming down over the field at no more than 25 feet. As the leader racked his plane up in a violent right climbing turn, something happened. Maybe a hundred people saw the whole thing, and I'll bet you would have gotten a hundred slightly different versions, if you had asked them all what happened. Of course, I know what happened. As he horsed the plane up, he forced it into a high-speed stall, it buffeted and the right engine tore loose. The plane essentially came to an abrupt stop in the sky from well over 300-mph, fell into a flat spin and splatted in from about 100 ft. It burned and the pilot was killed instantly. There was a report that the supercharger tore loose from the engine and flew through a Quonset hut, end to end, and grazed the elbow of a GI asleep on a table outside.

The second pilot sort of milled around for a while, looking the situation over and slowly flew off in the direction of his base. The next day, a truck from the night fighter base came and got the remains of the plane and hauled all that was left away in one load. There wasn't enough left of the pilot to bury. That sort of thing casts a pall over a base, even if you don't know the pilot. It was discussed in rather hushed tones at chow that night.

The Air Force had made it a practice to provide rest camps for their combat crews, so that after a specified number of missions crews would be pulled out of combat and given a week off. They tried, as best they could, to make the rest facilities as little like a military establishment as possible. In WW II, we called it "rest leave", now it is R&R. Same thing.

Although the war was over, we were still sent on rest leave, because we were still flying a lot. And, I suppose, they were phasing out the rest camps along with all other combat related activities, but needed to keep them operating as long as there were personnel in the theater. For our area, there were two places we could go, Rome or Capri. We had no choice; we went where we were sent. We all had preferences, but no one ever turned down rest leave because he didn't get his choice.

Approaching Capri

In early June, I was tapped for rest leave at Capri. I would have really preferred Rome, I thought, but Capri it was. I knew next to nothing about Capri, except from a popular little song of the Thirties, "It was on the Isle of Capri that I met Her." That certainly didn't prepare me for what I found.

This is what the encyclopedia says about Capri.

Capri (ancient Capreae), island, south central Italy, at the entrance of the Bay of Naples, near the city of Naples. It is about 6 km (about 4 mi) long and about 2 km (1.5 mi) at its widest point. Limestone cliffs, 274 m (900 ft) high, rise from the sea in the east; Monte Solaro, in the west, the highest point on the island, is 585 m (1920 ft) above sea level. The town of Capri, 136 m (450 ft) high, is an Episcopal see. From the town 784 steps, carved in the rock, lead upward to Anacapri. To the west of the town of Capri is the Grotta Azzurra (Blue Grotto), a cavern, entered from the sea by a narrow opening not more than 91 cm (3 ft) high, but which inside is of magnificent proportions. Elliptical in form, it is 53 m (175 ft) long, 30 m (100ft) at the widest part, and 12 m (41 ft) high; the water in the cavern is 15 m (48 ft) deep. Stalactites hang from the roof and sides. The blue color within the grotto is caused by the light passing through the water. Capri contains relics of prehistoric ages and numerous remains of Roman times, including the ruins of the 12 villas built by the emperor Tiberius, who resided in Capri for ten years. No springs or streams are on Capri, but it has abundant rainfall and is fertile, producing olive oil, wine and fruit. The tourist trade provides the principal source f income for the islanders. Area, 10,4 sq. km (4 sq. mi); population (1990 estimate) 7400.

I was paired with another 1st Lt. pilot named Miller. I only knew him casually, but he seemed an all right guy. He was not a carouser, and we got along quite well. Had either of us wanted to carouse, we couldn't have done it on Capri. It was a rest area in the most complete sense. There was not much to do there but hike around the island, take a boat tour, swim or check out the shops, of which there were few. If there were bars and nightclubs, we didn't go looking for them.

Our accommodations were in a pre-war resort hotel that the Army had restored to its earlier splendor. Our room had twin beds with real sheets and pillows. There was also a tile bath with shower. And there was maid service. We didn't have to make up our beds, clean the bath or police up the room. For a week we lived like a tourist on holiday. This, of course, was the idea. We were supposed to use that time to completely forget about the war and enjoy ourselves. The fact that the war was over in Europe didn't relieve a sense of concern about our immediate future, but this time off did help. We were able to more or less put it out or our minds and just relax.

Capri town from our hotel

We flew to Naples from Fano and were taken by ferry out to Capri. At the ferry landing, we boarded an inclined railway, much like the one in Chattanooga, but not as long. That was not the only way up to the town of Capri, but it was the most convenient. As we boarded the cars, there was a band playing a song I had heard as I was growing up. I knew it as "Funiculi, Funicular." I have an idea that it was a refrain from some Italian opera, but it was familiar. It turns out that the inclined railway is called a Funicular in Italian. It seemed that is the way visitors to Capri are always greeted.

I don't remember a lot about what we did that week other than just laze around and look the island over. That was the idea, I suppose.

One day Miller and I went down the waterfront and, instead of taking the big motorized tour boat, rented a small boat and a boatman and he took us part way around the island. He used a long stern mounted sweep like those you see on the Venetian gondolas. That seemed like a rather tedious way to propel a boat, but he made it move right along. He took us to the Blue Grotto and took us inside. We had to wait our turn because only a few boats at a time could go in. The opening is so small that the passengers in the boats have to lie down and pull the

Entrance to the Blue Grotto

boat in with a chain attached to the entrance. Once inside, it opens up into the very large cavern described above. The opening into the cavern below the water level is very large, and the light coming in through that gives the water a brilliant blue color, like it has been mixed with ink. At the back of the cavern is what looks like a tunnel sloping up into the island. Our guide said that it did go all the way to the surface, and that smugglers and slaves had used it in the ancient days, also, by people trying to get away from the Germans during the recent war.

Around the town square there were several little shops dealing in souvenirs and bric-a-brac for the tourists, in this case, GI's. I only bought

a couple of things, a ring carved out of aluminum from a German airplane, so the shopkeeper said, and a baby dress made from parachute nylon. The lady who ran the shop was very fluent in English, and was a

Miller having a milkshake at a local soda shop

great help when I told her about my baby daughter that I hadn't seen. She told me that the dress had been made locally and was all hand sewn. It was just the thing for Betty, I thought. I had no idea that it would fit, but I bought it, anyway. It turned out that I got it home just before Betty outgrew it. We had her picture made in it and put it away. I'm not sure she ever wore it but that one time.

One afternoon, late in the week, the hotel cooks built a roaring fire in a big beehive oven out on the lawn back of the hotel. We could see the activity from our third floor balcony, but had no idea what was going on. I didn't even know that the device had anything to do with cooking until I saw them stoking up the fire. They got the fire going and went away and left it until the wood burned down to coals. Then they raked out the oven, swept off the bottom of it, put a cover over the door and went away. That seemed a strange thing to do. I supposed that they had decided not to do whatever it was they had started out to do.

About four o'clock in the afternoon, there was another burst of activity. The cooks were back with tables set up on the lawn and they were busily making something to eat. They were pouring whole canned tomatoes on

215

large, flat rounds of raw dough, and covering it with grated cheese. This went into the oven for about five or ten minutes and then was brought out, cut up into wedges and we were all summoned down to eat it. I had no idea what I was eating, but it was delicious. I would never have believed that GI canned tomatoes could taste so good. No one ever told us what we were eating, and it was not until years later when the pizza craze hit the U.S., that I realized that I had had my first pizza in 1945, on the beautiful little isle of Capri. About every time I eat pizza now, I think of Capri.

Hotel courtyard where we had pizza

Seven days and we were back to the monotony of squadron life. It was beginning to look like I might be over there long enough to get another rest leave. Things didn't seem to be going much of anywhere.

Sometime in June, Ely came down with appendicitis and was hospitalized in Ancona, about 52 kilometers (31.2 mi) down the coast. One Sunday, we checked out a jeep and all the crew went down to see him. For some reason, I was selected to be the driver. That was the first and last time I ever drove a jeep. I know why they were called "kidney killers." They had no springs, to speak of, and it seemed to have a mind of its own when it came to hitting all the potholes in the terrible Italian roads. It also had next to no brakes, I soon found out. But, despite its seeming desire to kill us all, we made it there and back. We had a good visit with Ely, and left him in good spirits. But then, Ely was always in good spirits, no matter the situation. Unfortunately, that was the last time any of us saw him, because before he could get out of the hospital, we had shipped out. As it turned out, he would not have gone with us had he not been in the hospital. Tail gunners were the armorers on a B-25, and as such, were not actively engaged in aircraft operation, except in combat. They were sending tail gunners home in a group by other means of transportation.

Very shortly after our visit with Ely, we got our orders back to the states. We were assigned aircraft #43-27724, a B-25J-2, to fly back home. This plane was built in 1943, so it had seen some combat. The orders were to take it to Hunter Field and turn it in.

Just before loading to go home. l. to r.: Crouse-co-pilot, Dromgoole-pilot, Harbeson-bombardier, Flynn-Engineer, Gaines-radioman.

Chapter XVII

IT'S HOME AGAIN, HOME AGAIN, JIGGEDY-JOG

Ready to leave for home

On 30 June, we took off for Naples on our first leg back along the Southern ATC route. We had with us a Capt. P. J. Grant, from the Adj. General's office. As some of the non-combat personnel came up for rotation, they were offered the chance to ride back home with one of the returning crews. P. J. was in the ground echelon of the 379th, in what capacity, I don't remember, and was a welcome passenger. He was a lawyer by profession and an extremely pleasant fellow to have around. We hit it off very well. The same could not be said for the next passenger we picked up in Naples.

For some reason, the Army decided that returning crews needed to have a qualified navigator aboard. Somehow they seemed to feel that we needed help to get back that we didn't need to get over there, so the ATC would supply us with a navigator. Strange is the working of the military mind.

We drew a cocky little 2nd Lt. from the Eight Air Force. He had gotten overseas late and had only gotten in a few easy missions and the war ended on him. He hadn't gotten his fill of flying, so he applied for transfer to the ATC. He got started off on the wrong foot with us from the very beginning. We didn't think we needed him, since it was just a matter of flying the reverse of the route we had flown, sans navigator, six months before, but he assured us that we would get lost very soon without his expert navigating. He immediately began to put down the mediums as toys, and assured us that our war was just a side show compared to what the Eighth had been in. The B-17 was the plane that had won the war and we were very lucky to have him to keep us out of trouble. He was one of these guys that you couldn't verbally insult. They just went over his head.

We decided that we would give him a chance, since the orders were to take him, so we integrated him into the crew as best we could. We let him plot the courses and set up the ETA's, and let him play with his little sextant to shoot the sun to confirm our course. All the time, Charlie was to surreptitiously check him out and let us know when he screwed up. He would have been mortified if he had known that a mere bombardier was back checking him.

The first legs, Naples to Tunis, Tunis to Marrakech, Marrakech to Dakar were relatively uneventful. We didn't get lost and we hit our ETA's pretty much on time. No better than we had with Charlie navigating, but the little guy seemed happy, and we had begun to tune out his bragging about the mighty Eighth. P. J. would needle him occasionally, but that was the way P. J. was.

The morning we were to go from Dakar to Roberts Field, a squall was blowing in from the ocean. It was pretty localized, but you could see it was big. Our take off was to be delayed until it could blow over, but it looked like it was going to delay us enough that we would have to remain another night in Dakar. This was unacceptable. We wanted to be on our way home. At the last minute, it began to look like the storm was going to veer north and not hit Dakar head on, and you could see clear weather under the cloud bottom. We talked the air traffic controller into letting us take off and stay under the clouds, instead of climbing to our assigned 9,000 ft. He cleared us out at minimum altitude until we were clear of the storm.

The bottom of the clouds was about 500 ft., so Joe took off and leveled off at 50 ft. and away we went. We cleared the storm in about fifteen minutes and were in perfectly beautiful weather, and out of sight of Dakar. This was a perfect time to do what all pilots love to do, fly low and fast.

The first part of this leg was along the coast, so Joe eased on down to about 25 ft. and went tearing down the coast of Africa at about 200 mph. Our little navigator buddy had never flown this low except on takeoff and landing, and he was bug eyed. He completely forgot to navigate and stared out at the surf and sand just outside the window. As we turned inland, we stayed right on the treetops, dodging an occasional mahogany tree sticking up out of the canopy. We picked up a river that paralleled our course for a while, so Joe dropped down to just off the water and we went wheeling along looking straight out the window at the trees. By this time, the navigator was getting a little green and begging Joe to get up out of the river. When we blew over small sailboat with our prop blast, he about died. He asked us if we did this sort of thing often, and lying in our teeth, we assured him we did it all the time. We didn't hear much about the inferiority of the B-25 after that.

Flying that close to the ground gets a little tiring after a while, and we had thoroughly impressed our passenger, so we climbed on up to our cruising altitude for the rest of the leg into Roberts Field. Roberts hadn't changed much. Everyone there was still yellow from atabrine. There was nothing memorable that I can recall about the night there. We were all so tired that we hit the sack early. We had a long over water leg the next day and needed our rest.

The navigator really seemed to be eager to have this over water stretch so he could further impress us with his navigational abilities. There would be no landmarks, so we would have to rely on his sun shots and time and airspeed calculations to get us to Ascension Island. What he didn't know was that we had an ace-in-the-hole in case he went astray, the radio compass.

In retrospect, it is sort of mind-boggling how confidently we set out on this leg. Ascension Island was still just as tiny as ever, in middle of the Atlantic Ocean, all by itself, no alternates in case something happened. It would be so easy to miss the island completely with only a small error in course. At least, this time we should have no concern about German subs leading us off, since there shouldn't be any, anymore. With a confidence born of our youthful ignorance and the knowledge that we had been there before, off we went.

Charlie checked the navigator's course and was satisfied, although the kid still didn't know he was being monitored by a mere bombardier. The day was perfect. A few clouds, no adverse winds, just miles and miles of ocean. From time to time the navigator would get out his sextant and take a sun shot and check or correct our course. He seemed to be having a ball, doing his calculations and perusing his charts.

As soon as we could pick up the radio beacon from Ascension, we began to home in on it without the navigator's knowledge and ignored his plots. Fortunately, that station had a range of about 750 mi, so we picked it up a long way out. We had been on the beam for a couple of hours when the navigator shot the sun and gave us a course correction that would have made us miss our landfall completely. We wouldn't have even seen the island. Joe shook his head and pointed to the radio compass and grinned. The navigator was thoroughly hacked off, and allowed as how we could all go to hell. We could go ahead and get lost. He wasn't going to navigate for us any more, if we didn't have any more confidence than that in him. Pointing out that his course would have gotten us all drowned, including him, didn't mollify him much. Losing his navigational skills was not much of a loss to us, we felt. We had made the reverse trip without him, and were pretty sure we could get back home without him.

The trip over had taken us 21 days, what with maintenance and weather delays. So far, we were right on schedule to make it back to the states in eleven days, one leg per day. Not only was the weather better in the summer, but we had a tried and true airplane that had had all the bugs wrung out of it and had had the advantage of having been maintained by highly skilled combat mechanics. It was purring along like a champ.

Ascension Island had changed some in the six months since we were through there before. The main change was in the chow they were feeding. They had gotten cold storage units set up so there was fresh meat, eggs and whole milk, instead of powdered milk, powdered eggs and C rations. There were also fresh vegetables! It was there that I first heard of hydroponic gardening. The Army had set up a system of hydroponics large enough to provide tomatoes, onions, beans, peas, radishes, lettuce and potatoes for the whole base and all the transients. It was great! It was said that most of the permanent party experienced bouts of diarrhea from too much fresh lettuce when it first became available. Some strange cravings develop when one is deprived of things we tend to take for granted. You would think that such things as ice cream or milk shakes would be at the top of everyone's cravings list. You would be surprised to learn that lettuce or anything green were the things you seemed to miss most.

When we landed at Natal, we were instructed to stay in our plane with the windows and hatches closed until base personnel could disinfect us. Disinfect us? What did they think we were, lepers? It turned out that they were taking precautions against tse tse flies and other African pests that the Brazilians didn't want in their country. We sat on the end of the runway in the broiling tropic sun for about thirty minutes before the guys with the pyrethrum bombs could spray down the inside of the plane. It got pretty darned hot.

The next leg up to Belem was uneventful, but the leg to Georgetown was not. You remember that I told about the thunderstorm we experienced between Georgetown and Belem on the way over. Such storms must be a year round occurrence in that area, because there was a squall in line pretty much the same place as six months before. This time, we could see it coming and we swung out to sea and went around the end of it. We had learned our lesson. One of the other crews flying the same route made the mistake of trying to fly through. They made it, but the pilot had to be helped out of the cockpit, he was so weak and scared. He just sat there and shook for about ten minutes after he parked. There were loose rivets all over the plane. It is a good thing the B-25 is such a controllable and sturdy machine. Not all our combat aircraft could have gotten through, unscathed.

The next two legs were uneventful. We took off, flew to our next stop, sacked out and took off the next day. We flew directly from Puerto Rico to Hunter Field in Savannah, where we had started our saga just over six months before. There we turned in our trusty steed, never to see her again. It was a little sad.

Our POE (port of embarkation) was Charleston, SC, so we were loaded on a C-54 and flown from Savannah to Charleston. There we turned in all our combat gear and I bought my fleece lined flight jacket for $15. It turned out to be a lifesaver in college when I couldn't afford to buy a civilian type coat. I still have it in storage, a bit worse for the wear, but full of memories. I would liked to have kept my .45, but couldn't talk the quartermaster into writing it up as lost, and they wouldn't sell it to me.

As we off loaded from the C-54, we were met by some nice ladies from a local church with milk and cookies. We were each handed a pint of ice cold, fresh milk and a handful of warm cookies, and welcomed home like the conquering heroes we were. Seeing those pleasant, smiling faces, and hearing those soft southern accents made me know that I was home again. That experience has endeared Charleston to me ever since. It has made that city one of my favorite places to visit in the whole world.

The Army didn't waste any time with us. They must have known we were coming, because our orders were ready and all of us were assigned to the Reception Center nearest to our home for overseas leave orders. Mine was Ft. McPherson in Atlanta. I was granted 30 days leave plus 2 days travel for R & R, after which I was to report back to Ft. Mac for further assignment. My orders were dated 11 Jul 45 and I was due back at the Reception Center no later than 13 Aug 45.

We had left Fano on 30 Jun and had turned in our plane at Hunter on 10 Jul. We made the 11-stop trip in 11 days. We didn't stay more than one night anywhere. I think the fact that we were going home may have had some bearing on our not wanting to lay over.

Chapter XVIII

BACK TO CIVILIAN LIFE. NORMALCY?

The prospect of getting home to see Laverda, Betty and the rest of my family was almost overwhelming. I had just completed a great adventure and was faced with the possibility that a still greater one was in store. The thing I wanted most at that moment was to get on the first train to Rutherford. Although we had been apart only six months, so much had happened in that time that it seemed almost a lifetime. I realized that many men had been away from home and family for years, and might have years more before them, and I felt bad for them. But, there was nothing I could do about that; so, my own situation was of more immediate concern.

I don't remember a lot of detail about my homecoming, just that I think I got into Rutherford about mid morning, and no one knew just when I was to arrive. Most of us coming back from overseas moved so fast that we didn't have time to notify the folks back home. We were sort of scheduling our travel as we went along.

I stopped by the bank to see Jab and get some transportation out to see Laverda. He didn't see me come in but one of his tellers, Martha McCullough, did and called out to him. He just about jumped over the counter and grabbed my hand and about crushed my knuckles. A few tears were shed, too. I think he was proud of me, but he couldn't show it too openly. It would have spoiled his image.

I wasn't sure where Laverda was, at her home or with my folks. Jab lent me his car and told me she was with her folks. He told me to get on out there and he would get home somehow. I made tracks out there as fast as that old 35 Chevy would take me. She knew I was coming in any day, and was on the lookout for me. When I stopped in front of the house she hit the ground running and we met at the car door. After we had hugged and kissed and cried a little, she took me straight to see our baby. I know she must have been disappointed in my reaction to Betty. She expected me to grab her up and hold her, but I didn't. This was a totally new experience for me. I didn't know anything about babies. For all I knew, she might break, or I might drop her. I had missed the last three months of pregnancy, the birth and the first 31/2 months of her life. This was going to take a little getting used to. Here was this little stranger that had somehow gotten plopped down in our lives and nothing was ever going to be same again. I was having to make an abrupt transition from devil-may-care flyboy to a papa with new responsibilities. It was almost more than I could handle at that time. Little babies have a way of getting into your heart very quickly, and I was soon picking her up and holding her and even changing diapers. Fatherhood began to overtake me very quickly.

Ah! Fatherhood

The next thirty days went by in a blur of activities. We spent time both at the King's and the Crouse's. We also managed to get in a belated honeymoon of four days in Gatlinburg. Neither of us had ever heard of Gatlinburg, so when my sister Madge suggested it, we had to look it up on the map. Madge had worked some in Oak Ridge, and knew something about East Tennessee. At the time, I knew absolutely nothing about Oak Ridge, or had any inkling of what might be going on there. Neither did Madge, for that matter. She just knew it was an enormous defense operation. The name made no impression on me.

We rode a bus up to Gatlinburg and arrived there without a reservation anywhere. In 1945, Gatlinburg was only just beginning to burgeon as a resort town. There were a few motels and hotels, some shops and a few restaurants, although all building had stopped with the beginning of the war and had not begun again. Not knowing anything about the town, we just asked around and someone recommended the Greystone Hotel, because it was new and still under construction. I pretended that we had called ahead for reservations, and when they found out I was a serviceman on leave they found us a room. We had a room with three meals a day for $10 a day! The food was superb and plentiful, and you would never get a deal like that these days for twenty times that price.

There was very little to do there but roam the few shops, hike and ride horses. The hotel didn't even have a pool. There was a place in the Little Pigeon River where someone had piled up some rocks to make a shallow pool, but very little swimming could be done. Mostly we just ate, hiked and relaxed. It was an unwinding time.

Four days was about all Laverda could stand to be away from Betty, who was in the care of her mother. She was sure Mrs. King was not looking after her properly. After all, she had only raised 11 of her own. What did she know? Four days was enough for me, too. I was not used to doing nothing for long at a time.

Relaxing at the Greystone

My sister Dee was an avid listener to the war news on the radio, because her husband, Dave, was still in Europe. Sometime during my leave she heard that a bomb more powerful that any ever before had been exploded and it had the potential to end the war. She asked me about it, and I told her we had heard about all sorts of doomsday weapons and secret machines that were going to end the war, and had come to pay very little attention to such rumors. I dismissed it as just another of thousands of rumors, and thought no more about it. Then, just before I was to leave to return to active duty, the word about the bombing of Hiroshima and Nagasaki was released, and the end of the war was thought to be eminent. That news was welcome, but it didn't change the fact that I was still in the Army and was due back in Ft. McPherson on 13 Aug. Soldiers tended to not pay much attention to what was going on in the war away from where they were. Whatever was going to happen was going to happen and I had my orders.

I reported back to Ft. Mac and picked up orders to proceed to Seymour Johnson Field, Goldsboro, NC, for further assignment. I was put in charge of a shipment of about nine officers, with orders to see that they got there safely. The day we were to ship out happened to be VJ Day. **THE WAR WAS OVER!!! Now what?**

When the news was announced, staid old Atlanta went bonkers. The streets filled with people and cars. Whistles blew, horns sounded and sirens screamed. Complete strangers hugged complete strangers, and if you had on a uniform, everyone wanted to shake your hand, buy you a drink, take you to dinner, or just talk about how happy they were the war was over. I was standing on a street corner just watching the milling crowds when a young girl, about sixteen, came up and struck up a conversation. I thought, "Does your mama know that you are talking to a complete stranger, and a serviceman, at that?"

I'll bet that under different circumstances she would never have done that.

Lots of people did lots of unconventional things that night. I just mused about how the world had changed, and wondered what lay in store for me. Did I want to stay in the service? I sort of liked the life and the pay was excellent. I hadn't gotten my fill of flying, and there were all sorts of new planes coming on line. But there were thousands of 1st Lt. pilots that would like to make the Army Air Force a career. Did I have a chance? Was I qualified enough to be attractive to the Army? Then there was my family to consider. Would it be fair to subject them to life in the military, even in peacetime? I was pretty sure, even before going to Seymour Johnson that all these questions would have to be answered there. It was unlikely that the Army would want to retain many of the run-of-the-mill aviators. They would want rank and experience, of which I did not have enough.

We had been briefed on the GI Bill, and its applications and advantages. Mostly the educational privileges had been emphasized, and most of the guys I knew planned either to go back to college or to enroll as soon as they got out. That seemed like a likely course for me, since I had harbored a desire to be a chemical engineer, even back in high school. Questions, questions, questions, all sorts of questions. Pretty soon I was going to be faced with some tough decisions.

One of the guys I was responsible for looked me up in the afternoon and said he was not going to Goldsboro on the train with the rest of us. He had met a girl that afternoon that wanted to party and he was going to party with her. He declared that she had promised that she would drive him up to Goldsboro in time for him to report in by midnight the next day. I didn't have the authority to order him on the train, so I told him that if he didn't make it I would tell the MP's that he didn't make the train and I thought he was AWOL. He vowed he would not be AWOL, but that he couldn't miss out on an opportunity like this. I figured that if he wanted to take the chance, it was his problem. I wasn't going to cover for him. As it turned out, he did get in just before midnight, and we were both off the hook. Under the circumstances, it probably would not have made much difference anyway. About all the Army would have done was dock some of his pay since we were all probably going to get out soon.

I spent the next three weeks in Goldsboro exploring my options, doing a little flying, but mostly hanging around the PX and O Club. Most of us looked into the possibility of making the military a career, but the Army could not promise us more than about a year more, at best. There were a lot of bull sessions about what we ought to do, and the general consensus was that we ought to get out and get on with our lives. The military option was too tenuous. I decided to get out.

There were so many of us there that it took quite a while to process us out. The paper work moved a little slowly, but by the end of August I was given my orders to return to Ft. McPherson, which was now called a Separation Center. I reported there and was processed out, given my discharge papers, my "ruptured duck," (Honorable Discharge lapel button) and sent on my way home on 12 Sep 45. **I WAS A CIVILIAN, AGAIN!!**

I figured that if I was ever going to get a college education, it had to be now. There was no sense waiting. I routed myself home through Knoxville, went straight to the Business Office of the University, identified myself and declared my intention to enter that institution of higher learning. I was one of the first of thousands that showed up there over the next several months as beneficiaries of the GI Bill of Rights. They seemed very happy to see me, and when I left there I was officially a first quarter freshmen.

All I had to do was go home, get my family and report back there in time to register for the Fall Quarter, around the 21st.

THUS ENDETH MY MILITARY CAREER (2 years, 5 months, 29 days)

MISSION LOG

Mission 1 Jan. 31, 1945 Chuisaforte(W) RR Bridge 3 hr, 40 min
    Pilot-Fitzsimmons (box lead)   Milk run – no flak

Mission 2 Feb. 5, 1945 San Michele   3 hr, 50 min
    Pilot-Fitzsimmons (box lead)   Milk run – no flak

Mission 3 Feb. 14, 1945 Brenner Pass   4 hr, 15 min
    Pilot-Fitzsimmons (box lead)   Anti-flak – 3 holes

Mission 4 Feb 17, 1945 Dogna Town Bridge   5 hr, 15 min
    Pilot-Fitzsimmons (box lead)   Flak – inaccurate

Mission 5 Mar. 3, 1945 Solarno RR Div.   4 hr, 30 min
    Pilot-Fitzsimmons (box lead)   Milk run – no flak

Mission 6 Mar. 4, 1945 Solarno RR Div.   4 hr. 35 min
    Pilot-Jones (box lead)   Milk run – no flak

Mission 7 Mar. 9, 1945 Ora RR Div.   4 hr
    Pilot-Shirley (wing)   Flak – one hole

Mission 8 Mar. 10, 1945 Ora RR Div   4 hr, 30 min
    Pilot-Shirley (wing)   Flak & **HOW** –
                                          no holes

Mission 9 Mar. 12, 1945 Posthumia RR Br. (Yugoslavia) 3 hr, 55 min

Pilot-Allison (group lead)   Milk run – no flak

Mission 10 Mar. 14, 1945 San Margherita   3 hr, 50 min
    Pilot-Jacobs (element lead)   Flak – inaccurate

Mission 11 Mar. 16, 1945 Campo(N) RR Br.   4 hr, 35 min
    Pilot-Jacobs (element lead)   **WOW! – 17
                                                                 HOLES**

Mission 12 Mar. 17, 1945 Cittadella RR Br.   3 hr, 20 min
    Pilot-Jacobs (element lead)   Milk run – no flak

Mission 13 Mar. 20, 1945 Bologna Area   2 hr, 30 min
    Pilot-Jacobs (element lead)   Nickeling – no flak

Mission 14 Apr. 1, 1945 Crema RR Br.   4 hr
    Pilot-Jacobs (element lead)   Milk run – no flak

Mission 15 Apr. 5, 1945 Steinach RR Br.   4 hr, 40 min
    Pilot-Dromgoole (wing)   Milk run – no flak

Mission 16 Apr. 8, 1945 San Michele RR Fill   2 hr, 25 min
    Pilot-Dromgoole (wing)   Milk run – no flak

Mission 17 Apr. 9, 1945 Imola front line support   2 hr, 55 min
    Pilot-Dromgoole (wing)   Frags(Beaucoup
excitement) no flak

Mission 18 Apr. 10, 1945 San Patrizio front line support 1 hr, 50 min
    Pilot-Dromgoole (wing)   Frags(didn't drop)
                                                                 Scant flak-no holes

Mission 19 Apr. 11, 1945 Lavezolo front line support 2 hr
    Pilot-Dromgoole (wing)   Frags, milk run-
                                                                 no flak

Mission 20 Apr. 14, 1945 San Ambrosio RR Br.   4 hr
    Pilot-Dromgoole (wing)   Milk run – no flak

Mission 21 Apr. 15, 1945 Pradura de Sasso   2 hr, 30 min
   Pilot-Dromgoole (wing)   Frags – no flak

Mission 22 Apr. 16, 1945 Portomaggiori   1 hr, 30 min
   Pilot-Dromgoole (wing)   Frags – no flak

Mission 23 Apr. 17, 1945 Bologna Road Br.   2 hr, 25 min
   Pilot-Dromgoole (wing)   Milk run – no flak

Mission 24 Apr. 17, 1945 Pradura de Sasso   2 hr, 5 min
   Pilot-Dromgoole (wing)   Frags – no flak

Mission 25 Apr. 19, 1945 Calliano RR Br.   4 hr, 35 min
   Pilot-Dromgoole (wing)   Scant to moderate
                                                     flak – no holes

Mission 26 Apr. 20, 1945 San Ambrosio RR Fill   2 hr, 50 min
   Pilot-Crouse (wing)   Scant, inaccurate
                                                     flak

Mission 27 Apr. 21, 1945 Ineffective sortie   2 hr, 10 min
   Pilot-Dromgoole (wing)

Mission 28 Apr. 21, 1945 Ficarolo Ferry Landing   2 hr, 10 min
   Pilot-Dromgoole (wing)   Scant, inaccurate
                                                     flak

Mission 29 Apr. 22, 1945 Ficarolo Ferry Landing   2 hr, 15 min
   Pilot-Dromgoole (wing)   Scant, inaccurate
                                                     flak

Mission 30 Apr. 22, 1945 Occhiobello Ferry Landing   2 hr,15 min
   Pilot-Dromgoole (wing)   Scant, inaccurate
                                                     flak

Mission 31 Apr. 23, 1945 Ostiglia Ferry Landing   2 hr, 15 min
   Pilot-Dromgoole (wing)   Milk run – no flak

FINITO -ETO

MEDITTERANEAN THEATER
OF OPERATIONS

SELECTED PICTURES FROM THE 310ᵗʰ BOMB GROUP HISTORY

(These pictures are from Kevin Arnwine whose father was a gunner in the 379ᵗʰ Squadron. Bill Poole and the National Archives also provided some.)

Target bound over Italy

Over the Apennines

Landing echelon from the no. 2 ship

Good strike on a typical target

Typical box formation on the way to target

Bombs Away!

A good concentration of bombs

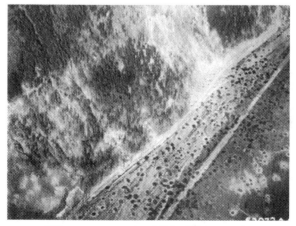

Efforts to cause a landslide did not work.
This target was hit numerous times

Corsica in winter. Not very inviting to an old southern boy

Typical tent city for a nomadic bomb group

Bombs away over the Po valley. Target unknown

BEKANNTMACHUNG

Der Oberbefehlshaber der deutschen Armeegruppe Süd-
west, Generaloberst Heinrich von Vietinghoff, hat sich mit
sämtlichen unter seinem Kommando stehenden—deutschen und
faschistischen—Truppen übergeben. Er hat dementsprechende
Befehle erteilt, denen unverzüglich Folge geleistet werden muss.

Ihr habt den Kampf sofort einzustellen und auf Eurem
gegenwärtigen Standort verbleibend, weitere Anordnungen
abzuwarten.

H. R. ALEXANDER
Feldmarschall
Alliierter Höchstkommandierender
Mittelmeer-Kriegsschauplatz.

Propaganda leaflet. We dropped them on a "nickeling" mission.
Why they were call that I have no idea

Landing approach-echeloned to the right for a left overhead

Unloading fragmentation bombs

Bombed out railroad bridge-not a roller coaster

Inspection before an awards ceremony

Celebrating a milestone. This crew was from the 379th squadron
and those are donuts

Judging from the craters the bombing may have been a bit inaccurate

INCIDENTAL COMBAT TALES

As I went through the war, I learned or encountered any number of interesting things that bore no particular relationship to me, but might be interesting reading to others. These were in the nature of sidelights, cultural phenomena, apocryphal stories and **outright** lies, often referred to as "combat tales." Every person who ever served in the military has many of these and usually shares them only with other ex-military types. Persons who have not been there seem to quickly get bored, and you can see a glazed look come into their eyes, indicating loss of interest. I have noticed this condition in my own children, which is one reason I have not made much effort to regale them with "combat tales."

I don't harbor any particular resentment that what my veteran buddies and I find fascinating and hilarious doesn't resonate with them. I would probably get bored with my grandchildren's conversational exchanges after a time, too. I believe that otherwise disinterested persons might enjoy reading some of these things more than listening, because you can stop reading, but it sometimes difficult to turn off a garrulous old man.

ONE WAY TO FOIL AN Me-109

I have a friend from college and the Oak Ridge National Laboratory who flew in the 310th before I was in it. His name is Marion L. Picklesimer, better known to his friends as "Pick." Pick was assigned to the 310th when it was first organized in South Carolina in 1942, and went overseas with it for the invasion of North Africa. He always liked to needle me about how easy I had it in 1945 compared to the tough days in North Africa. He told me one tale about a maneuver they once used to outfox the German fighters after leaving a target. I always thought it was just another one of his exaggerations until I read the same story in a history of the 310th.

On one mission, an eighteen ship effort, the target was bombed successfully before the fighters jumped them, and as usual, they headed for the deck as fast as they could get there. This was standard procedure in those days. The idea was to get away from the target area as fast as possible. Also, as usual, the fighters were waiting for them as soon as they cleared the flak. The group leader called for all the ships to form on him pretty much in line abreast, right on the deck. Pick said they were seldom over 25 feet off the desert floor. They were so low that the prop wash was kicking up dust off the ground. This prevented the fighters from diving through the formation, as they liked to do at altitude. It also presented eighteen top turrets with 36 fifty-caliber machine guns bearing on any incoming Jerry. Any time a fighter made a pass it had to pull up over the formation making it a broad target at a time it couldn't shoot back. It was pretty frustrating to the Germans. One pilot got so frustrated that he tried coming down on the deck behind the formation and overhauling it. This didn't work either, because he got caught in the prop wash of eighteen planes and was flipped into the ground before he could get off a shot. The wash from a B-25 had the reputation of being the most violent of any plane in the U.S. inventory, and that group leader used it as a defense mechanism. You used whatever worked.

B-25 vs. P-38

This title seems a bit incongruous. Those two planes were supposed to be on the same side. This episode also supposedly happened in North Africa as a result of a heated discussion between a P-38 pilot and the pilot of a B-25. It all began in a bar one night when a dispute began about the comparative maneuverability of the two planes. This on the face of it is a pretty silly argument, because no bomber is ever designed to out maneuver an attacking fighter, but, as things often happen when young fliers get together, words were exchanged, claims were made and challenges issued. The 25 pilot declared that he could turn inside a 38, and the fighter pilot rose to the bait and dared him to a fly off. The die was cast.

The next day the contest took place over the bomber base. They took off and squared off where everyone could see them. The B-25 pilot lowered his gear and flaps and flying as slowly as he could, began to turn in a circle, with P-38 right on his tail. Tighter and tighter and slower and slower they went until finally the 38 fell into a stall while the 25 kept flying. The fighter guys stood for the drinks that night.

This is not to say that every pilot of a B-25 could out turn a P-38, but that particular pilot did it to that particular fighter pilot, because the bomber pilot was especially good, and knew just what he could do with his plane. Admittedly, this was a very special case where the only dispute was whether one plane could out turn the other. Maneuvering of this type would never take place in combat.

THE F-5 MANEUVER

While I was on rest leave at Capri, I met one of the members of Class 44G from Mather. He had been one of the lucky ones who went into photo reconnaissance flying the F-5, a stripped down, camera equipped P-38. In the time I was getting in 31 combat missions, he had flown five recon missions. That's the way it was in reconnaissance, you flew seldom, but you flew a long time when you flew.

He told a couple of tales of the "Photo Joes" that bear repeating. When one of their pilots flew his last mission, he was expected to put on a show for the squadron when he came home. According to my friend, each one tried to outdo the last one, and there was always great anticipation as it came time for the conquering warrior to get back.

This one day everyone was gathered at the field because one of the old timers was ending his tour and they were expecting a show to end all shows. My friend had his camera out so he could get some footage of this exhibition. The pilot made his obligatory drag of the field doing rolls before he really began to wring it out, then the show started. He did everything one could do with a 38 plus a few things no one had seen before, including an engine out buzz job. One of his last passes was balls out, high speed run topping 400 mph with a straight up rolling climb out. This took him almost out of sight, but they could see him roll over for another pass. Straight down he came, and as he came sailing across the field the last time, they realized that he had both props feathered. He flew his pattern and landed dead stick. My friend completely forgot to even aim his camera.

Another F-5 pilot reported coming home from a mission over Yugoslavia and as was the custom, as soon as he cleared land, dropped down on the deck for his run down the Adriatic. They did this because most of the mission consisted of climbing to maximum altitude, above 40 thousand feet, flying straight and level for several hours and then coming home with very little excitement. This allowed them to let off a little steam and feel like real pilots, not truck drivers.

This pilot said he was as close to the water as he dared get when he saw two strange parallel streaks in the water along his course. Curious to see what it was, he speeded up a bit and pretty soon overhauled another F-5 on its way home and the pilot had it so close to the water that it was actually kicking up spray and leaving a wake. That's low flying, folks

BIG FRIENDS, LITTLE FRIENDS

One of the guys I met in training in Greenville that had flown in the 5th Air Force told about coming home from a particularly rough mission one day when they had been pretty well shot up. Three of them were escorting a wounded 25 and were right on the deck, thinking to stay low so the Japs would have trouble making passes. They were sure they were as low as they could get without going into the water, when some guy began going crazy on the radio. They finally figured out that he was trying to get them to see the P-38 with one engine out flying along between the B-25's and the water. The fighter jock figured the safest place for him at that time was underneath some big friends with big guns.!

HELP

Sometime during the fighting in North Africa, a P-40 pilot got into a fracas with several Me-109's and was sorely in need of assistance. He got on the horn and began to scream for help. Almost immediately he got a response from a P-38 pilot who asked him his location so he could join him. When he reported that he was in a certain area, and that it was in North Africa, the 38 pilot answered back and said, "Sorry, Mac. I can't help you. I'm over southern France."

What they had just experienced was one of those weird anomalies that take place in radio transmission when the conditions are just right. There is what is called the "sporadic E-layer" way up in the stratosphere that acts as a reflector of radio waves. Transmissions bounce off of it without loss of power so that oftentimes signals that shouldn't go more than a few hundred miles are received thousands of miles from their source. This happened to a Navy pilot in the South Pacific when he called for help and was answered by a commercial pilot on his approach to La Guardia Field.

TOM PHILLIPS

Tom was one of those extraordinary individuals that never met a stranger, and was perfectly at ease in any company. He could immediately relate to the most unlearned dirt farmer and very soon be talking to him about his crops, or fit in with the most sophisticated of business people or politicians. It was amazing. He put that talent to good use in his business dealings after college.

He came in and sat down just like we had known each other all our lives, and very soon, it began to feel like we had. We were both Air Force veterans, and had served in Italy, he in the 15th Air Force and I in the 12th. Right away, we had that in common and it served to start a bond that just grew stronger the longer we knew each other. We spent that night swapping stories of our experiences, talking into the wee hours. He finally bedded down on the sofa in our living room sometime after midnight, and thus, began a friendship that flourished until his death from cancer in 1965. Along the way, he married Madge and became my brother-in-law.

I learned a great deal about Tom that night as we exchanged combat tales. He had attended Union University in Jackson, TN, where he had played football before he went into the Air Corps. He had trained in B-24's and took one over to Italy to the 15th AF. True to the way the military does things, they immediately took him out of B-24's and checked him out in B-17's which he flew until shot down and captured by the Germans.

Tom was a big man, a shade under six feet and weighing in at 230 pounds. He was the ideal heavy bomber pilot, placid temperament, iron willed, very sure of himself and not inclined to take undue chances. It was a shame he didn't get to fly more missions because he was destined for leadership, if anyone ever was. I never flew with Tom, but I did ride in a car with him many times and if the way he flew was anything like the way he drove, you can bet that B-17 did just what he told it to. He was the picture of supreme confidence when he took hold of the wheel, and you just knew he was in complete control. I can see him in my mind's eye at the controls of a 17, headset cocked up on one ear, massive left hand overwhelming the wheel, right hand gently adjusting the throttles to keep his place in formation and eyes fastened on his lead ship. This may seem somewhat romantic, but time tends to do that to one's perception.

I don't remember how many missions Tom flew, but it wasn't many, something less than ten, it seems. He had been on a mission to a target in Austria, as I recall, when his plane was badly shot up by flak. He was trying to get back home but the plane was on fire and losing altitude fast.

It was obvious that they weren't going to make it, so his only option was to abandon ship, because there was no place to land and the plane would never last for a crash landing, anyway. Somewhere over northern Italy, he gave the bailout signal and all the crew jumped. Tom was the last to go, as any good captain is. He said he was standing between the seats holding the plane under control as best he could while the co-pilot was getting ready to jump. He was taking way too much time getting himself all set, so Tom was just about to boot him in the butt when he finally jumped. Tom was right behind, because he didn't have a lot time left before it would be too late. Because they were so low, he pulled his ripcord as soon as he cleared the ship. At that point he was traveling through the air much faster than was recommended for opening a chute, but he felt he had no choice. The chute opened, but three panels were ripped out, making its efficiency marginal, at best. To compound his troubles, he had just picked up the first chute he came to when leaving for the mission and it was the smallest the Air Corps stocked, made for little guys, not 230 pound hulks. He was coming down way too fast, and the stupid airplane had circled around and crashed directly below him, burning. He said he tried everything he had been taught about how to control a parachute, and some that weren't in the book, and managed to miss the plane by about 100 feet.

When he gathered his wits about him, he got up and discovered he was covered by the rifles of a squad of Hitler Youth. They were kids in their mid-teens who had been thoroughly indoctrinated to hate their enemies and give them no quarter. Fortunately, they were commanded by an over aged regular German army sergeant, who knew the Rules of the Geneva Convention regarding treatment of prisoners of war. Tom said you could see the hate in their eyes and hard young faces.

When he left the plane he had gashed one of his legs pretty badly and could feel the blood running down into his shoe. He bent down to inspect it when he heard the unmistakable sound of a rifle bolt being slammed home. Tom said, "I stood at attention and would not have moved if my leg had fallen off at the hip."

The sergeant quickly gained control and upbraided the kid for his action. He treated Tom and the other officers they had captured with the respect the German soldiers had for their officers. That may have been all that saved Tom.

After rounding up the rest of the crew, the Germans escorted them all to a railroad station where they were taken to a holding camp. Tom was put in solitary immediately and fed only bread and water. He said the lights were left on all the time, but he was able to sleep some. There were all kinds of noises from the other cells, shouts and screams and curses that seemed to come from other prisoners. It left the impression that some of them had been there for a very long time. In retrospect, Tom said, he wondered if those things were staged by the Germans to break the new prisoners down. The walls of his cell were wood and had all sorts of graffiti on them, names, dates and crude calendars depicting the number of days some prisoners had been there. The length of time it appeared that some had been in solitary bothered Tom more than anything else.

After six days a German Army major who spoke perfect English with an American accent took him out for interrogation. Up until then Tom had only been asked his name, rank and serial number, and that was all he had given them. The interrogation began with the major offering him an American cigarette, which Tom gratefully took. When he finished the first one he was given another, and finally the whole pack. The major then proceeded to tell Tom his group and squadron number, his commanding officer's name, rank and serial number and any number of supposedly confidential bits of information. This was supposed to break down the prisoner's resistance to giving up all he knew, since the Germans already knew so much. Tom figured that since they knew all that, then they probably knew anything else he knew, so why bother telling them what they already knew. He just repeated his name, rank and serial number and told the major that was all he was going to get. He explained to him that he was only a lieutenant and lieutenants in the U. S. Army were the last to know anything. The major threatened to put him back in solitary, but it was only a threat. It was obvious that it would not be worth the effort to break Tom, since he couldn't tell them much they didn't already know. He was shipped off to a stalag, where he spent the next 11 months.

When he was captured Tom weighed 230 pounds, and when he was released he was down to 135! That was a 95-pound loss in just 11 months. He said his diet consisted of moldy black bread and potato or cabbage soup, twice a day. Occasionally, there was some sort of ersatz oleo that resembled rancid lard. They had the clothes they were shot down in, and they were worn day and night. When they were able to wash them, they had to wrap up in their threadbare blankets until they were dry. Only when the International Red Cross inspection teams came around did they get any new clothes or blankets, which were immediately taken away from them when the team left.

They were allowed an occasional letter out, heavily censored, of course. Once in a while packages from home got in, just to demonstrate how compassionate the Nazis were, but they were stripped of anything edible. Just before the Red Cross teams would show up, special goodie packages would be distributed and they would get candy, cigarettes, writing paper, soap and shaving stuff. These occasions were so infrequent that they provided essentially no relief at all. Somehow, the Nazis always knew when the teams were coming in, although it was supposed to be unannounced. The teams were made up of people from neutral countries, i.e. Sweden and Switzerland, who were for the most part cooperating with the Germans more than the Allies.

When the movie "Stalag Seventeen" came out, Tom went to see it to see just how much the motion picture folks had distorted the facts. He came out very surprised just how realistic it really was. Most of the dramatic parts were fanciful, but the depiction of the barracks life, he said was fairly much on the money.

There had been proven instances of infiltration of the camps by American born Nazis, such as played by Peter Graves, so the inmates were always on the alert for anything not quite Yankee enough. There was once a new young guy put in the compound that no one would have anything to do with, and it nearly drove him crazy. He was an outcast, and he couldn't figure out why. Finally, someone told him that it was because he was wearing black shoes and they had picked up on an infiltrator once who came in wearing his German army shoes. It turned out that the man was a genuine American prisoner who had first been picked up by the Italian partisans who took his good GI combat boots and gave him a pair of Italian shoes, which happened to be black. The Italians would have returned him to his own lines, but they were ambushed by the Germans who took the American.

The Germans allowed the prisoners to play some athletics like soccer and basketball, so teams were organized between barracks. In Tom's barracks there was a kid who had been a star college basketball player, but he was so malnourished that he didn't have the strength to play a whole game. They decided to pool the barracks Hershey Bars from their Red Cross packages before the camp tournament and feed them to him so he could keep up his energy to lead the barracks team. It worked, because Tom's barracks won the camp trophy.

Near the end of the war, the German guards were fairing very little better than the prisoners, as far as food went. They were invalided regular army, replacing the SS guards, who had gotten out while the getting was good. Some of the more levelheaded and compassionate of them began to share what little they had with the prisoners, hoping to garner a little good will before the Allies showed up. It was a case of too little, too late. No one gained back any weight before they were finally liberated.

NIGHT BAIL OUT

This is a tale Tom told me about the experience of one of his prison camp acquaintances. It seems he had been on a night reconnaissance over Austria when his plane was shot up by flak. On the way back south, the crew had to bail out over the Alps in pitch-black darkness. There was a heavy overcast, dark of the moon and no ground lights, so he could see absolutely nothing, although he knew he was over mountains. In getting out of the out of control plane, he had fractured some ribs and was in considerable pain. His chute opened all right and he came down into he knew not what. He came to a sudden stop when his chute caught in the branches of a tree. As he hung there he contemplated his situation. There was no way of knowing just how high off the ground he was. He might be a hundred feet up, two feet up or hanging out over a thousand foot precipice. He didn't know. It was about midnight so he had several hours to go before it would be light enough to see anything.

At first, he thought he would just sweat it out until he could see but he kept passing out because of the pain in his ribs. The longer he hung there, the more excruciating the agony became. He had just about reached the limit of his endurance, so he decided that anything was better than suffering any longer. He decided to take a chance and slip out of his chute harness anyway. He was ready to fall a thousand feet just to get some relief, even if it meant his death. So, he unbuckled, slipped out of the harness and fell----about six inches!!

THE WAGES OF SIN

In my squadron there were a couple of unhappy co-pilots that had once been P-47 hotshots. They were good, if disgruntled pilots and their story is worth retelling.

It seems that four of the fighter jocks were on rest leave in Naples when they did what a lot of aviators did when away from combat. They got drunk. In their drunken carousel, they stole an MP jeep and took it for a ride around the Italian countryside. Somewhere along the way, they broke into a barn and found some pink paint, which they proceeded to apply to the jeep. They now had the only pink colored army jeep in existence. As usually happens in an escapade such as this, they wrecked the jeep and were pretty thoroughly beaten up. When they got out of the hospital, their punishment was to pay the farmer for the damages to his barn and the loss of his paint and to pay the Army for their jeep. As if this wasn't enough, they were then exiled to a medium bomber outfit as co-pilots, never to see their beloved Jugs again. They acted like they would have rather been in the stockade than flying B-25's. We thought they got let off pretty lightly, and that they had distinctly improved their flying lot.

VINO IS NOT FOR NOVICES

I have never been inclined to imbibe in alcoholic beverages. My mother was dead set against them and my father only drank a little bourbon in eggnog at Christmas time. It was seldom around our house, so there was never a temptation to try it. I was so thoroughly indoctrinated with evils of "demon rum" by Mama that I just left it alone. One of my greatest fears was being made to look foolish, and as I saw just how foolish drunks could be, that added to my resistance to it. I didn't find it particularly difficult to stay sober in the Army, even when many around me seemed to find going out on pass and getting sloshed made you a man. I felt like it took more of a man to say no than to give in.

In Italy wine drinking was a way of life. They had a saying, "Water is for washing and milk is for babies." Table wine was put up in twenty-gallon demijohns and hauled around on two wheel carts. It was just a part of the culture to share a glass of vino with friends for any occasion. This once led me into a slightly embarrassing situation in Fano. I had taken some shirts to a local tailor to be taken in at the waist, and he with several of his friends and an American captain were celebrating sundown with a glass of wine. He insisted that I join with them, despite my protestations that I didn't drink. The Italians didn't speak English, so I couldn't make them understand that it wasn't my custom to drink anything alcoholic. The captain spoke a little Italian, but he didn't seem to be able to make them understand either. I'm not sure he tried very hard.

I could see that there was hardly any left in the demijohn, so rather than offend the tailor I agreed to a small glass. The tailor emptied the demijohn into my glass, and what looked like just a few drops in the big bottle, turned out to be a whole tumbler full. What was I to do? I was due at the ball field to play a game in just few minutes, so, foolishly, I drained the glass far too quickly, offered my "Ciao" and left for my ball game. The day was hot and the vino went to my head quickly. On the way to the ball field I began to see two roads and not knowing which one to choose, I tried to stay between them. That worked because I made it to the game without falling in the ditch.

R.H.I. P.

During the war the rapid promotions that took place created many strange and humorous situations. One that was told and retold all through the AAF involved a fighter pilot and an AAF ground pounder. It seems this fighter pilot back from combat was stooging around near a base in the Southwest. He was having a ball buzzing everything in sight and making machine gun noises on the radio, singing, making ribald comments to other fighter pilots in the air. He was violating every radio discipline rule in the book, and this got under the skin of the major in charge of the airfield that day. The major got on the horn and began chewing him out and ordered him back to the field for disciplinary action. The pilot radioed back and asked, "Who the hell are you, Mac?"

The officer in the tower said, "I'm the ground executive officer for this base. My name is Major Smith."

The fighter jock answered back, "Well, Roger Dodger, you old codger. I'm a Major, too."

****

Another similar incident happened at another air base when a P-47 pilot called in for clearance to land. When he got clearance, he proceeded to beat the field up thoroughly. This was permissible overseas, but was a serious no, no stateside. When he pulled into the flight line and parked, there was a very officious captain waiting for him. The captain proceeded to read him the riot act about how it was against the rules to buzz the field and that he was in serious trouble with the airfield commander, Maj. Anderson. The pilot got out of the cockpit, dressed in his summer slacks and a tee shirt. He looked about twenty years old. Meanwhile, the captain was chewing him out.

The pilot reached back into the cockpit and pulled out his shirt and put it on and the captain was stricken dumb in mid syllable. The kid was a Lt. Colonel. He said, "What was it you were saying, Captain?'

Throwing him a snappy salute, the captain said, "Welcome to Shaw Field, Sir."

THE BISCUIT GUN

Planes that have no radio, such as the Cub and Stearman, require some means of communication with the ground to authorize take offs, landing and go arounds. This was accomplished with an aimable light in the control tower. This was a large device that looked like a small lard can with a pistol grip and trigger attached to it. It swung from the ceiling by a cord and could be pointed in any direction. It was actually a focused, high intensity light that, when aimed at plane, could be seen only by the pilot of that plane. It had two interchangeable filters, one red and one green, so that it projected either a red or green beam.

Tower control monitored all traffic and used the light to direct our activities. When you were on the end of the runway ready to take off, you looked to the tower for a signal. If all was clear the operator would flash you a green light and you were "go for takeoff." (A little space age jargon, there.) A red light meant, "hold." You also looked for a green light when approaching the field to enter the landing pattern. A red light meant stay out of the pattern or go around. It worked very well, if you always remembered to check the tower.

The device had been nicknamed the "biscuit gun," because some wag in the past had claimed it was used to shoot biscuits up to a panicked cadet, who couldn't work up nerve enough to land his plane. This was to keep him from starving until he could figure out how to get back on the ground.

WHO DAT?

Radio discipline was emphasized from the beginning of our Basic Flight Training through the rest of our tour of duty. It was especially pertinent in combat, where radio silence was the order of the day among the bombers. It was thought that the presence of several hundred heavy bombers could be kept secret from the Germans by eliminating or severely curtailing radio traffic. Vain hope. The Germans knew exactly when our missions took off, how many planes were aloft, and, usually, where they were headed. Nevertheless, the brass insisted on no plane to plane transmissions after takeoff This was a real headache and a bother to the crews up there who could see the Jerries ack ack and fighters headed right for them. They couldn't see the point.

The story is told about one long, especially boring mission when a very large group of bombers was cruising along at altitude, experiencing no opposition, at all. The tedium finally got to an obscure co-pilot, somewhere in the formation, and he keyed his mike and quietly inquired, "Who dat?"

Immediately, there was a response, "Who dat, say, Who dat?"

From another source in the formation, "Who dat, say, Who dat, when I say, Who dat?"

This nonsensical exchange cascaded through the whole formation with the leader going bananas try to get them to shut up. Since there was no way to know who started this rigmarole, the whole group got chewed out at the end of the mission, but you don't ground a whole combat group for violating radio discipline. It did have the effect of pointing out the absurdity of such rigid radio silence rules, and they were relaxed after that.

LITTLE THINGS RELIEVE THE TEDIUM

Adjusting to the discipline of military life is always difficult, especially if you are young Americans with no cultural influence toward the necessary regimentation of such a life. They always pushed the envelope, to use an Air Force expression, seeing what they can get away with before the authorities would react. One such incident comes to mind in my journey through the rigors and alternate boredom of Army training.

All throughout my training, until I became an officer, we went everywhere in a marching formation. Oftentimes we went at "double time", a 240 steps a minute jog. Once, while stationed at Santa Ana, we were double timing to class there came from deep in our formation, this mournful "WHOOooooo, WHoo, WHOOooo."

It was the sound of a steam whistle, perfectly imitated by one of the cadets. He had been listening to the "chk, chk, chk, chk, chk," sound of our GI shoes on the pavement and watching the pumping of our arms as we ran, and they reminded him of a locomotive. Unable to resist the temptation and knowing the DI would not be able to pinpoint the source, he let loose with his interpretation of Norfolk and Western's Old No.17 chugging it's way up the grade into Bluefield.

The DI couldn't have disciplined him if he had wanted to, because he was laughing too hard. This incident led to a further refinement of our formation when it was discovered that if we all scuffed our foot on the first cadence count, it sounded even more like a train. CHUFF, chuff, chuff, chuff; CHUFF, chuff, chuff, chuff. We would be jogging along and someone would start the sound effect and the human whistle would sound off, and there we would go down the street of Santa Ana Army Air Base, the Squadron 55, Flight A Express. This exercise cracked up everyone the first time they heard it. Full colonels were even seen to suppress a smile as we went by.

One of the songs we sang as we marched was "Someone's in the Kitchen with Dinah," which ended with the refrain,

"Dinah won't you blow your horn?" In our formations, this was always punctuated with, "Whoo, WHOOooo

AXIS SALLY

Early in the war, both sides began an active propaganda campaign to demoralize the troops on the other side. There were any number of ploys designed to do this, but the most public was the radio activity of the Lord Haw Haw's, Axis Sally's and Tokyo Rose. Lord Haw Haw turned out to be a turncoat Britisher who nightly broadcast to the British from somewhere in Germany. He taunted the British about their defeats and what was going to happen to them when the Nazis invaded. He kept this up for most of the war, but seemed to have nil effect on their morale.

When America got into the war, they came up with Axis Sally. She may have been an American, or a German with an American accent. I don't know. There may have also been more than one Sally, because the Americans in England heard one and we in the Med. heard another. Her broadcasts consisted of telling us all about who was just coming into the theater, where they were going, what our mission target was to be the next day, and how the 4F's and returning servicemen were getting it on with our wives and sweethearts back home. It was so patently phony that it was laughable. We liked to listen because she had a pretty good band led by Otto, and a girl trio called the Three Doves of Peace, who sounded remarkably like the Andrews Sisters. They played good dance music and jazz. They came in stronger than the Armed forces Radio in Naples.

Tokyo Rose was American-born Japanese who was impounded by the Japanese and forced to broadcast for them. Apparently, it didn't take much persuasion, because investigation after the war determined that she was, at least, a semi-traitor, and she served some time in jail.

None of the broadcasters had a noticeable effect on the morale. They were of more entertainment value than anything else.

DRASTIC MEASURES

One last improbable tale involves a somewhat dubious method of flight instruction that I heard of while in Primary flight training. The story goes that there was one instructor who would employ a rather bizarre means of forcing a cadet to pay attention to his flying and practice the techniques he was being taught. This was usually used on students who obviously had the capabilities but were just a little sloppy and carefree. This instructor felt that they needed some sort of dramatic attention getter that would force them to perform the way he was sure they could.

He had been known to unscrew the control stick and throw it overboard to get the student to sharpen his attention and make him fly right. This was a highly questionable thing to do because he might just get a student who would freeze or go bonkers resulting in a terrible mess on the landing field.

The story goes that one of his students, being forewarned of this instructor's idiosyncrasy, removed a stick from another plane and stashed it in his cockpit before his session with this nut. Sure enough, during the flight the instructor pulled his stunt and dramatically tossed his stick over the side. The student then went through the motions of unscrewing his stick and, getting the instructor's attention, tossed his spare over. The instructor promptly bailed out.

The student finished the session and came in and landed, becoming the first cadet in history to start a session dual and finish it solo with only one landing.

AND NOW, THE REST OF THE STORY (apologies to Paul Harvey)
In the narrative of my combat experiences I related the happenings of 9 Apr. 45 involving the dropping of fragmentation bombs on some planes in our bombing formation. At the time of that writing I did not know or remember whose crew it was that caught the frags and was not sure about the details and results.

To refresh the recollection of the readers, we were on a mission to bomb a troop concentration at Imola, Italy using fragmentation bombs. Due to some sort of mix up, one box dropped their bombs through the formation below them. Most of us below escaped damage by scattering or by dumb luck. One plane, however, was hit by as many as eight bombs. Only by a miracle and remarkable piloting did the crew survive.

Since that time I have managed through the magic of cyberspace to make contact with some of my squadron mates, one of whom was the pilot of that ship. His name is Bill Poole and he has graciously provided the details and permission to relate them here. I shall quote directly from the letter he wrote me about the incident so as to be sure of accuracy. This letter is in response to one I wrote him recounting some of my experiences, one of which happened to be the Imola raid. I quote:

257

"Interestingly, eight each 25# frags hit the aircraft. Only one had fallen far enough to arm, and this unit landed in the area near the rear of the left engine and cleaned the entire flap off and put many holes in the rear wing spar as well as pushed in the side of the aircraft and blew all the radio equipment of the port side as well as hitting George Jollie, many, many times taking his left leg. George, as well as his wife are both departed now. We visited with both at the Colorado Springs Convention in 1991 for a half day. I am in touch with one of the two daughters. We drove to the meet and took the folks out for a drive and lunch.

Continued: All bombs excepting a seventh fell through the aircraft and downward. The seventh hit in the accessory section of the left engine, shearing the alloy fuse off with the iron nose of the bomb. The shearing included the firing pin, which was exactly centered in the bomb where it belonged when all the commotion was over. I suppose the tapped opening for the fuse was about ¾ of an inch. The threaded part of the fuse was in place inside the bomb, with that nasty looking firing pin looking squarely out of the hole in the nose of the bomb. (*This meant the bomb was armed and ready to go off when discovered after the landing; my note*)

One other item: I had the crew go back a number of times and verify if George was dead or alive and assist him if possible. All said he was dead. The entire floor had what appeared to be ¼ inch of blood. Then all the people reported that they could not see any damage. I really think they were scared out of their senses. George told me in 1991 that he knew everything that was happening but could even move his eyes. I asked the crew if they wished to ride home or jump. They desired to fly home and we were close as you know.

All instruments were out and I planned a high approach approx. 2500 feet on the downwind. Signaled flaps down and the aircraft started to rotate toward upside down and fortunately for us there was sufficient pressure in the accumulator to reverse the flaps. Only the right side was coming down. Most of the left side was missing. I really have always believed my glider experience saved us in respect to anything having to do with flying the aircraft and I was flying by the seat of [*sic*] pants. We were recipients of 100 miracles that afternoon and I am the first to profess.

The drag was obvious so I made a 180 degree approach aimed over the canal and Lombardy poplar trees with touch down on the graded earth well short of the runway. No tire on the left main gear, full throttle to hold the aircraft straight. Requested the gear be raised and cut power and switches proceeding into a large ground loop. The gear collapsed sideways lowering us to the earth as easy as a powder puff! (yet another miracle). The live bomb could have easily shaken loose in the accessory section had we come down with a bang. I rounded out at about 170 mph, estimated and stalled immediately upon round up which have always thought was probably about 150 mph estimated. We had no knowledge of the live bomb until April 10 when the pictures were taken."

Bill Poole and his broken bird

The picture shows Bill and a friend standing where the rear of the left engine nacelle should be with the radio compartment completely blown out and the area riddled with holes from the frag bomb. You can see the top turret popped out of its mount and a noticeable bend in the fuselage. So, now you know the rest of the story. (Once again, apologies to Paul Harvey.)